Protest Dialectics

Protest Dialectics

STATE REPRESSION AND SOUTH KOREA'S DEMOCRACY MOVEMENT, 1970–1979

Paul Y. Chang

Stanford University Press
Stanford, California

Stanford University Press
Stanford, California

Library of Congress Cataloging-in-Publication Data

Chang, Paul Y., author.
 Protest dialectics : state repression and South Korea's democracy movement, 1970-1979 / Paul Y. Chang.
   pages cm
 Includes bibliographical references and index.
 ISBN 978-0-8047-9146-5 (cloth)
 ISBN 978-1-5036-1012-5 (pbk.)
 1. Social movements--Korea (South)--History--20th century. 2. Protest movements--Korea (South)--History--20th century. 3. Political persecution--Korea (South)--History--20th century. 4. Authoritarianism--Korea (South)--History--20th century. 5. Korea (South)--Politics and government--1960-1988. I. Title.
 HN730.5.A8C3729 2015
 303.48'4095195--dc23

                           2014044063

 ISBN 978-0-8047-9430-5 (electronic)

Typeset by Bruce Lundquist in 10/14 Minion

for mother and brother,
in memory of father

CONTENTS

ILLUSTRATIONS

PHOTOGRAPHS (following page 138)

Park Chung Hee campaigning, 1971

Korea University students demonstrating, 1971

Riot police confronting Seoul National University students, October 2, 1973

Pastor Pak Hyŏnggyu speaking at a Thursday Prayer Meeting, n.d.

Dong-A Ilbo Declaration of Action for a Free Press, October 24, 1974

Lawyer Kang Sinok arrested, 1975

Chaeya leaders meeting, November 5, 1973

Women workers from the Y. H. Trading Company being dragged out of the
New Democratic Party building, August 11, 1979

ACKNOWLEDGMENTS

Many people helped me complete this book. I am indebted to Gi-Wook Shin, who believed in the project from its inception and over several years generously provided feedback and resources to help it come to fruition. This book would not have been possible without his support. At Stanford University, it was a great privilege to study with Doug McAdam, Susan Olzak, and Morris Zelditch Jr., who lent their methodological and theoretical expertise when the project was beginning to take shape. A special word of gratitude goes to Litze Hu who taught an unlearned undergraduate student the intricate joys of social science research.

I am especially thankful to Jonathan Bolton, Paul S. Cha, Gru Han, Hajin Jun, Charles Kim, Helen Jin Kim, Se-Woong Koo, Dennis Lee, Namhee Lee, Timothy S. Lee, Dale Lim, Hannah Lim, Leslie Paik, Albert L. Park, Juhwan Seo, Hijoo Son, and Dae-Han Song for reading and commenting on early drafts. Their invaluable feedback is reflected throughout the book. Strange as it may sound, there may be no better way to solidify friendships than by coding data together and I want to acknowledge the many people who helped me create the Stanford KDP Events Dataset: Haewon Ahn, Min Chi, Young-taek Choi, Sena Kim, Serim Kim, Yunjung Kim, Dennis Lee, Jaemin Lee, Kangsan Lee, Hannah Lim, Yi Sook Lim, Yoen-sook Lyu, Hyunjung Min, and Chan S. Suh. I owe much to Sena Kim, Dennis Lee, and Hannah Lim for their painstaking work putting together the bibliography, formatting tables and figures, tracking down facts, and standardizing the Romanization of Korean names and terms. Ho-Ryong Lee provided access to the archives at the Korea Democracy Foundation, on which much of this book is based.

The Korea Institute at Harvard University is a warmly supportive intellectual community and I thank Carter Eckert, Nicholas Harkness, Sun Joo Kim, and David McCann for encouraging me in the very last stages of writing; and Myong-suk Chandra, Jina Kim, and Susan Laurence for their incredible administrative help. I am also glad to work next door to Alexandra Killewald, who has a knack of reminding me at the most opportune times that everything is going to be all right. Michelle Lipinski, my editor at Stanford University Press, was steadfast in her encouragement and patience as she shepherded the book through reviews and revisions. Mariana Raykov skillfully carried the book through production.

I was fortunate enough to receive manuscript preparation grants from several institutions. Research for this book was supported by the Academy of Korean Studies (Korean Studies Promotion Service) Grant funded by the Korean Government (Ministry of Education) (AKS-2007-CA-2001). I thank Heather Ahn at Stanford University's Korean Studies Program for managing the AKS grant. Additional support was provided by the National Research Foundation of Korea Grant funded by the Korean Government (NRF-2013S1A3A2055081) and I thank the grant's principal investigator, Changrok Soh, and manager, Jeong-Woo Koo. I am also grateful to Steven Bloomfield at Harvard University's Weatherhead Center for International Affairs for providing the funds to host a book workshop, and to Marina Ivanova for helping me organize it.

As the book was coming together, several people allowed me the opportunity to share my tentative findings. Gi-Wook Shin gave me the first chance to present the arguments publicly, at a luncheon seminar of the Stanford University Korean Studies Program. I am thankful to several others for inviting me to present the book at their various colloquia and workshops: Dukjin Chang (Seoul National University's Department of Sociology), David Kang (USC's Korean Studies Institute), Jeong-han Kang (Yonsei University's Department of Sociology), Namhee Lee (UCLA's Center for Korean Studies), and Orlando Patterson (Harvard University's Workshop in History, Culture, and Society). My sincere appreciation goes to David Cunningham, Carter Eckert, Sun-Chul Kim, and David S. Meyer for offering extensive feedback on the manuscript during the book workshop sponsored by the Harvard Weatherhead Center. Excerpts from an article that appeared in *Social Forces* (vol. 87, no. 2, pages 651–677) are scattered throughout the book and I thank the journal's editors for permitting me to reprint the materials here. I am also grateful to Hank Johnston at *Mobilization* for allowing me to reprint tables and figures from an article published in 2013 (vol. 18, no. 1, pages 19–39).

Finally, I mention those who continue to sustain my work and life in intangible ways. For their friendship I thank Johnny Cho, Gideon Choi, Michael Chung, Chrissy Kim, Daniel Kim, Jason Kim, John Kim, Jeong-Woo Koo, Chung Kwon, Gerald Lew, Dale Lim, Jaemin Suh, Sean Torre, and the rest of the boys from

Fullerton, California. The many late–night conversations I had with Dale Lim were critical to the shaping of this project. My stepfather, Myunjin Paik, is a student of Western continental philosophy and I thank him for sharing his books and showing me what dedication to work looks like. The last and deepest word of gratitude goes to my wife, Seah Lee, for pulling me out of valleys and reminding me that there are peaks yet to come. If only a small amount of her faith rubs off on me, I will consider myself blessed.

ABBREVIATIONS

ACL	Anti-Communist Law
AKC	Amnesty Korean Committee
ASC	Army Security Command
CBS	Christian Broadcasting System
CGC	Capital Garrison Command
DRP	Democratic Republican Party
ED	Emergency Decree
EPB	Economic Planning Board
EYC	Ecumenical Youth Council
FKTU	Federation of Korean Trade Unions
JOC	Young Catholic Workers (*Catholic Jeunesse Ouvrière Chrétienne*)
KCIA	Korean Central Intelligence Agency
KDF	Korea Democracy Foundation
KSCF	Korean Student Christian Federation
NCCK	National Council of Churches in Korea
NDP	New Democratic Party
NDYSA	National Democratic Youth and Student Alliance
NMHDC	National Movement Headquarters for a Democratic Constitution
NSL	National Security Law
PMCDR	People's Movement Coalition for Democracy and Reunification
PRP	People's Revolutionary Party
SCNR	Supreme Council for National Reunification

SNU   Seoul National University
UIM   Urban Industrial Mission
UNTCOK   United Nations Temporary Commission on Korea
USAMGIK   United States Army Military Government in Korea
WCC   World Council of Churches
YMCA   Young Men's Christian Association

NOTE ON ROMANIZATION

Korean names and words were Romanized using the McCune-Reischauer system. Exceptions were made for authors who have published in English (for example, Ahn Byung-Mu and Lee Ho-Chul) and for other names, places, and organizations with standard or official English spellings (such as Park Chung Hee, Seoul, *Sasangge Monthly*, and Kyungpook National University). Following Korean custom, surnames precede given names, excluding names that reference English language publications.

Protest Dialectics

INTRODUCTION
Protest Dialectics and South Korea's
Democracy Movement

Those who expect to reap the blessings of freedom, must . . . undergo
the fatigues of supporting it.

Thomas Paine, *The American Crisis*, September 12, 1777

The promise of a democratic Korea was made on August 15, 1948, with the official founding of the Republic of Korea, or South Korea. Established with the support of the United Nations, South Korea represented one of the first demarcations of the political line that would come to define the emerging world order in the aftermath of World War II. It was to be a beacon of democracy and capitalism juxtaposed to what was then the real viable alternative of world communism. The following month, the Democratic People's Republic of Korea, or North Korea, was founded and these two states, occupying a small peninsula in East Asia, became symbols for a larger Cold War that engulfed the world in the postwar period.

It is a curious thing, then, that South Korea did not transition to democracy until forty years after its founding. June 29, 1987, was a watershed moment in South Korea's political development. Against the backdrop of a hot summer's day that burned even brighter due to the violent street protests that had occurred in the weeks before, Roh Tae Woo, chosen successor to President Chun Doo Hwan, announced the reinstitution of direct presidential elections. The June Declaration was a significant political turning point and South Korea is now a celebrated case of democratization during the "third wave of democracy" (Huntington 1991). Today South Korea enjoys a relatively stable, if not always peaceful, democratic polity.

The content, and indeed the very necessity, of the 1987 June Declaration for political reforms would have surprised observers of Korea in 1948. The victory of the Allied Powers in World War II, and the subsequent presence of the United States in East Asia, brought to the region new political and economic forms. Countries occupied by the United States, including most importantly Japan, were to be democratic capitalist polities acting as bulwarks against the spread of communism. Demarcated by various focal points throughout the world—initially Greece and Turkey—the policy for "containment" outlined by George F. Kennan and declared by U.S. President Harry S. Truman in the Truman Doctrine on March 12, 1947, marked the beginning of the Cold War.

It was uncertain in the immediate postwar period how this new U.S. foreign policy was to affect the Korean peninsula. Statements about the fate of Korea at the various conferences of the world's superpowers during and after World War II were ambiguous.[1] But with the agreement for a shared trusteeship and the subsequent occupation of the Korean peninsula in 1945 by the Soviet Union in the north and the United States in the south, Korea became increasingly important to America's containment policy. Indeed, as Bruce Cumings notes, the partitioning of Korea in 1945 was "the first postwar act of containment" (1981: 117). After Korea's liberation from Japanese colonial rule (1910–1945), it was readily assumed that it was to be a single nation governed by democratically elected leaders. But in 1948 Kim Il Sung and the northern Korean leadership refused to allow the United Nations Temporary Commission on Korea (UNTCOK), which was to oversee the formation of an independent Korean government, to enter its sphere of influence (Armstrong 2003: 133), and the failure of the UNTCOK to hold a peninsula-wide presidential election all but secured the formal division of the Korean nation.

The UN-sponsored election in 1948 was held only in southern Korea and brought to power Syngman Rhee, who was to dominate South Korean politics until 1960, when large student demonstrations forced him to abdicate. Although the Republic of Korea "officially espoused liberal democracy as its form of government from the outset" (Kang 2002: 6), in the *realpolitik* context of the Cold War, national security and economic development took precedence over freedom and liberty. Democracy gave way to dictatorship and South Korea was ruled by authoritarian leaders until the reinstatement of direct presidential elections following the June Declaration in 1987. Although there were times when a democratic South Korea seemed likely—most notably during the Chang Myŏn government in 1960–1961 and the "Spring of Seoul" in 1980—these moments proved to be ephemeral as successive military generals forcibly took political charge. The democracy promised in 1948 would evade South Koreans for four decades, sacrificed for the sake of security and development. In the end, democracy was not to be something granted but had to be won by a burgeoning contentious civil society that emerged and evolved within the context of authoritarian rule.

THE DARK AGE FOR DEMOCRACY?

This book examines South Korea's democracy movement in the 1970s, a period considered by many to be the "dark age for democracy" in Korea (Lee M. S. 2010; Lee 2006; Yi 2011). Partly because the 1970s is characterized as a "dark age," most studies of South Korea's democratization have focused on social movements in the 1980s, when in the summer of 1987, traditionally docile segments of society, including the middle class, joined antigovernment protests.[2] There are, for example, several important studies on the Gwangju Uprising[3] and the impact that Gwangju had on the radicalization of social movements in the 1980s (Lewis 2002; Lee 2007; Shin and Hwang 2003). Other writers have looked at specific sectors of the 1980s democracy movement, including the activism of particular social groups—students (Park 2008; Lee 2007), farmers (Abelmann 1996), white-collar laborers (Suh 2009)—and the rise of the *minjung* (people's) culture that provided master symbols and narratives that structured the discourse of the movement (Lee 2007; Wells 1995a). Justifiably, analysts point to democratic transition in 1987 and further consolidation in the 1990s as central steps in Korea's[4] democratization (Kim 2003; Diamond and Kim 2000).

But before Gwangju in 1980 and democratic transition in 1987, numerous events in the 1960s and 1970s laid the groundwork for the democracy movement in the 1980s. The large protest cycle in the summer of 1987 was in no way spontaneous and was instead the culmination of a movement that spanned more than two decades. The 1970s was a particularly important period when many social groups joined students, the primary movement actor in the 1960s, in the fight against dictatorship. The impact of events discussed in this book—such as the 1973 Theological Declaration of Korean Christians, the *Dong-A Ilbo* Declaration of Media Freedom in 1974, the Minch'ŏng and People's Revolutionary Party cases in 1974 and 1975, the Declaration for the Salvation of the Nation in 1976, and the Tongil Textile and Y. H. Trading Company's women workers' struggles in 1978 and 1979—extends beyond that period in that they motivated the politicization of diverse sectors of Korean society and shaped the trajectory of state-society relations in the 1980s. I bring to light these and other stories that unfolded as the promulgation of the Yusin Constitution in 1972 "transformed the presidency into a legal dictatorship" (Eckert et al. 1990: 365).

The narrative of the 1970s as democracy's "dark age" obfuscates important material and discursive developments that facilitated South Korea's transition to democracy and became the foundations for contemporary civil society. I present a comprehensive analysis of social movements in the 1970s to show how these foundations were laid.[5] By focusing on the 1970s democracy movement I do not intend to underestimate the importance of events that preceded the Yusin period (1972–1979). Most significant was the April 1960 student revolution, by which students and other segments of Korean society forced Syngman Rhee to resign his presidency. The revolution that began on April 19, 1960, established a model for future antigovernment protests, providing an all-too-rare moment of success for people's movements in South Korea.

Also, when South Korea and Japan began a dialogue with the goal of re-establishing diplomatic relations, students across the nation again took to the streets in large protests. Though their efforts did not stop the two countries from normalizing relations in 1965, both the 1960 and 1964–1965 protest cycles are part of the lore of democratization narratives in South Korea and were in tangible ways important for movements in the 1970s.[6] Still, the 1970s presented to dissidents an altogether different authoritarian structure compared to that of the 1960s—one that would require a sustained movement for democracy. As Hae Gu Jung and Ho Ki Kim point out, the 1970s democracy movement "was different from that of the past . . . it now became resistance to the Yushin system itself, namely an antiestablishment movement" (2009: 7).

The reasons that a sustained democracy movement emerged in the 1970s are quite simple. Although some suspected that his supporters had tampered with the electoral process during the elections in 1963 and 1967, President Park maintained a semblance of democracy in the 1960s by establishing relatively independent executive, legislative, and judicial branches of government, and by holding regular direct presidential and general elections. Thus it is incorrect that "for the next 18 years (following the coup d'état in 1961) Park would rule the country with an iron hand" (Lee M. S. 2010: 58). Compared to the Yusin period, the 1960s represented a distinct political situation, one that Hyug Baeg Im characterizes as "soft authoritarianism" or "a brief democratic interlude" (2011: 234). But after Park Chung Hee forced the National Assembly to amend the constitution in 1969 to allow him to run for a third presidential term, and after he replaced the democratic constitution with the Yusin Constitution in 1972, it became clear to all that he had no intention of upholding democratic principles. The Yusin Constitution institutionalized authoritarianism and, consequently, dissident communities mobilized to change foundational political structures rather than address ad hoc government policies.

PROTEST DIALECTICS

In a 1959 article published in the leading Korean intellectual journal *Sasangge Monthly* (*World of Thought*), Quaker leader Ham Sok Hon criticized college education for "imprisoning" the minds of students, who by only reading books are blinded to the necessity of engaging in their country's social and political life (Ham 1959).[7] Ham's exhortation foreshadowed the important role that students would play in bringing down Syngman Rhee's government through the April 1960 student revolution. From the vantage point of hindsight it is thus surprising that the same journal that was a platform for democratic participation in the 1950s then endorsed Park Chung Hee's military coup d'etat in 1961, declaring in the June issue that "the Military Revolution of May 16, 1961, constitute[s] the last effort to save the nation from the dire predicament it faced" (quoted in Park 2011: 379). The contributors to *Sasangge Monthly* were not the only ones to harbor hope in Park's new government, and it is no less surprising that in another influential journal, *Kidokkyo sasang* (*Christian Thought*), Hyŏn Yŏnghak—a leading member of the progressive Christian community— declared his support of Park Chung Hee's economic policies: "Succeed or fail, we must see [the Park Chung Hee government's] Five-Year Plan to completion, even if we have to fix its flaws and inadequacies along the way, because of the utmost urgency of establishing our own autonomous economy" (Hyŏn 1962: 51).

The hope that Park Chung Hee would "save the nation" quickly deteriorated, however, as progressive intellectuals became increasingly critical of Park's policies, including the normalization of relations with Japan in 1965 and the amendment of the constitution to extend his rule in 1969. By 1970 *Sasangge Monthly* had completely reversed its initial "positive appraisal" (Park 2011: 379) of Park Chung Hee when it published Kim Chiha's poem "Ojŏk" ("Five Bandits") in the May issue,[8] and Chang Chunha, the journal's founding editor and publisher, emerged as a leading critic of Park's rule. Similarly, Hyŏn Yŏnghak had a radical change of heart, becoming during the Yusin period a proponent of Minjung Theology, which advocated "liberation from the oppression" of the very economic policies he had endorsed in his 1962 article.

The initial support that the contributors to *Sasangge Monthly* and *Kidokkyo sasang* lent to Park Chung Hee at the outset of his rule and their eventual antigovernment stand represent not only the changing attitudes of progressive intellectuals and theologians but also the shifting relationship between state and society throughout the 1960s and 1970s.[9] Just as the authoritarian nature of Park Chung Hee's government evolved over the course of the eighteen years he ruled South Korea—from military government (1961–1963) to the "democratic interlude" (1963–1972) and finally to formal authoritarianism (1972–1979)—so too did the voices critical of Park's regime. As Park moved increasingly closer to autocratic rule, these critical voices became louder, eventually developing into a sustained social movement for democracy. In turn, after the formation of a formal authoritarian state in 1972, Park responded to antigovernment protesters with new repressive laws and tactics. In short, the repressive capacity of the Yusin regime and the movement for democracy developed in tandem, each influencing the trajectory of the other. If South Korea in the postliberation period is characterized by a "strong state and contentious civil society" (Koo 1993: 231), this book shows how, through specific historical processes, the state became "strong" and civil society "contentious."

Data Sources

This book draws on several types of data to track the emergence and evolution of the democracy movement during the highly repressive Yusin period. Focusing on the relationship between state repression and mobilization, I use a mixed methods strategy to analyze qualitative and quantitative data (Tashakkori and Teddlie 1998). Qualitative sources include Korean and English language archives and sourcebooks: the Korea Democracy Foundation's "dictionary" of protest events (*Minjuhwa undong kwallyŏn sakŏn sajŏn*) and movement organizations (*Minjuhwa undong kwallyŏn tanch'e sajŏn*), the UCLA Archival Collection on Democracy and Unification in Korea, and the eight volume *1970s Democracy Movement* (*1970-yŏndae minjuhwa undong*) published by the National Council of Churches in Korea.

In addition, throughout the empirical chapters I present excerpts from twenty in-depth interviews I conducted with individuals who participated in antigovernment protests in the 1970s. The interviewees were active in different dissident networks during the Yusin period, such as pastors and laypersons from the progressive Christian community, members of the first generation of human rights lawyers, journalists from leading newspaper *Dong-A Ilbo* who began the media freedom movement, and progressive intellectual groups. The oral histories derived from the interviews offer rich accounts of how individuals experienced important events in the 1970s. They are invaluable for the simple reason that the generation that participated in the democracy movement in the 1970s is aging and many important figures have already passed (see Appendix A for further detail of data sources and interviewees).[10]

To better understand the overall temporal trajectory of the democracy movement, I complement the qualitative sources with analyses of a novel quantitative protest and repression events database that is part of the larger Korea Democracy Project (KDP) at Stanford University. The Stanford KDP is a collaborative effort to take stock of South Korea's democracy movement in the postliberation period. At the heart of the Stanford KDP are several datasets that record various attributes of events related to the democracy movement. I analyze the Stanford KDP Events Dataset (1970–1979), which includes characteristics of nearly three thousand protest and repression events. Although the data are not without some of the limitations found in most protest events datasets, to my knowledge they represent the most exhaustive effort to systematically quantify characteristics of protest and repression events related to South Korea's democracy movement in the 1970s (see Appendix B for the dataset codebook).

Analytic Approach and Outline of Chapters

I analyze the qualitative and quantitative data deductively using a conceptual framework derived from recent theoretical developments in social movement research. The analysis begins with the reasonable, if not always obvious, assumption that social movements change over the course of their trajectories. Simply put, movements move. Some scholars have taken note of this, arguing that social movements "are seldom static; thus to study them is to study SM [social movement] change" (Gale 1986: 205). In order to study change, however, we need a diachronic view of movement evolution that accounts for the dynamic nature of contention over time (Meyer and Staggenborg 1996). To better understand how the democracy movement evolved throughout the Yusin period, I adopt what Tahi L. Mottl describes as "a unified movement-countermovement perspective to conflict" (1980: 623).

Sociologists have long argued that state actors fundamentally affect collective action because they control the material conditions that define the possibilities for mobilization (Skocpol 1985; Zwerman and Steinhoff 2005; della Porta 1996; Earl 2003; Davenport, Johnston, and Mueller 2005). This is particularly true for authoritarian systems such as Park Chung Hee's Yusin government: authoritarian regimes, relative to their democratic counterparts, exercise greater control over the polity because power is centralized (Davenport, Johnston, and Mueller 2005; della Porta 1996; Earl 2006; Goldstone and Tilly 2001) and they hold a "monopoly on violence" (Weber 1919, reprinted in Gerth and Mills 1946: 77). If there is general agreement about the role that repression plays in defining authoritarian systems (Almeida 2003, 2008; Davenport, Johnston, and Mueller 2005; Johnston 2005; Earl 2003, 2006; Goldstone and Tilly 2001; della Porta 1996; Osa 2003; Rasler 1996), it is less clear what the consequences of repression are for social movements.

Research on comparative social movements has revealed a "paradox" regarding the impact of repression on mobilization (Brockett 1995, 2005). Whereas some argue that repression discourages social movements (Olzak, Beasley, and Olivier 2003), because of the additional costs associated with dissident activity, others insist that it increases grievances and, subsequently, motivation to participate in protests (White 1989; Khawaja 1993, 1994). In reviews of this literature, researchers have puzzled over the fact that "both threats and opportunities can mobilize activism" (Meyer and Staggenborg 1996: 1645). As David S. Meyer and Suzanne Staggenborg ponder, "for some challengers, increased political openness enhances the prospects for mobilization, while other movements seem to respond more to threat than opportunity" (1996: 1634).

Still others have argued for a nonlinear relationship between repression and protest. But even here, the directions of nonmonotonic patterns are contested. Some argue that the relationship takes on an inverted U shape: lower levels of repression might offer the opportunity to engage in various forms of collective action, but if the repression becomes severe, the costs of participation might be too high and thus lead to demobilization (Brockett 2005; Muller 1985; Weede 1987). Others suggest the reverse: repression is a threat to movement participants and initially deters protest activity. If, however, this repression is determined to be unjust, the same repression can lead to the radicalization of a movement and facilitate further protest (Opp and Roehl 1990; Rasler 1996).

These conflicting findings have led some to the unhelpful conclusion that "there are theoretical arguments for all conceivable basic relationships between government coercion and group protest and rebellion, except for no relationship" (Zimmerman 1980: 191; quoted in Lichbach 1987: 267). Although the relationship between repression and mobilization is indeed complicated, past studies have primarily analyzed the most simple indicator of movement vitality: aggregate counts of protest events (Olzak, Beasley, and Olivier 2003; Rasler 1996; Opp and Roehl 1990). As Dean Hoover and David Kowalewski recognize, however, quantitative studies that rely on overall protest event counts as the main variable of analysis "are limited by their use of single dimensions of dissent and repression" (1992: 156). Although repression might increase or decrease (or both) the number of protest events, a more thorough understanding of a movement's trajectory is possible if we consider the possibility that repression has multiple, and sometimes divergent, consequences for mobilization.

One helpful way to disentangle the relationship between repression and protest is to disaggregate movements into their various components and assess how repression impacts individual parts such as protest "form" (McAdam 1996), tactical adaptation (Ennis 1987; McAdam 1983; Olzak and Uhrig 2001), and internal movement dynamics, including alliances and schisms (Almeida 2005; Meyer and Corrigall-Brown 2005; Bystydzienski and Schacht 2001). That is, we can shift our focus away from the total *quantity* of protest events to the substantive *quality* of movement characteristics. Mara Loveman (1998), for example, has shown that activists in Latin America were motivated to establish social movement organizations during heightened periods of repression. In addition, several studies have shown that movement actors will alter their tactical strategies to adapt to repressive contexts (McAdam 1983; Lichbach 1987; Moore 1998), while others have found that high levels of repression influence the articulation and development of movement ideologies (Davenport and Eads 2001). Thus, expanding organizational capacity, tactical adaptation, and ideological development are just a few of the unintended consequences of repression that studies employing simple event counts miss.

This book is an attempt to contribute to this growing literature on the differential impact of repression on social movements. The democracy movement that emerged during the Yusin period would wax and wane through the 1970s in what Myung-Lim Park has described as "an endless cycle of repression and resistance" (2011: 398). I provide a detailed account of how this "endless cycle" unfolded by specifying the conditions that contributed to the increasing severity of state repression, which in turn influenced the mobilizing strategies of antigovernment dissidents. The arguments laid out in the book highlight the importance of combining quantitative and qualitative data sources to analyze disaggregate components of mobilization, because state repression did not so much quell the democracy movement as it shaped its trajectory in significant ways.

The empirical chapters are organized into three parts. In Part 1, I assess the larger political context from which the democracy movement emerged. Chapter 1 tracks the transformation of Park's leadership as he shifted from ruling within the parameters of a democratic system to establishing a formal authoritarian structure in 1972. His pursuit of national security and economic development led to two important policy decisions in the 1960s. Fearful that America's commitment to South Korea's national security would be compromised by the redistribution of military resources to Southeast Asia, Park agreed to U.S. President Lyndon B. Johnson's request for Korean participation in the Vietnam War. In addition, as the United States winded down its assistance program to Korea, Park turned to Japan as a source of financial resources. The normalization of relations with Japan in 1965 and the reparations received from reestablishing diplomatic ties were intended to boost the government's economic drive but faced widespread criticism from Korean society. Intent on pushing through normalization, Park Chung Hee reverted to using the military to put down student demonstrations, reflecting his increasing reliance on coercive tactics to silence political dissent. This authoritarian tendency culminated in the Yusin Constitution in 1972.

The Yusin Constitution formalized authoritarianism in Korea. In Chapter 2, I discuss the repressive structures that undergirded Park's dictatorship, including the military and the Korean Central Intelligence Agency. In addition, guided by a fairly nuanced and evolving repression strategy, Park consolidated the authoritarian system by enacting additional political control laws that allowed him to ignore basic rights and bypass *habeas corpus* codified in his own Yusin Constitution. The promulgation of presidential Emergency Decrees, along with the National Security Law and the Anti-Communist Law, reflected a greater capacity for structural repression. Temporal analysis of aggregate protest data shows that increasing state repression had a profoundly negative impact on the ability of dissidents to stage public protests. Initially targeting student dissidents who were considered to be the largest threat to social stability, the Yusin regime continued to expand its repressive coverage of the democracy movement.

The chapters in Part 2 trace the emergence of the democracy movement from the context of the authoritarian political system established with the passing of the Yusin Constitution. In Chapter 3, I explain how students, motivated by a proud history of political engagement, made multiple attempts to organize a nationwide movement against Park Chung Hee's government. After a relatively quiet period following the 1960 student revolution and the 1964–1965 protest cycle against the normalization of relations with Japan, Park Chung Hee was pressured to respond to the reemergence of the student movement in 1971. Because he assumed power in 1961 in the wake of the student revolution, Park was well aware of the potential of student demonstrations to cripple social stability and challenge his rule. Increasing state repression was fueled by his determination not to let large student protests develop into the kind of revolution that brought down Syngman Rhee's government in 1960. The consequences of repression were dire: the mass arrests of student protesters led to the rapid demobilization of their movement at two critical junctures in 1971 and 1974.

If the analysis stopped here, the macro quantitative indicators would corroborate the interpretation that state repression was highly effective in stifling protest and that the 1970s were indeed a dark period for Korean democracy. The fall of the student movement, however, motivated the politicization of new social movement groups and in Chapter 4 I discuss the emergence of Christian activists, who replaced students as the salient actors in the movement after 1975. The participation of Christians in antigovernment protests was critical to the survival of the democracy movement and for various reasons the state was less effective at repressing them than at repressing secular groups. The diversification of movement actors also included journalists and lawyers, and in Chapter 5 I explore how and why they became key contributors to the democracy movement in the latter part of the 1970s. Although each group addressed different aspects of Park Chung Hee's authoritarian government, both journalists and lawyers came to the fore of the movement as the severity of state repression reached new heights. The chapters in Part 2 thus detail the differential impact of state repression as it led to the demobilization of some movement groups while politicizing others.

The diversification of actors participating in antigovernment protests triggered important changes in the democracy movement. The chapters in Part 3 assess how the movement evolved as dissidents adapted to new repressive measures by the state. In Chapter 6, I argue that state repression unintentionally motivated the development of protest strategies and the movement's ideology. Because different groups relied on tactics that were specific to their own community norms, the demise of the student movement and the entry of new movement actors altered the overall character of the movement. Similarly, whereas the initial goals of the movement in the early 1970s revolved around democratic and economic reforms, new actors further diversified the issues that were raised in antigovernment protests. In short, the diversification of movement participants subsequently led to the diversification of their tactical repertoire and the discursive challenge that dissidents raised against the Yusin government. These developments, it is important to note, occurred when the overall number of protest events plummeted after the systematic repression of the student movement in 1974 and the promulgation of Emergency Decree 9 in 1975.

In Chapter 7, I explore an additional unintended consequence of state repression. The diversification of movement actors provided the opportunity to create alliances and coalitions, which in turn strengthened the solidarity of the movement. Movement solidarity was primarily driven by the repression strategies employed by the state against dissenting groups. The impact of outgroup contention on ingroup solidarity was evident in the formation of loose alliances between diverse sectors of the democracy movement. These informal alliances led in turn to formal coalitional organizations that brought together Christians, journalists, lawyers, laborers, oppositional politicians, intellectuals, and students. Some of the alliances first established in the 1970s, most notably between students and workers, set the stage for the important relationships that defined the democracy movement in the 1980s (Lee 2007).

In the concluding chapter I discuss the legacy of the 1970s democracy movement to South Korea's democratization. Although the Yusin system ended with Park Chung Hee's death in 1979, social movements active during his rule continued to have consequences for the democracy movement in the 1980s. Subsequent movements inherited from the 1970s several important pillars of mobilization, including a generation of leaders who came of age during the Yusin period, organizational models, and master symbols that defined movement ideology. This is not to overlook significant differences between activism in the 1970s and activism in the 1980s: the latter involved a process of radicalization after the shock of the massacre in the 1980 Gwangju Uprising (Lee 2007). The purpose instead is to remember that "perhaps movements are never really born anew. Rather, they contract and hibernate, sustaining the totally dedicated and devising strategies appropriate to the external environment" (Taylor 1989: 772). It is the hope of this book to tell the story of those who sacrificed much— and in some cases all—for the possibility of democracy in South Korea, and to give due credit to them for planting the seeds that matured into the vibrant civil society in South Korea today.

MOVEMENT CONTEXT

Part 1

1 THE MAKING OF THE AUTHORITARIAN STATE

Today, at this place, I clearly say to you all that this will be the last
political speech where I ask you to vote for me as president.

Park Chung Hee, campaign promise, April 25, 1971

A recent flurry of scholarship has taken stock of Park Chung Hee and the "Park Chung Hee era" (Lee 2012; Kim and Vogel 2011; Kim and Sorensen 2011; Lee 2006). Contemporary evaluations of Park Chung Hee's tenure as South Korea's leader tend to focus on two main themes: economic development and dictatorship. Studies of development, for the most part, paint Park Chung Hee as orchestrator of the economic "miracle on the Han" (see among others, Lee 2006; Kim 2004), while scholarship on Korean politics identifies him as first in a line of military dictators who established a harsh autocracy that lasted until democratic transition in 1987 (Park 2011; Kim J. H. 2011).[1] Both emphases in the literature are critical to understanding the trajectory of South Korea's modernization in the postliberation period, and it is fitting that Park's legacy has motivated the application of new terms, including the apt "developmental dictator" (Lee 2006). This chapter sets the stage for the analysis of South Korea's democracy movement by highlighting the *transformation* of Park's government as repression became an increasingly essential feature of his ruling strategy.

There were in fact three distinct phases of Park Chung Hee's rule. He first ruled South Korea under the banner of a military government, from 1961 to 1963, before transitioning to a period of "democratic interlude" or "soft authoritarianism," when the legitimacy of his presidency was based on democratically held elections in 1963 and 1967 (Im 2011: 234). In the third phase, Park reverted back to formal authoritarianism after unilaterally promulgating dramatic constitutional revisions that suspended direct presidential elections and ensured his lifelong rule. After the promulgation of the Yusin Constitution in 1972, however,

Park increasingly relied on repressive measures in direct response to the growing voices of dissent that challenged his leadership. Indeed, the core components of Park Chung Hee's authoritarianism "were continually evolving entities" (Kim B. K. 2011a: 4) that developed over the eighteen years of his rule. Understanding these transformations requires a temporal assessment of the historical events that culminated in the Yusin regime.

THE "DEMOCRATIC INTERLUDE" (1963–1971)

In April 1960, the First Republic of South Korea came to an end when Syngman Rhee abdicated the presidency following the April 19, or "4.19," student revolution. The subsequent government under Chang Myŏn and Yun Posŏn proved to be ephemeral, and on May 16, 1961, a "second-tier leader," two-star Major General Park Chung Hee, successfully executed a coup d'état and established the Supreme Council for National Reconstruction (Kukka Chaegŏn Ch'oego Hoeŭi) in place of the government (Han 2011: 35).[2] Partly because Park Chung Hee's coup restored order and stability at a time when the nation seemed to be plunging into social chaos amid growing political demonstrations, hyperinflation, and spikes in the crime rate (Kim 2004: 45), student activists and the greater part of society initially maintained a "wait and see" attitude. In addition, after a short deliberation about the advantages and disadvantages that Park Chung Hee represented to American interests in Korea and East Asia, "the United States accepted the coup as a fait accompli" and did not interfere with Park's power grab (Kim and Baik 2011; see also Brazinsky 2007) .

Park Chung Hee, for his part, attempted to garner public support by claiming that the "5.16 Military Administration"—marking the day of the coup—was merely a temporary government and promising to reinstitute democratic procedures in due time. Responding to the increasing demand from both the Korean people and the United States to follow through on his promise, Park Chung Hee announced the reestablishment of civilian rule by means of a presidential election scheduled for October 15, 1963. Park promptly retired from the military and ran successfully, thus becoming the president of South Korea's Third Republic.[3]

At this early stage, it was still important for Park Chung Hee to build legitimacy for his government and win the support of the Korean people. Park was acutely aware of the powerful potential of student mobilization to facilitate social change, and he argued that his own "May Revolution" was a continuation of the 4.19 student revolution. In his inaugural address on December 17, 1963,

Park Chung Hee presented a narrative that linked his May 1961 coup d'état with the 4.19 revolution:

> Our fiery democratic convictions overthrew dictatorship in the April Revolution. This was succeeded by the May Revolution, which rejected corruption and injustice, restored the national spirit, and made possible the construction of the new republic which comes into existence today. Our unavoidable historical task in this decade, as initiated in the course of the April and May Revolutions, is the modernization of the fatherland in all fields—political, economic, social and culture. . . . On this meaningful occasion, I therefore propose a great reform movement to materialize our national ideals as demonstrated by the April 19 and May 16 Revolutions. . . . (Park 1970: 286)

Ignoring students who insisted that "the 4.19 and 5.16 Revolutions cannot coexist,"[4] Park Chung Hee was able, as he began his first term, to establish social stability and restore some faith in a democratic Korea. The reinstitution of the democratic process, evidenced in the 1963 presidential election, contributed to the feeling that Park would uphold the democratic system. This feeling was also engendered by several speeches Park gave in the 1960s on the importance of further consolidating democracy in Korea. On May 27, 1965, for example, upon returning from a visit to the United States, he exhorted the Korean people to become better democratic citizens:

> The flower of democracy does not bloom, if there is no attempt to realize it. Before one preaches democracy, one should first be a good democratic citizen. We Koreans should recognize again what democracy is and discipline ourselves to be democratic citizens. Without this effort, democracy and the construction of democratic society is impossible and the flower of democracy will not bloom. (Park 1970: 315)

At the start of his first term, then, hope remained that Park Chung Hee's presidency would be the kind of democratic government that had been promised to the Korean people in 1948. But within a few years this hope, along with invocations of the 4.19 student revolution, would dissipate, when Park Chung Hee pushed through controversial policies that reignited large protests. The commitment to send South Korean troops to participate in the Vietnam War and the unpopular decision to normalize diplomatic relations with Japan were driven by the two central concerns of Park Chung Hee's government: national security and economic development.

Participation in the Vietnam War and
the Normalization of Relations with Japan

It is important to situate Park Chung Hee's decision to deploy South Korean troops to Vietnam in the larger context of the international Cold War. Although the role that the United States played in the founding of the Republic of Korea in 1948 and in the Korean War (1950–1953) reflected the importance of South Korea to America's East Asian foreign policy, U.S. commitment to its small ally was at times doubted by the South Korean leadership. This was especially true in the period leading up to the Korean War, when top American political leaders debated the extent to which they would go to protect South Korea in the case of a communist incursion. Most notably, U.S. Secretary of State Dean Acheson reiterated in January 1950 America's commitment to protecting Japan while leaving South Korea outside the U.S. defense perimeter.[5] When this scenario was made known, it triggered a "deeply ingrained fear of abandonment" in South Korea (Lee M. Y. 2011: 404). Although America's subsequent involvement in the Korean War reassured South Koreans that the United States was indeed committed to protecting its ally, Korean political and military leaders never forgot the shocking possibility of Dean Acheson's initial proposal.

In the 1960s, America's involvement in the Vietnam War led to the redistribution of its military resources in the Asia-Pacific region, and plans were put in place to dispatch a significant number of U.S. troops from South Korea to Vietnam. Fears that the reduction in U.S. troops would compromise South Korea's national security were compounded by a significant decline in U.S. military aid to Korea, "from an annual average of $232 million during the 1956–1961 period to $154 million for the 1962-1965 period" (Lee M. Y. 2011: 405). Eager for America to maintain its commitment to South Korean security, Park Chung Hee informed President John F. Kennedy during their summit meeting in Washington, D.C., in 1961 of his willingness to dispatch Korean soldiers to Vietnam (Lee M. Y. 2011: 409). A formal request for Korean participation in the Vietnam War was made by President Lyndon B. Johnson a few years later, on May 1, 1964, and by the following September, Park Chung Hee had sent nearly two thousand noncombat troops to Vietnam (Kim J. H. 2011: 173).

Within a year, South Korea sent combat troops as well, and at peak deployment there were fifty thousand Korean soldiers in Vietnam, making South Korea the country "with the second-largest number of military troops after the United States" (Lee M. Y. 2011: 404). From 1964 to 1973, some three hundred thousand Korean soldiers participated in the Vietnam War (Cumings 1997:

THE MAKING OF THE AUTHORITARIAN STATE 19

321). In return, from 1965 to 1972, the United States rewarded South Korea with roughly a billion dollars in financial support, as well as with assurances that it would not reduce the number of American military troops stationed in South Korea (Lee M. Y. 2011: 425; Cumings 1997: 321).

The "extraordinary" rewards (Katsiaficas 2012: 142) that South Korea would reap from its participation in the Vietnam War did not, however, preclude significant opposition from institutional politicians when Park Chung Hee submitted to the National Assembly the bill for dispatch of combat troops. When it came time to vote, legislators from the opposition parties boycotted the session, but Park's Democratic Republican Party (DRP; Minju Konghwadang) occupied enough seats in the National Assembly to pass the bill anyway. Park's complete disregard for minority party members and his unwillingness to engage in dialogue and debate were early signs that he would not entertain challenges to his policies. This authoritarian tendency became more evident when Park initiated the process of reestablishing diplomatic relations with Japan. Both the bill for the dispatch of troops and the bill for normalization of relations with Japan were presented to the National Assembly on July 14, 1965. The latter bill was more controversial than the dispatch bill, and a majority of opposition party members resigned their parliamentary positions en masse in protest of Park's efforts to normalize relations with Japan.

The motivation to reestablish relations with Japan was predicated on similar anxieties that prompted South Korea's entry into the Vietnam War. Because "his rule coincided with a sharp decline in annual U.S. economic aid" (Lee M. Y. 2011: 407), Park Chung Hee needed alternative sources of capital to fuel his economic programs. Although the successful normalization of relations with Japan in 1965 secured "$800 million in grants and preferential loans as reparations for Japanese colonial wrongdoings" (Lee M. Y. 2011: 425), this sparked the first large wave of protests since Park Chung Hee took power in 1961. Park was accused by various segments of Korean society, including opposition party members, intellectuals, and students, of selling out the country by conceding to a "humiliating agreement" (kuryokchŏk in hyŏpchŏng) with Japan.[6] Beginning in March 1964, students nationwide staged protests that were the largest since the April 1960 revolution. Park responded to this "explosion of student protests" (Kim B. K. 2011a: 25) by declaring martial law on June 3, 1964, and deploying military personnel to the cities to violently put down student demonstrations.[7] Park's disregard for the legislative process when pushing through the troop dispatch bill, and his use of the military to quell student protesters during the

Japan normalization process, unequivocally confirmed his authoritarian tendencies and his willingness to apply violent repression strategies to oppositional forces. The crackdown on student protests in 1964 and 1965 set precedence for state-society relations in the years to come as Park Chung Hee moved the country increasingly toward a formal authoritarian state.

Toward Formal Authoritarianism

Having successfully put down the demonstrations against normalization with Japan and secured Japanese and U.S. foreign capital commitments to support his economic programs, Park Chung Hee finished his first presidential term. Bolstered by the significant economic growth that his policies created, Park beat past president Yun Posŏn in the 1967 presidential election, winning just over 51 percent of the popular vote. He began his second term in July 1967, intent on continuing and expanding the economic programs he deemed necessary to modernize South Korea. Park was keenly aware of the two-term limitation for presidents that the existing constitution imposed and, unwilling to relinquish power, he orchestrated a constitutional amendment in 1969 that would allow for a third term. The proposed amendment was met with fierce opposition from minority party members in the legislature. Realizing that Park Chung Hee's DRP had the necessary two-thirds majority to pass the amendment, opposition party members staged a sit-in rally in the plenary session hall of the National Assembly. Choosing to sidestep the challenge rather than face it, members of the DRP met on September 14, 1969, "at 2:27 AM in an annex building to pass its bill" (Kim B. K. 2011b: 156). The meeting took all of six minutes. The constitutional amendment allowing Park Chung Hee to run for president in 1971 was finalized after a national referendum conducted in October 1969 showed that 65.1 percent of the Korean people approved of the amendment (Kim B. K. 2011b: 156).

Park Chung Hee's manipulation of the constitution to prolong his rule further confirmed suspicions that his promise to foster democracy in South Korea was just rhetoric. For many observers, the push for extra-constitutional extension of the presidency was becoming all too familiar and some noted the similarities between Park's 1969 power play and Syngman Rhee's rule. Writing in the period after the 1969 amendment and before the 1971 presidential election, David C. Cole and Princeton N. Lyman, who in the mid-1960s had been in Korea acting as economic advisors to Park's government, warned that "the unwillingness of the president to step aside at the end of his second term, which repeats the pattern of Syngman Rhee, raises the possibility that he will try to remain in office indefinitely" (1971: vi). The students and citizens who maintained a "wait and see" attitude when Park assumed control in 1961 now saw his true will to power. Students again led the charge and organized large protests demanding that Park step down as president. In the fall of 1969, student protesters and the police squared off in what were often violent exchanges, and it wasn't until Park closed down thirty-eight universities on September 10, 1969, that social order on university campuses was restored (Kim B. K. 2011b: 156). In addition to forcefully repressing student criticisms, Park Chung Hee justified the constitutional amendment by arguing that a third term was necessary for the continuation of economic progress.

Repression and justifications aside, Park insisted that if he was democratically elected again in 1971, it would be his last term, because he would relinquish power at the end of the third term. This was indeed a salient campaign promise, made in a speech given on April 25, 1971, just two days before the election:

> It is said that "if we vote for President Park again, he will make an authoritarian system and President Park will be president until he dies." Today, at this place, I clearly say to you all that this will be the last political speech where I ask you to vote for me as president. (Minjuhwa Undong Kinyŏm Saŏphoe 2006)

Belying Park Chung Hee's campaign promise to relinquish power at the end of the third term, scholars argue that before the presidential election in 1971 he already had concrete plans in place to prolong his rule indefinitely. In his thorough analysis of the three-year period from the constitutional amendment in 1969 to the election in 1971, Hyug Baeg Im (2011) has shown that Park Chung Hee consolidated his power within the DRP by demoting and purging second-tier leaders who might have entertained hopes of succeeding him at the end of his second term. In what amounted to a dizzying array of political moves, Park imperiously "cleared the road towards his lifelong presidency" by "undermining the power bases of all major DRP leaders" (Im 2011: 242). These steps set the stage for formal authoritarianism in 1972 as Park Chung Hee moved "incrementally but consistently" toward the Yusin Constitution (Kim B. K. 2011a: 30).

The first step was to weaken the mainstream faction of the DRP that supported Kim Chongp'il, who had orchestrated the coup d'état in 1961 and was Park's long-standing second in command. Because the mainstream faction was loyal to Kim Chongp'il and expected that he would be the DRP's presidential candidate in 1971 after Park's second term, they were against the constitutional amendment in 1969. Park reacted to their insolence by "purging Yang Sun-jik, Ye Ch'un-ho, Chŏng T'ae-sŏng, and Kim Tal-su of the mainstream faction from the DRP," even though this action jeopardized the two-thirds majority that the DRP enjoyed in the National Assembly (Im 2011: 240). Park complemented this move by strengthening a separate DRP faction that led the charge for the constitutional amendment: the so-called Gang of Four, consisting of Kim Sŏnggon, Paek Namŏk, Kil Chaeho, and Kim Chinman (Im 2011: 240; Sohn 1989: 30).

After securing the amendment, however, Park Chung Hee turned on the Gang of Four under the pretense that they disobeyed his orders when they criticized his appointment of O Ch'isŏng as Interior Minister. Park knew that with Kim Chongp'il out of the way, the Gang of Four, as the new leaders of the DRP, harbored hopes of replacing him in 1975 at the end of his third presidential term. The punishment for harboring these hopes and disobeying Park's order to support O Ch'isŏng was severe. Kim Sŏnggon and Kil Chaeho were tortured by the Korean Central Intelligence Agency (KCIA, Chungang Chŏngbobu), after which the power of the Gang of Four was broken (Sohn 1989: 30). These drastic moves had the effect of "eliminating all second-tier leaders who might have had any ambition to succeed him" (Kim B. K. 2011a: 30) while concentrating the power of the DRP in the hands of Park Chung Hee.

Although Park won the presidential election in April 1971 with 53.2 percent of the vote—beating oppositional candidate Kim Dae Jung by fewer than a million votes—it was during this time that Park solidified his resolve to transition to formal authoritarianism (Nohlen, Grotz, and Hartmann 2001).[8] The surprising popularity of Kim Dae Jung in the elections, even though limited access to media and other restrictions were imposed on Kim's campaign, was a "personal defeat for him" (Sohn 1989: 32) and signaled to Park Chung Hee that the democratic system could not be relied on to ensure his rule. Compounding these anxieties were the results of the general elections that were held one month after Park won the presidential election. Park's DRP secured its majority standing in the National Assembly but lost a significant number of seats to the opposition New Democratic Party (NDP; Sinmindang) and no longer retained the necessary two-thirds margin to pass another constitutional amendment. This outcome was indeed a sobering shock, and after the general elections, Park realized that he "could only resort to extra-constitutional measures to stay in power after his third term expired in 1975" (Im 2011: 246).

THE YUSIN REGIME (1972–1979)

On October 17, 1972, Park Chung Hee declared martial law and deployed the military to secure central locations in Seoul in preparation for implementing the "Reforms for National Resurrection" (Park 1973: 25). In this special presidential declaration (Taet'ongnyŏng t'ŭkpyŏl sŏnŏn), Park promulgated four "extraordinary measures" that outlined the process of transitioning to a formal authoritarian government (Park 1973: 31):

1. As of 1900 hours on October 17, 1972, the effects of certain Articles of the Constitution shall be suspended: the National Assembly shall be dissolved, and the activities of all political parties and other political activities shall be suspended;

2. The functions provided for in the suspended Articles of the present Constitution shall be performed by the Extraordinary State Council (Pisang Kungmu Hoeŭi). The functions of the Extraordinary State Council shall be carried out by the State Council under the present Constitution;

3. The Extraordinary State Council shall announce by October 27, 1972, draft amendments to the present Constitution with the view of peaceful unification of the nation. The draft amendments to the Constitution shall be put to a national referendum and be affirmed within one month from the date of their announcement; and

4. In case the draft amendments to the Constitution are affirmed, the constitutional order shall be normalized by the end of this year at the latest in accordance with the procedures set forth in the Constitution as amended.

The "draft amendments" mentioned in the special declaration were in essence an entirely new constitution that Park Chung Hee had been planning throughout 1971. Earlier that year, Park Chung Hee instigated the "Good Harvest Project" (p'ungnyŏn saŏp), which brought together key figures—KCIA Director Yi Hurak, Minister of Justice Sin Chiksu, KCIA Deputy Director Kim Ch'iyŏl, Senior Secretary of Political Affairs Hong Sŏngch'ŏl, and other legal and academic advisors—who were entrusted with drafting the amendments (Im 2011: 243). Following the special declaration on October 17, the process moved rather quickly. The public announcement of the Yusin Constitution occurred on October 27 as planned, and the national referendum was held on November 21 under martial law. After the votes for the referendum were counted, Park Chung Hee justified the Yusin Constitution by declaring, "It is now clear that the people, through the exercise of their sacred sovereign right, have demonstrated that they are the prime force to push through the revitalizing reforms" (Park 1973: 34–35).

The actual substance of the amended constitution contradicted the rhetoric that Park Chung Hee spouted in his special declaration on October 17, when he expressed his "profound conviction that free democratic institutions in this country should be fostered and developed more soundly, substantially and efficiently" (Park 1973: 31). Although he admitted that "we can hardly find any other political system better than the free democratic one," apparently he was able to find one after all. The Yusin Constitution fundamentally transformed Korea's political system by limiting the democratic process in several key ways. Most drastic was the suspension of direct presidential elections in favor of indirect elections through an electoral college. The Supreme Council for National Reunification (SCNR; T'ongil Chuch'e Kungmin Hoeŭi Taeŭiwŏn) consisted of 2,359 members who, on December 23, 1972, voted to elect Park Chung Hee as the first president under the new system. Only two members of the SCNR did not vote for Park Chung Hee, and it was evident to all observers that the electoral college was only a facade of a democratic institution, one that would rubber-stamp Park's elections (Minjuhwa Undong Kinyŏm Saŏphoe 2006). Presumably, with the shift from direct to indirect presidential elections, Park Chung Hee kept his 1971 campaign promise that he would not ask South Korean citizens to vote for him in any future elections.

In addition to denying citizens the right to vote for the president, the Yusin Constitution also extended the length of a single presidential term to six years and, more important, lifted the limit on the number of terms that could be served. Given the SCNR's power to elect the president and the possibility of unlimited presidential terms, the Yusin Constitution for all practical purposes ensured Park Chung Hee's lifelong rule.

Having established the political procedures necessary to ensure indefinite rule, the Yusin Constitution further concentrated power in the presidency by compromising the independence of the legislative and judicial branches of government. After the National Assembly was allowed to reconvene, Park Chung Hee exercised the power to appoint one-third of its members directly, which effectively guaranteed a legislative majority for Park's own party. In addition, the Yusin Constitution did away with the Council on the Nomination of Justices, a semi-independent body that was responsible for appointing judges at the central and local levels. Park Chung Hee was now able to appoint unilaterally the Chief Justice of the Supreme Court, who then had the power to select the other

Supreme Court justices as well as lower-court judges. In short, though there were conspicuous manifestations of Park Chung Hee's authoritarian tendencies in the 1960s—including most notably his willingness to use the military to suppress public protests and his disregard for the democratic process when dealing with the National Assembly—the promulgation of the Yusin Constitution removed all semblance of democratic governance by creating an authoritarian political *structure* that led to "the most repressive seven-year period" in modern South Korean history (Minjuhwa Undong Kinyŏm Saŏphoe 2006).

Justifying Yusin: Economic Development and National Security

The transition to a formal authoritarian regime was facilitated by Park Chung Hee's use of coercive force to silence criticism from institutional politicians as well as from society at large. On the same day that he announced the four "extraordinary measures" that outlined the plan for establishing the Yusin Constitution, the military, at the behest of the Army Security Command, implemented a dual strategy of (1) arresting opposition politicians on trumped-up charges of illegal fundraising for Kim Dae Jung during the 1971 elections, and (2) placing soldiers in key areas around Seoul to preempt public demonstrations (Kim J. H. 2011: 188). In addition to this exercise of material power, however, Park waged a discursive campaign aimed at justifying his new government. In several speeches, including one delivered on Independence Day, August 15, 1973, Park argued that "we adapted the true values of democracy in such a way that they could serve our own traditions and prevailing conditions most suitably . . . so that the democratic system could operate more effectively" (Park 1973: 51). The Yusin Constitution, according to Park, was "Korean-style democracy" (*Han'gukchŏk minjujuŭi*) and appropriate for the unique challenges that South Korea faced, including the necessity to develop the economy and protect national security.

Economic development was a primary concern for Park Chung Hee from the very beginning of his rule. Soon after the military coup in 1961, Park established the Economic Planning Board (EPB), which implemented a series of five-year economic plans (5-kaenyŏn kyŏngje kaebal kyehoek) with the larger goal of industrializing South Korea. These efforts resulted in a 7.8 percent rise in the gross national product by the end of the first five-year plan (1962–1966) and another 10.5 percent increase by the end of the second five-year plan (1967–1971; Oh 1991). Park cited this "miracle of the Han" to justify his leadership because "he needed economic progress to defend his political base against those who regarded his seizure of power as illegitimate" (Vogel 1991: 51). Starting in

1969, however, the economy began to falter, partly because of a world recession sparked by growing concern over a global oil shortage, a problem that
peaked in 1973 (Merrill 2007). The global oil crisis was particularly devastating
to the U.S. economy: its gross domestic product (GDP) dropped to 0 percent
growth in 1970 and Americans saw their gas prices go from thirty-five cents a
gallon to ninety cents in the 1970s.[9] The combination of economic recession
and rising inflation led to new American protectionist policies, including taxes
on imports, which compromised Korea's export-dependent economy. Because
the U.S. market accounted for 40 percent of exports, between 1969 and 1973—a
period directly corresponding to Park Chung Hee's move toward formal authoritarianism—GDP growth in South Korea slowed dramatically for "the first
time since Park embarked on export-led industrialization" (Im 2011: 248, 250).

The extraordinary powers invested in Park Chung Hee through the Yusin
Constitution were presumably a necessary response to the economic crisis.
Earlier, on August 3, 1972, Park had already promulgated the Emergency Decree for Economic Stability and Growth (Kyŏngje ŭi sŏngjang kwa anjŏng e
kwanhan kin'gŭp myŏngnyŏng), which relieved the debilitating private curb-
market loans of the chaebŏls, Korea's large conglomerates (Kim and Park 2011:
285). Park Chung Hee interpreted the results of the national referendum on the
new constitution as "overwhelming popular support" for continuing his strong
leadership and declared in a speech commemorating the ninth Export Day on
November 30, 1972, that the new "revitalizing reforms" would "ensure our national prosperity by boosting and solidifying our national strength" (Park 1973:
130). Prioritizing the economy over democracy, Park "emphasized that without
'economic equality,' political democracy is no more than an 'abstract, useless
concept'" (Oh 1999: 52). Even more poignant was Park's reasoning that developing nations sometimes "have to resort to undemocratic and extraordinary
measures in order to improve the living conditions of the masses. . . . One cannot deny that people are more frightened of poverty and hunger than totalitari-
anism" (quoted in Oh 1999: 53). In response to the economic crisis in the late
1960s and early 1970s, Park secured the power to unilaterally set economic policies and manipulate market conditions.

In addition to arguing that the Yusin Constitution was necessary to continue the successful economic policies of the 1960s, Park Chung Hee was motivated in no small part by his growing anxiety over South Korea's national
security. Although U.S. commitment to South Korean security was predicated
upon the latter's strategic role in America's Asian foreign policy, the war in Viet-

nam diverted attention away from Northeast Asia to Southeast Asia as the most important "hot spot" in the Cold War. American involvement in the Vietnam War in the 1960s necessitated the reallocation of military resources to Vietnam, which in turn weakened South Korea's military defense. This, as already discussed, motivated Park Chung Hee to deploy South Korean troops to Vietnam in exchange for security guarantees and financial incentives. Notwithstanding these guarantees, the United States reduced its troop presence in South Korea "from 64,000 soldiers in 1969 to 40,000 in 1972," which exacerbated Park's concerns about Korea's security (Lee M. Y. 2011: 422).

Perhaps more significant than the reduction of troop levels was the shifting American attitude toward both allies and communist nations. Shortly into his first year as president of the United States, Richard Nixon (in office 1969–1974) publicly declared that American allies should prepare to be responsible for their own military defense. For South Korea and Park Chung Hee, the Nixon Doctrine, declared in Guam on July 25, 1969, signaled a significant departure from the policies of the John F. Kennedy and Lyndon B. Johnson administrations (in office 1961–1963 and 1963–1969, respectively): in the 1960s, the United States had granted large military and financial assistance for the purpose of transforming its small East Asian ally into a bulwark against communist expansion.

Nixon's administration followed through on its new foreign policy strategy by instigating détente with China, starting with National Security Advisor Henry A. Kissinger's clandestine visit to China in July 1971 and President Nixon's visit the following year. In addition, when the Yusin Constitution was promulgated, Kissinger had already opened a dialogue with North Vietnam to secure America's "'honorable' exit from the Vietnam War" (Kim J. H. 2011: 176; Im 2011: 259). These were indeed monumental events in the Cold War that prompted Park Chung Hee to make a special statement on June 23, 1973, in which he suggested that "the era of Cold War after World War II has come to an end" (Park 1973: 44).

Park Chung Hee's anxieties about these "profound changes" in the international situation were not completely unfounded. As Joo-Hong Kim points out, "the coming of détente at the level of great power relations was, however, joined by an opposite trend of rising tensions on the Korean peninsula" (2011: 176). Through a series of North Korean provocations in the late 1960s, South Korea and Park Chung Hee were reminded of how quickly the Cold War could turn hot. On January 21, 1968, North Korean commandos crossed the demilitarized zone and penetrated to within one kilometer of the presidential Blue House in an attempt to assassinate Park. Just two days later, on January 23, the North Korean

Navy attacked and captured the USS Pueblo, a U.S. Navy intelligence ship, claiming that the American vessel had entered its territorial waters (Liston 1988). Later in the year, on October 30, North Korean soldiers again infiltrated South Korean territory, leading to military skirmishes in the villages of Uljin and Samcheok. The following year, on April 15, 1969, North Korea shot down a U.S. reconnaissance plane over the East Sea; and on December 11, 1969, a Korean Airlines plane that had four crewmembers and forty-six passengers on board was hijacked.

The heightened sense of threat posed to South Korea's national security by North Korean aggression was in stark contrast to the détente unfolding between the democratic and communist superpowers. Although on October 24, 1973, in a speech commemorating the twenty-eighth anniversary of the founding of the United Nations, Park acknowledged that "the world is now entering a new age of peaceful coexistence from the post-World War II Cold War era," peace was an elusive goal on the Korean peninsula (Park 1973: 198). Park Chung Hee took the Nixon Doctrine to heart and attempted to reinforce the nation's defense capabilities to compensate for the reduction of American aid and military presence in South Korea. The Yusin Constitution was part of this nation-strengthening plan, and it was made clear in the special declaration on October 17, 1972, that the potential impact of the changing international situation on South Korea's national security was the main motivation for the new constitution:

> The international situation surrounding us has undergone profound changes.
> . . . Under these circumstances we must guard ourselves against the possibility
> that the interests of Third World or smaller countries might be sacrificed for the
> relaxation of tension between powers. . . . The present Constitution, various laws
> and ordinances and the present political structure itself were all fixed in the cold-
> war era under the East-West bipolar confrontation. . . . In the face of the current
> situation, however, it is more than natural that a series of Revitalizing Reforms
> should be carried out to build up a new structure which can best adapt itself
> to the needs of the newly-developing situation. Bearing in mind the necessity
> and inevitability of such a great reformation, and facing squarely the political
> realities in this country, I have arrived at the conclusion that this sort of refor-
> mation cannot be materialized by ordinary means. (Park 1973: 25–29)

Irrespective of whether the Yusin Constitution was truly necessary to buttress security, the North Korean provocations in the late 1960s played readily into the hands of Park Chung Hee, who attempted "to mobilize public support by heightening people's fear" of external threats (Im 2011: 240). Although many would agree with Hyug Baeg Im that "it was the removal of constitutional restrictions on the number of presidential terms more than any threats of societal resistance, domestic political instability, industrial conflict, and economic crisis that appears to have motivated Park's move to the *yushin* regime" (2011: 257), it is not clear that economic growth, national security, *and* Park's will to power were mutually exclusive motivations for the new government. What is clear, however, is that Park's insistence during his 1973 New Year's message that Yusin was not incompatible with democracy—that "the new Constitution provides explicitly that the establishment of political parties shall be free, and the plural party system guaranteed . . . that the basic order of our government is derived from the democratic principle which guarantees the political freedom of the people"—was mere empty rhetoric (Park 1973: 185).

In the years following the establishment of the Yusin Constitution, Park Chung Hee continued to justify the authoritarian system. On February 12, 1975, for example, the government conducted a national referendum to gauge whether Korean citizens supported or objected to "the presidential majority policy" (UCLA Archival Collection: Box 42, Folder 3). Although the 1975 referendum, like the one in 1972, was meant to show objectively that the majority of citizens supported the Yusin system, the government resorted to using a wide variety of tactics to ensure supporting results, including the mobilization of school children and teachers to encourage positive votes, and threats by regional government officials who "made it clear that any district that had a significant negative vote would receive reduced government aid following the referendum" (UCLA Archival Collection: Box 42, Folder 3). Legitimating his government through rhetoric and referendums was clearly not enough to assuage the growing criticism of Park Chung Hee's new ruling structure. After the promulgation of the Yusin Constitution, Park increasingly relied on repressive measures to subdue dissident groups that challenged his rule, further limiting the already restricted political opportunities afforded by the new constitution. Indeed, the establishment of the Yusin regime was just the start of a longer process of consolidating authoritarianism in South Korea.

2 CONSOLIDATING AUTHORITARIANISM

The basic order of government is derived from the democratic principle which guarantees the political freedom of the people.

Park Chung Hee, New Year Message, 1973

The extraordinary measures codified in the Yusin Constitution marked a new era in South Korean political history. Although Syngman Rhee relied on ad hoc authoritarian tactics to exercise power, his government was organized within the parameters of a democratic system, however compromised, and it wasn't until the Yusin Constitution that the *structures* for authoritarian rule were established. Central to this authoritarian structure was the expanded capacity for repression in the form of new political control laws. To better understand why the period between the implementation of the Yusin Constitution in 1972 to Park's death in 1979 came to be known as the most repressive period in South Korea's history (Lee 2006), it is important to appreciate the continuing evolution of Park Chung Hee's rule.

After the Yusin Constitution installed the political structures that undergirded Park's authoritarian government, the state relied on old and new repression strategies intended to control and discipline society. During the Yusin period (1972–1979), Park continued to rely on effective state organs, such as the military and the KCIA, while turning to new presidential Emergency Decrees to quell the emerging movement for democracy. These repressive structures constituted the backbone of Park Chung Hee's regime, and the promulgation of the constitutional reforms was only the beginning of a process that Hak-Kyu Sohn has called the "consolidation of the Yushin system" (1989: 65). In short, Park's new Yusin government continued to grow ever more repressive in response to the rising critical voices against it.

REPRESSIVE STRUCTURES:
THE MILITARY, KCIA, AND POLITICAL CONTROL LAWS

Ruud Koopmans (1997) provides a useful typology of state repression strategies that differentiates *structural* repression from *situational* repressive tactics. The former identifies the institutional mechanisms that limit political freedoms, which are broadly applicable to varied situations, while the latter constitutes the specific ways in which state organs deal with "on-the-ground" antistate protests (Chang and Vitale 2013). Although the two types of repression are related—for example, when new repressive laws justify police responses to public protests—Koopmans's typology allows us to distinguish between the sources and applications of state repression. The coercive capacity of Park Chung Hee's Yusin regime was significantly enhanced by repressive state organs that reflected the institutionalization of authoritarian power and were used to implement a far-reaching strategy of disciplining antigovernment groups in Korean society.

By the time Park Chung Hee rose to the rank of major general, the South Korean military constituted a powerful force in Korea. The primary catalyst for its growth was the Korean War (1950–1953), during which "Korean forces had increased from 65,000 to over 700,000 men" (Cole and Lyman 1971: 22). Even after Park Chung Hee retired from the military to run as a civilian in the 1963 presidential election, the armed forces were a continual source of support for him. Park turned to trusted military colleagues to staff key bureaucratic and political positions in his government, and in the 1971 National Assembly elections alone, retired generals accounted for 46.6 percent of Park's DRP candidates (Kim J. H. 2011: 186). As Joo-Hong Kim notes, these "officers-turned-bureaucrats took on the role of a royal guard for the *yushin* regime within the state bureaucracy" (2011: 193).

In addition to providing Park with a pool of loyal supporters to work in his government, the military also played a central role in securing social stability during critical junctures throughout his tenure. Delegating his orders through the two key military control units, the Army Security Command (ASC) and the Capital Garrison Command (CGC), Park declared martial law five times during the 1960s and 1970s, and deployed military troops into the cities three different times after issuing garrison decrees (Kim J. H. 2011: 168, 171).[1]

Martial law, declared on June 3, 1964, and a garrison decree on August 26, 1965, stifled the contentious mobilization against the South Korea–Japan normalization treaty. Soon after, Park faced another cycle of protests following the constitutional amendment that allowed him to run for president a third time in 1971. Reacting to the large student protests that occurred before and after the 1971 presidential election, Park Chung Hee issued a second garrison decree on October 15 of that year. The military was deployed to universities where major demonstrations took place, and semipermanent quarters were established near campuses so that soldiers could quickly confront students in what were often violent exchanges. The 1971 garrison decree led to the arrest of more than a thousand students.

It wasn't until the very end of his presidency, on October 20, 1979, that Park Chung Hee issued the third garrison decree. Preceded by another proclamation of martial law on October 18, the third garrison decree was Park's response to the massive demonstrations that had erupted in the cities of Busan, Masan, and Changwon. Just six days after the garrison decree, however, Park Chung Hee was assassinated and the military, led by General Chun Doo Hwan, stepped in to restore order in the aftermath of Park's unexpected death. Evidently, throughout Park's rule (and after), the "armed forces served him both as the ultimate guarantor of political order in times of crisis and as a stable supplier of loyalists and supporters to man the key institutions of his political regime" (Kim J. H. 2011: 168).

Although the military played an important role at critical periods, Park Chung Hee relied most consistently and heavily on the KCIA to monitor society. The KCIA was created on June 19, 1961, by Park's interim military administration under the leadership of Kim Chongp'il. Unlike its American counterpart, the KCIA was designed at the outset to coordinate both domestic and international intelligence gathering. Indeed, the KCIA monopolized almost all information on national security and even possessed considerable power over other segments of government, including the military's ASC and CGC (Kim J. H. 2011: 168, 171). Designated the central state organ in Park's strategy to defend South Korea from communist threats, the KCIA's power to investigate individuals and organizations accused of antiregime activities was nearly unlimited.

The KCIA was led consecutively by a series of high-ranking military officers in the Republic of Korea Army who were personally loyal to Park Chung Hee: Kim Chongp'il (KCIA director from 1961–1963, one-star brigadier general, and main architect of the 1961 coup), Kim Hyŏnguk (1963–1969, one-star brigadier general), Yi Hurak (1970–1973, two-star major general), Sin Chiksu (1973–1976, major general), and Kim Chaegyu (1976–1979, three-star lieutenant general).[2] Because the KCIA occupied a central position in the repressive apparatus of the

Yusin system, its directors were granted privileged access to Park Chung Hee and, according to Byung-Kook Kim, could "knock on his door anytime day or night, if necessary" (2011b: 147).

The KCIA exercised extraordinary powers and its activities often went beyond legally defined objectives and jurisdiction. In 1968, for example, KCIA agents kidnapped Korean citizens living in West Germany and brought them back to South Korea to charge them with violating Korea's National Security Law (NSL). This incident set a precedent for the 1973 kidnapping in Tokyo, Japan, of Kim Dae Jung, the main opposition candidate against Park Chung Hee in the 1971 presidential election.[3] In addition to carrying out the kidnappings, the KCIA also spearheaded one of the boldest attempts to influence a foreign government: in what became known as the 1976 "Koreagate" scandal, KCIA agents illegally lobbied and bribed U.S. congressmen in an effort to win favors for the Korean government.[4] Although Koreagate was a debacle for Park Chung Hee's government, leading to the defection of some key KCIA agents and strained relations with the United States, the incident reflected the incredible scope of KCIA programs. During the Park Chung Hee era, as Byung-Kook Kim puts it, "behind every major political plot stood the KCIA" (2011b: 155).

International escapades notwithstanding, the KCIA was most effective when surveilling domestic actors who represented threats to Park Chung Hee's rule. The sources of that threat, whether institutional politicians or dissident students, did not matter. So many dissidents were taken to be interrogated at the KCIA facility in the Seobinggo district, at the foot of South Mountain (Namsan) in central Seoul, that activists would joke that they were checking into the "Seobinggo Hotel VIP room." The euphemism belies the terror the KCIA represented as it frequently spied on, harassed, investigated, detained, and tortured participants in the democracy movement. The KCIA was responsible for the most egregious human rights violations in the 1970s, including the People's Revolutionary Party case discussed in Chapter 3. It was, simply put, the most feared and despised institution during the Park Chung Hee era.

In addition to relying on repressive organs such as the military and the KCIA, Park Chung Hee's Yusin regime also enacted "political control laws" (chŏngch'i kyujepŏp). The two most notorious of these were the NSL and the Anti-Communist Law (ACL).[5] Based on the Law for the Maintenance of Public Security, which was in effect during the Japanese colonial period (1910–1945), the NSL was created in 1948 by the First Republic of South Korea under Syngman Rhee to "restrict antistate acts that endanger national security and to protect the nation's safety and its people's lives and freedom" (Kukka Inkwŏn Wiwŏnhoe 2002). The NSL targeted individuals who the government believed were communists or sympathizers of the communist regime in North Korea, but it was also freely used to arrest and incarcerate dissidents who mobilized for a democratic South Korea. For those in the democracy movement, the NSL was a salient symbol of state structural repression.

To further strengthen the state's ability to suppress communist elements in South Korea, Park Chung Hee's interim military administration passed the ACL on July 3, 1961, immediately after his coup d'état. Although the ACL "overlapped the National Security Law in many respects . . . [it] permitted a very wide interpretation of socialism, and thus, even more than the National Security Law, could restrict academic freedom, freedom of thought and conscience, and the freedom of political and social activities" (Seo 2007: 135). Throughout the 1970s, the NSL and the ACL served as legal tools for arresting and prosecuting antigovernment dissidents.[6] A comprehensive study of the government's use of the NSL and other political control laws—conducted by the National Human Rights Commission of Korea (Kukka Inkwŏn Wiwŏnhoe) and cosponsored by the Association of Family Members of Democracy Movement Practitioners (Minjuhwa Silch'ŏn Kajok Undong Hyŏbŭihoe)—showed that from 1970 to 1979, 1,229 and 3,082 individuals were arrested under the NSL and ACL, respectively (Kukka Inkwŏn Wiwŏnhoe 2002: 23).

CONSOLIDATING AUTHORITARIANISM: THE EMERGENCY DECREES

As Park Chung Hee's Yusin regime framed dissidents as communists and arrested them under the NSL and the ACL, it continued to promulgate new laws to address specific situations as they arose. The power to enact emergency measures "for the maintenance of 'national security' and 'public peace and order'" was stipulated in Article 53 of the Yusin Constitution (Kim J. H. 2011: 188). These presidential Emergency Decrees (EDs; *kin'gŭp choch'i*) were ad hoc laws that did not need the approval of the National Assembly and, even more than the NSL and ACL, came to symbolize the repressive capacity of Park's government. Indeed, the EDs were such a salient component of the Yusin system that the 1970s is sometimes referred to as the "ED era" (*kin'gŭp choch'i sidae*). As scholars have pointed out, Park Chung Hee's first use of the EDs in the mid-1970s reflected a noticeable change in his style of leadership toward more heavy-handed repression, which in turn corresponded to significant political and personal events.

Along with the growing domestic democracy movement, the most important event during this time was America's exit from the Vietnam War beginning in 1973 and culminating in the fall of Saigon in 1975. The defeat of the United States and the victory of communism in Vietnam weighed heavy on the minds of all South Koreans, who, having experienced their own civil war, knew better than most the consequences of communist aggression. In addition to the ever-present security threat posed by North Korea and the shock of Vietnam, Park Chung Hee also experienced a deep personal loss when a Japan-born Korean, in sympathy with North Korea, attempted to murder Park but instead killed Park's wife, Yuk Yŏngsu, on August 15, 1974. According to Byung-Kook Kim, following the death of his wife, "Park lost his acumen, vigilance, and discipline, became frequently fatigued with work, and withdrew ever more into his deeply introverted personality" (2011b: 165).

The promulgation of the first two EDs marked the beginning of the process of consolidating Park Chung Hee's authoritarian control over society. Criticisms of his Yusin Constitution surfaced almost immediately after it was announced in October 1972. On December 24, 1972, Chang Chunha, founding editor of the influential *Sasangge Monthly*, and several prominent leaders in the progressive community began a no-confidence campaign against the constitutional reforms in the form of a "one-million signature" drive (Seo 2007: 190). Chang's stature as a leading public intellectual helped to popularize this conspicuous challenge to Park's government.[7] The no-confidence signature campaign, mostly organized by high-profile intellectuals and religious leaders, continued through 1973, when it was buttressed by the reemergence of large student demonstrations starting in October. By the end of 1973, Park Chung Hee faced threats on multiple fronts, which motivated his government to enact the first two EDs.

ED 1, issued on January 8, 1974, disallowed criticism of the Yusin Constitution generally, and forbade antigovernment petition drives specifically. ED 2, promulgated on the same day, designated the General Emergency Martial Court to process cases of individuals arrested under the first ED, a move that gave Park Chung Hee greater control over the judicial process. Central figures in the signature campaign, including prominent novelist Lee Ho-Chul[8] (interview with Lee Ho-Chul, December 16, 2004), were arrested for violating ED 1. Clearly, the first two EDs were a direct response to the no-confidence petition drive and the reemergence of student protests.

Student demonstrations did not subside after EDs 1 and 2. Instead they grew in size and scope through the winter of 1973 and spring of 1974. As detailed in

Chapter 3, student leaders made a concerted effort to establish a national front by creating networks among schools in different regions of the country. Pursuing a preemptive strategy, Park Chung Hee issued ED 4 on April 3, 1974, the same day that students across the country were to hold the largest nationwide day of protest since the establishment of the Yusin government.[9] ED 4 criminalized student political organizing and allowed "the KCIA, ASC, and CGC's military police to launch wholesale arrests of student activists" (Kim J. H. 2011: 192). In addition, to break the organizational foundations of the student movement, ED 4 illegalized the National Democratic Youth and Student Alliance and detailed a list of punishments for anyone who was involved in or supported this nationwide network of student activists. The mass arrest of student protesters following ED 4, and the forced closure of Korea University—a hotbed of activism—following ED 7 on April 8, 1975, crippled the student movement in the latter half of the 1970s.

The demobilization of the student movement after ED 4 became a catalyst for the politicization of new social movement actors. The severity of the repression of students alarmed many segments of Korean society as stories of torture spread through dissident networks. New groups joined the democracy movement, including progressive Christians, who emerged as the most active community engaged in public protests after ED 4 effectively stopped students from demonstrating. Additionally, as discussed in Chapter 5, state repression facilitated the politicization of journalists and lawyers who joined the democracy movement after the state censored newspapers sympathetic to the student movement and threatened lawyers who defended students arrested under the EDs.

Compounding the difficulty of facing an evolving constellation of antigovernment forces were, as mentioned earlier, significant developments in international politics, including most crucially the fall of Saigon in April 1975. ED 9, declared on May 13, 1975, was the broadly applicable answer to both the domestic and the international challenges that Park Chung Hee confronted. Among other things, ED 9 illegalized the spreading of "groundless rumors" about the government, debating the Yusin Constitution, collectively mobilizing against the government, and criticizing ED 9 itself. In essence, with its intentional vagueness, ED 9 "combined all of the past EDs into one law" and "even one wrong word could land you in jail" (Minjuhwa Undong Kinyŏm Saŏphoe 2006).[10]

The unique content and purpose of the various EDs are indicators of the relatively tight coupling between specific mobilization efforts and the government's responses to them. If the purpose of ED 1 was to discourage a particular protest tactic—the petition drive—EDs 4 and 7 were more thorough as they targeted an entire segment of the democracy movement—student activists. ED 9 represented the culmination of the ED strategy and its wide applicability was a logical response to the diversification of the democracy movement. "Legally" justified by the EDs, the government significantly expanded its capacity for repressing dissident movements through various coercive tactics, including arrest, torture, and murder.[11] In short, the antigovernment mobilization efforts of various dissident communities "influenced the forms and extent of state repression" (Yi 2011: 279), which in turn led to the further consolidation of authoritarianism in the 1970s.

Situational Repression Tactics

Legally backed by the NSL, ACL, and EDs, Park Chung Hee utilized the military, the KCIA, and the national police to suppress antigovernment protesters. The Yusin regime relied on a wide assortment of repressive actions, ranging from fairly mild tactics, such as threatening or criticizing dissidents, to extreme repression, including violence, torture, and execution. Table 2.1 summarizes the repression tactics of the Yusin regime as recorded in the Stanford KDP Events Dataset. Often the state would deploy riot police to demonstrations, sit-in rallies, employee strikes, and public declarations. The most common repression tactic used at protest sites was to arrest participants, which was often accompanied by violence. In addition to arrests and the use of violence, the state also relied on containment tactics, spoken threat, and interrogation, as well as several other strategies.

The Yusin regime strategically employed tactics tailored to specific social groups participating in the democracy movement. It often supported employers when they fired workers who attempted to organize democratic unions and fight for better working conditions. The state intervened directly in employer-worker disputes by deploying police to subdue labor strikes, at times shutting down factories altogether. Censorship was a repression tactic uniquely applied to journalists and others working in print media, such as writers and academics. Student mobilization, by contrast, was dealt with by temporarily stopping classes or closing schools and universities in order to limit students' ability to gather in large numbers. Deportation, another disciplinary measure, targeted foreigners who participated in the democracy movement. As Table 2.1 shows, the government often combined generally applicable repression tactics with more specific strategies to address different segments of the dissident community.

Table 2.1. Types of repression tactics and frequency

Severity	Repression Type	Frequency	Percent
Mild Repression			
	Denial of petition or request	14	.54
	Spoken critique or threat	126	4.84
	Government propaganda	2	.08
	Bribing	2	.08
	Subtotal: 144		5.54
Moderate Repression			
	Surveillance or spying	26	1.00
	Censoring	44	1.69
	Illegalization of movement organization	24	.92
	Harsher working conditions	34	1.31
	Cooptation	12	.46
	Subtotal: 140		5.38
Heavy Repression			
	Containment, disruption, or barricade	356	13.67
	Arrest or taken into custody	1,076	41.32
	Trashing office and confiscating files	14	.54
	Expulsion from school	62	2.38
	Interrogation or investigation	98	3.76
	Closing schools or stopping classes	128	4.92
	Wage cut or limiting funding source	16	.61
	Legal prosecution	20	.77
	Harsh treatment of prisoners	12	.46
	Firing from job or forcing resignation	130	4.99
	Closing down factory or company	16	.61
	Subtotal: 1,928		74.03
Extreme Repression			
	Violence	348	13.36
	Forced assimilation or brainwashing	16	.61
	Kidnapping	6	.23
	Sentencing to death	4	.15
	Killing	2	.08
	Deportation or denial of visa	10	.38
	Physical humiliation	6	.23
	Subtotal: 392		15.04
Total		2,604	100.00

SOURCE: Chang and Vitale 2013. Reprinted with permission of *Mobilization: An International Quarterly*. DATA SOURCE: Stanford KDP Events Dataset (1970–1979).

The Yusin government sometimes used creative tactics as well, including bribing dissidents and creating organizations that mobilized state supporters.[12] In one outlandish example, at some of the voting booths during the national referendum held on February 12, 1975, ostensibly to determine whether Korean citizens supported the Yusin system (see Chapter 1), the strings attached to the writing utensils used to mark whether one supported the constitution were purposely cut short so that voters could not reach the "not support" box (UCLA Archival Collection: Box 42, Folder 3)!

THE IMPACT OF REPRESSION ON PUBLIC PROTESTS

The application of tactics tailored for specific groups and situations shows that "states are purposive actors that are capable of acting strategically" (Moore 2000: 120). Relying on a diverse set of repression strategies, the Yusin regime became increasingly efficient at policing public protests. Jennifer Earl, Sarah A. Soule, and John D. McCarthy have conceptualized state repression decision making as a "two-stage process in which police must first decide to attend a protest event and then decide what actions to take once they are present" (2003: 585). To ascertain changes in levels of repression, it is helpful to consider the variable rate of the "repressive coverage" of protest events (Chang and Vitale 2013).

Figure 2.1 shows the annual rates of repressive coverage, calculated as the percentage of protest events at which police or other authority figures were

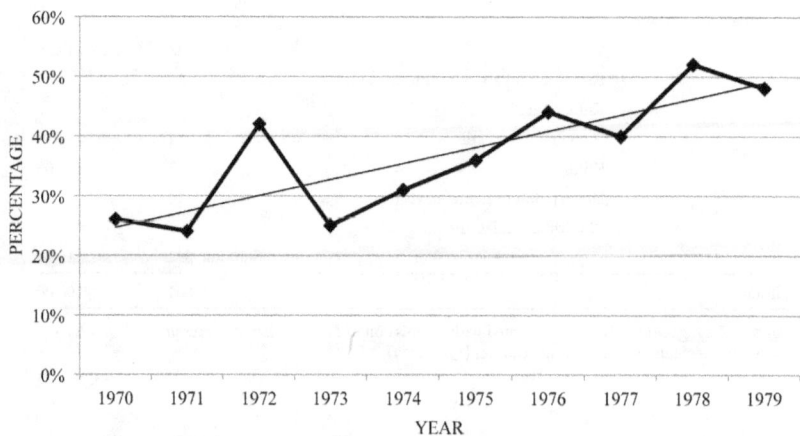

Figure 2.1. Repressive coverage of protest events

SOURCE: Chang and Vitale 2013. Reprinted with permission of *Mobilization: An International Quarterly*.
DATA SOURCE: Stanford KDP Events Dataset (1970–1979).

present. The graph makes it clear that, overall, the Yusin regime became more efficient at policing protest events. The spike in 1972 reflects the effects of the garrison decree in the fall of 1971 and the 1972 martial law, which were used to silence criticisms of Park Chung Hee's third presidential term and the passing of the Yusin Constitution, respectively. In 1973 and 1974, after martial law was lifted, the state was less likely, relatively speaking, to repress public protest. But soon, emboldened by the EDs and reacting to the diversification of dissident groups, the state stepped up its repression of protest events and in 1976 reached a level similar to the rate in 1972. This steady upward trend continued into the late 1970s, until 1978, when the Yusin regime reached the zenith of its repressive coverage of antigovernment protests.

The strengthening of the Yusin regime's capacity for repression through the promulgation of the EDs had a direct impact on dissidents' ability to stage protests. The annual counts of protest events during the 1970s show considerable fluctuation, and the regime's greater efficiency at policing protests clearly had a profound effect on the most public expression of the democracy movement. The number of protest events increased rapidly in 1971 before the promulgation of the Yusin Constitution, evident in Figure 2.2. Following a relatively quiet year in 1970, this spike was primarily driven by massive student demonstrations related to three popular issues discussed in Chapter 3. First, the suicide protest of Chŏn T'aeil, a garment factory worker, on November 13, 1970, ignited student

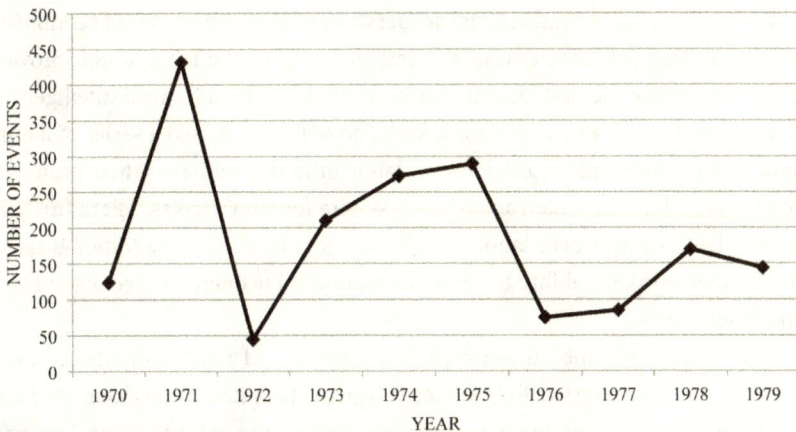

Figure 2.2. Annual counts of protest events
DATA SOURCE: Stanford KDP Events Dataset (1970–1979).

interest in labor issues and prompted students to protest for the rights of workers. Second, critical of Park's attempt to prolong his rule by amending the constitution to allow for a third term, students protested before and after the 1971 presidential election. Third, the government increased the number of mandatory hours for military training exercises on university campuses in an effort to subdue student mobilization. This new military training policy infuriated students, who took to the streets in large numbers.

The number of public protests fell precipitously in 1972, mainly due to the garrison decree that stifled student mobilization in the fall of 1971, and to the martial law declared by Park Chung Hee to support the Yusin Constitution. During most of that year, universities were closed down, curfews were stringently observed, and the military patrolled the city streets in full force: tanks and other heavy military equipment were placed in strategic locations throughout Seoul and other large urban centers. After martial law was lifted, from 1973 to 1975 the number of protest events steadily rose, but dropped again after the promulgation of the EDs, reaching its lowest points, except for 1972, in 1976 and 1977. If we were to limit our understanding of mobilization to include only macro quantitative indicators, such as aggregate counts of protest events, it is fairly clear that in the Korean case state repression was effective at subduing the democracy movement in the ED era.

The effectiveness of repression in discouraging public protests was most evident in the case of the labor movement. The government assumed that a cheap and docile labor force was necessary for industrialization and thus the control of workers was a fundamental cornerstone of Park Chung Hee's economic policy. As Jang Jip Choi notes, "the restructuring of the labor union movement was among the first tasks undertaken by the Korean Central Intelligence Agency" (1989: 30). As early as 1963, Park's government passed a series of labor laws that regulated the registration of labor unions, prohibited their political activities, and implemented an approval system for labor strikes.[13] Park further consolidated control over labor in 1970 and 1971 by enacting additional laws that limited workers' ability to mobilize around their interests (Seo 2007; Koo 2001; Ogle 1990).

The Temporary Special Act on Labor Unions and Labor Dispute Adjustment of Foreign-Invested Enterprises (Oegugin t'uja kiŏp ŭi nodong chohap mit nodongjaeng ŭi chojŏng e kwanhan imsi t'ŭngnyepŏp), passed on January 1, 1970, gave the government arbitration powers over disputes between Korean workers and companies holding foreign investments.[14] Furthermore, the Act on Special Measures for National Security (Kukka powi e kwanhan t'ŭkpyŏl choch'ipŏp), passed on December 27, 1971, prohibited labor strikes in cases of "national security."[15] Although according to Hagen Koo (2001: 159) the annual counts of union disputes remained more or less consistent throughout the 1960s and 1970s, the new labor laws significantly compromised the ability of workers to stage *public* demonstrations. Labor unrest increased in the late 1960s because of the impact of the global recession on South Korea's economy, and this large labor protest cycle continued into the early part of the 1970s. But as Figure 2.3 shows, with the implementation of the Yusin Constitution in 1972, public demonstrations organized by workers subsided as a proportion of the total number of protest events.

Some scholars note that the number of unions, and the number of members in them, grew in the 1970s, though that growth fluctuated from time to time. The increase in the 1970s in the number of unions (from 3,063 in 1970 to 4,394 in 1979; Koo 2001: 159; see also Choi 1989) and union members (from 490,000 in 1971 to 1,090,000 by 1979; Seo 2007: 219) reflects the development of the labor sector. But as George E. Ogle (1990: 77) perceptively points out, the cooptation of unions and the manipulation of union politics were important factors in curbing the effectiveness of union activities, and "union members increased without organizing by the labor movement" (Seo 2007: 219). Indeed, the sole national trade union at the time, the Federation of Korean Trade Unions (FKTU; reestablished in 1961),[16] was considered by most to be the central

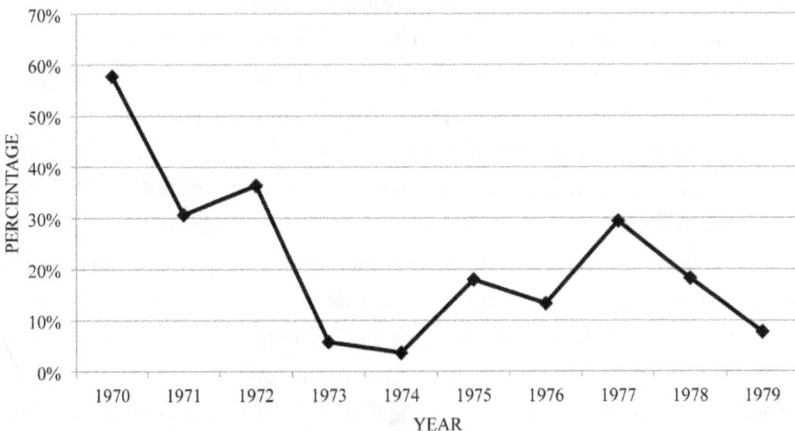

Figure 2.3. Percentage of public protest events by laborers
DATA SOURCE: Stanford KDP Events Dataset (1970–1979).

organ through which Park Chung Hee "successfully changed labor unions into company-controlled bodies under the protection of the state" (Choi 1988: 34; quoted in Lee 2006: 154).

If the 1980s labor movement was characterized by the struggle to achieve substantive material gains (Koo 2001), workers in the 1970s were still fighting for the right simply to organize around their own interests. Although important events occurred in the 1970s, such as the Tongil Textile Company and Y. H. Trading Company disputes that drew the attention of the larger public and motivated solidarity among the dissident community, these singular events belie the general trend of labor repression and cooptation during the Yusin period.

BEYOND EVENT COUNTS: REPRESSION AND MOVEMENT ADAPTATION

It is not surprising that authoritarian regimes, compared to democratic governments, have greater control over the political opportunity structure (Earl 2003: 59; see also Henderson 1991). After the Yusin Constitution was implemented in 1972, President Park Chung Hee not only secured the possibility of remaining president for life, but also was able to imperiously control South Korea's legislature and judiciary by directly appointing one third of the National Assembly and all of the Supreme Court justices. Although Park insisted that the Yusin Constitution allowed for a multiple-party political system, his DRP was so dominant in the 1970s that opposition parties were marginalized to the point of being irrelevant in institutional politics. Park buttressed his authoritarian regime by employing repressive state organs—the Korean military, the national police, and the KCIA—to suppress dissident movements while promulgating presidential EDs that provided "legal" justification for the mass arrest of antigovernment protesters. Through these various repression strategies, Park Chung Hee effectively wielded the power to discipline and punish.

Throughout the 1970s, dissident groups rose up to challenge Park Chung Hee's right to rule South Korea. Distinct from the large protest cycles in the 1960s that addressed specific policies, such as the normalization of relations with Japan and Korea's entry into the Vietnam War, the democracy movement that emerged in the 1970s targeted the authoritarian structure of Park's government. Demands for democratic reforms, however, invited repression from a government that was bent on staying in power. Emboldened by the powers vested in the authoritarian constitution, Park's government pursued extreme measures intended to discourage citizens from expressing grievances. With the passing of the EDs especially, the Yusin regime was able to police protests efficiently. During heightened periods of state repression, in 1972 and after 1975, the costs of participating in antigovernment activities increased significantly, and the number of protests dwindled as a direct consequence.

Evidently, state repression was effective at limiting public acts of contention. We would be remiss, however, if our story stopped here. In reaction to the institutionalization and consolidation of authoritarianism vis-à-vis the Yusin Constitution and increasing levels of repression, more social groups joined the democracy movement. Initially, the main actors challenging Park's rule were university students, who drew on a proud history of antigovernment mobilization, including most importantly the April 1960 revolution that pressured Syngman Rhee to resign his presidency. Recognizing the unique threat that students posed, Park Chung Hee specifically targeted them in his attempt to silence criticism against the Yusin government. The scope and severity of student repression, however, prompted important changes in the movement, including the politicization of new social movement groups. The diversification of participants in the democracy movement in turn transformed the qualitative character of antigovernment mobilization in the 1970s. As the following chapters lay out, the emergence of new movement actors and the subsequent evolution of the democracy movement were the direct results of a state repression strategy that first addressed the student movement.

MOVEMENT EMERGENCE

Part 2

3 THE RISE AND FALL
OF THE STUDENT MOVEMENT

It is said that the tree of democracy lives on by consuming blood.

Kim Sangjin, Seoul National University student, April 11, 1975

You still have many things to learn . . . Freedom to demonstrate is not democracy.

Park Chung Hee, addressing students, May 2, 1965

Immediately after a speech he gave at a student protest rally, Kim Sangjin, upon paraphrasing Thomas Jefferson's call to sacrifice, took out a knife twenty-two centimeters long and proceeded to stab himself in the abdomen. He then pulled the blade upward and to the right, cutting through his chest. As he fell to the ground, he asked his fellow students to sing South Korea's national anthem. He died in an ambulance on the way to the Seoul National University (SNU) Hospital (KDF Events Dictionary: 441; NCCK Archive Vol. 2: 650–662).

Kim Sangjin committed *seppuku*, a form of ritual suicide, in front of three hundred students in the quadrangle of SNU's College of Agriculture on April 11, 1975, just one day after the Yusin regime executed eight men in relation to the People's Revolutionary Party case. The SNU student rally occurred after EDs 4 and 7 were issued, when the state began its systematic repression of student protesters. Marking a critical turning point in the democracy movement, Kim Sangjin's death symbolized both the desperation and determination of students in the Yusin period.

After Korea's liberation from Japanese rule in 1945, students emerged as important agents of social change and were the catalysts for some of South Korea's most significant political transitions, including the April 19 (4.19) student revolution that pressured Syngman Rhee to abdicate in 1960, the 1980 Gwangju Uprising that "radicalized" the democracy movement (Lee 2007), and the mass protests that immediately preceded South Korea's return to democratic governance in 1987 (Kim n.d.; Shin et al. 2011). Park Chung Hee recognized the power of student mobilization at the very onset of his rule and initially argued that his coup d'état in 1961 was a continuation of the 4.19 student revolution. In the early years of his incumbency, Park viewed the 4.19 student revolution as a necessary correction for the corruption and ineptness of Syngman Rhee's presidency. His decision to hold a presidential election in 1963 in turn fueled students' hopes that the promise of a democratic South Korea would be kept.

With the reinstatement of presidential elections and the implementation of a constitution that limited the tenure of presidents to two terms, student demand for democracy subsided. A few years into Park's presidency, however, students again took to the streets. This time, their criticism was directed at specific policies pursued by Park's government. As discussed, a significant political issue in the 1960s was the normalization of diplomatic relations between South Korea and Japan. Driven by nationalist pride and resentment toward Japan, students accused Park Chung Hee of "selling out" to Korea's former colonizer and engaging in "humiliating diplomacy." Park Chung Hee responded quickly by declaring martial law on June 3, 1964, and violently suppressing student demonstrations against the planned normalization treaty. In addition, a garrison decree on August 26, 1965, preceded the deployment of military troops into the cities to "resolutely put-down" (Lee J. H. 2011: 451) student protests that erupted again after Park Chung Hee pushed the normalization bill through the National Assembly (ratified on August 14, 1965).

Although ultimately unsuccessful, the antinormalization protests were the largest demonstrations since the 4.19 student revolution and reminded the Korean government and society at large of the power of student mobilization. The student demonstrations in 1964 and 1965 were distinct from the 4.19 student revolution in that they were motivated by criticism of policy but did not challenge the foundational political structure of the government. This is a significant distinction that underscores the expectations that students had of the democratic system in the 1960s relative to the struggle to dismantle the authoritarian structure of the Yusin regime in the 1970s.

The power of the student movement was predicated upon students' ability to disrupt society through large public demonstrations. This power was a function of the stark growth in university enrollment in the postliberation period. According to Edward S. Mason and his colleagues (1980: 348), sheer growth in the absolute number of college students in the postliberation period—from 7,819 in 1945 to 296,640 by 1975—secured their importance in Korean society. Although intended by the South Korean government to be a vehicle for the "socialization of the population . . . into the basic attitudes of compliance with a strong central government" (Mason et al. 1980: 378), universities often provided

THE RISE AND FALL OF THE STUDENT MOVEMENT 51

the material (a place to gather) and cultural (exposure to political theory and ideology) resources for mobilizing large numbers of people.

The prodigious growth of the university student population might have provided the demographic foundations for their potential importance in Korean society, but numbers alone do not explain their politicization. In this chapter I trace the trajectory of students' participation in the democracy movement in relation to the consolidation of Park Chung Hee's authoritarian government. Although they are hailed as the "vanguard of democracy" in contemporary evaluations of South Korea's democratization, it is not true that "students continued to demonstrate until the collapse of the Park Chung Hee regime, mercilessly attacking the regime's morality" (Seo 2007: 150). Rather, a more nuanced analysis shows that the ebb and flow of student mobilization was directly dependent on the repressive response of the state.

Drawing on a celebrated tradition of social protest, students were the first actors to challenge Park Chung Hee's move toward authoritarian rule in the late 1960s. Well aware of their potential threat, Park Chung Hee crafted a repression strategy that directly targeted student dissidents. At two critical junctures, in 1971 and 1974, the state pursued a comprehensive strategy to eradicate the student movement that effectively reduced the total number of public protests. Although state repression negatively impacted students' ability to mobilize, they were able to sustain their movement by creating alliances with other dissident communities, including Christians and laborers, and by developing underground networks to disseminate antigovernment literature. In turn, students' continuing efforts to challenge Park Chung Hee's government prompted the state to enact additional repression policies that further contributed to the disciplinary power of the Yusin regime. In short, the consolidation of the authoritarian system and the rise and fall of the student movement occurred in tandem as each shaped their mutually dependent trajectories.

LEGACIES OF THE 1960S STUDENT MOVEMENTS

It is important to situate student mobilization in the 1970s within the larger context of student movements in the postliberation period. The student movement against Park Chung Hee's Yusin regime followed on the heels of the powerful protest cycles of the 1960s. At the time, the 4.19 student revolution in 1960 was the largest instance of student mobilization in Korean history. Also, student demonstrations in 1964 and 1965 against the plan to reestablish diplomatic relations with Japan were the first significant challenge to Park's rule. The 4.19

revolution and the antinormalization protests set important precedents and contributed to the 1970s student movement in several tangible ways.

First, students who participated in the protests that brought down Syngman Rhee constituted a distinct cohort that was shaped by its successful attempt at altering the political trajectory of South Korea. Those who participated in the antinormalization movement, however, were bound by a shared experience of state repression. Both the success of the 4.19 revolution and the failure of the antinormalization movement contributed to a contentious collective identity and a shared purpose among students, who believed that they possessed a moral mandate to protect the social and political development of the nation. Research on the consequences of political participation has shown that significant involvement in social movements solidifies, and at times radicalizes, the political views that actors held before joining a movement (Abramowitz and Nassi 1981; Fendrich 1977; Jennings 1987; McAdam 1988, 1989). Nancy Whittier points out that "one major outcome of mobilization is the formation of a political generation, a cohort of activists who are committed to the cause in enduring ways" (2004: 541). Although the students who participated in the 4.19 student revolution and the antinormalization movement had long since graduated and were in their late twenties and thirties by the time Park Chung Hee instituted the Yusin Constitution, a core group of them continued to support the democracy movement by playing advisory roles to students in the 1970s.

A second important legacy of the 4.19 student revolution and the antinormalization movement was the development of organizational strategies that became important models for the 1970s student movement. With the support of the opposition Democratic Party (Minjudang), students from several universities founded the National Student Committee for Fair Elections (Kongmyŏng Sŏn'gŏ Ch'ujin Chŏn'guk Haksaeng Wiwŏnhoe) on February 28, 1960. The goal of this organization of more than two hundred members was to ensure fairness in the 1960 presidential and vice-presidential elections (Chŏng 1995: 359–360). After the elections, the National Student Committee for Fair Elections publicized the irregularities that its members observed at several voting booths across the nation and helped mobilize the protests that culminated in the 4.19 student revolution. This organization was an early attempt to establish a national network led by the students themselves as they took a critical stand against government corruption.

Before the National Student Committee for Fair Elections was formed, the umbrella student organization that operated in the immediate postliberation period was the National Defense Student Corps (Hakto Hoguktan), officially launched on April 22, 1949, by the Ministry of Culture and Education. With Syngman Rhee as presiding governor, its purpose was to lead pro-government and anticommunist student rallies. Because the National Defense Student Corps was in essence an arm of Syngman Rhee's government, students sought to replace it with their own autonomous organization. The dissolution of the National Defense Student Corps in the aftermath of Syngman Rhee's resignation in 1960 allowed students to establish student-run organizations at their respective schools and to coordinate under the auspices of the National Student Committee for Fair Elections, which subsequently became the principal organizational structure for student mobilization in the 1960s and 1970s (Yi 2011: 179).

The advantages of nationwide coordination were also evident in the anti-normalization movement. After students staged independent protest events on March 24, 1964, at several key universities—SNU, Korea University, and Yonsei University—they moved to develop a national front against Park's plan to normalize relations with Japan. Central to this strategy was the formation of the Student Coalition Against the Korea-Japan Humiliating Talks (Han-Il Kuryok Hoedam Pandae Haksaeng Ch'ong Yŏnhaphoe) on May 22, 1964. It brought together students from thirty-two universities (Chinsil/Hwahae rŭl wihan Kwagŏsa Chŏngni Wiwŏnhoe 2010) and was instrumental in coordinating protests involving thousands of students on June 3, 1964. The scale of the protests prompted Park Chung Hee to declare martial law that day. Although the police and military arrested 1,120 students, incarcerating 348 of them, in what became known as the 6.3 incident, the power and efficacy of organizing nationwide networks were evident to the state and students alike. Student networks such as the National Student Committee for Fair Elections and the Student Coalition Against the Korea-Japan Humiliating Talks became models for the mobilizing strategies of student dissidents in the 1970s.

A third important legacy of the 1960s student movements was the simple fact that the 4.19 student revolution was successful in achieving its immediate goal of ousting Syngman Rhee.[1] This outcome contributed to the belief that civil disobedience grounded in the moral mandate to speak against illegitimate power was efficacious. As Doug McAdam (1982) argues in regard to the American civil rights movement, past movement success is a critical incentive for further mobilization because it contributes to the "cognitive liberation" of activists, who believe that change is possible. The 4.19 revolution was that kind of seminal moment in Korean student movement history and, as Sunjoo Han notes, it "gave the students a sense of political importance and power which they had not imagined or enjoyed before" (1980: 147). Although students were unable to stop South Korea and Japan from normalizing relations in 1965, the success of the 4.19 revolution loomed large over the students who fought Park Chung Hee's authoritarian government in the 1970s. As the underclassmen (*hubae*) of the 4.19 and 6.3 student protest generations, students in the 1970s, who inherited important organizational models and strategies from their seniors (*sŏnbae*), believed they too could change the political destiny of their country.

With this hope, students in the 1970s attempted to rekindle the spirit of the 4.19 student revolution and directly challenged Park Chung Hee's authoritarian rule. As Figure 3.1 shows, the number of student protests grew dramatically from 1970, reaching its highest point in 1971. Protest dwindled, however, following the state's closure of schools and the deployment of the military in and near university campuses in the fall and winter of 1971–1972. Unable to recover from the impact of the 1971 garrison decree, student protests reached their lowest point in 1972 in the context of martial law. After martial law was lifted, students again took to the streets, to challenge Park Chung Hee's new Yusin government.

Responding to this challenge, Park Chung Hee passed the first set of EDs, targeting various antigovernment movements. With ED 4, the state began the systematic repression of student leaders in what became known as the "Minch'ŏng incident." The arrest and incarceration of hundreds of student leaders significantly compromised the potential for student mobilization, which is reflected in the drop in the annual count of student protests. The promulga-

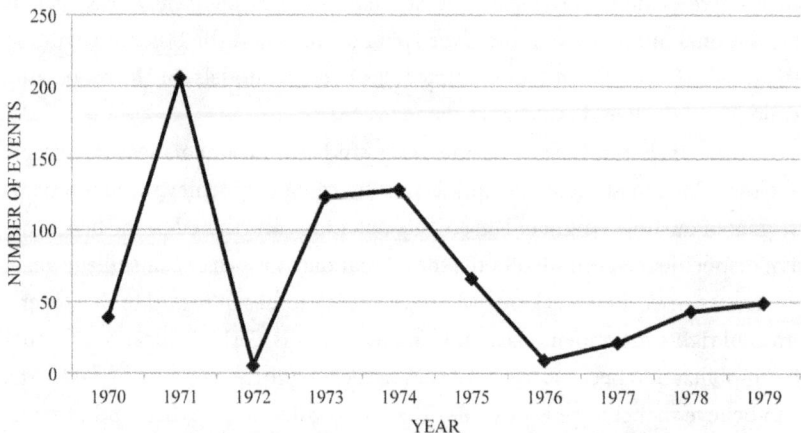

Figure 3.1. Annual counts of protest events by students
DATA SOURCE: Stanford KDP Events Dataset (1970–1979).

tion of ED 9 in 1975 raised the costs of antigovernment mobilizing further, and student protests nearly came to a halt in 1976. Although students attempted to regroup after 1976, the repressive conditions in the ED era made it difficult for them to stage the kinds of large protests they had organized in 1971. This quantitative macroanalysis of student protests clearly shows the negative effects of state repression on the student movement. But as discussed in the Introduction, aggregate counts of protest are only one way of understanding the trajectory of social movements. A more nuanced qualitative analysis reveals that although state repression limited the number of protest events, students were able to adapt in ways that are not captured by protest counts. To understand better the rise and fall of the student movement, we must look closer at the issues and strategies that students pursued in the 1970s.

REEMERGENCE OF THE STUDENT MOVEMENT (1970–1971)

Student protests subsided at the end of the decade after the South Korea–Japan normalization treaty in 1965 and Park Chung Hee's successful manipulation of the constitution in 1969 that allowed for a third presidential term. According to Yi Chaeo, the disappointments of not being able to stop the government from establishing formal relations with Japan and Park Chung Hee's blatant disregard for the democratic process "were so deep that the student movement lost its direction" (2011: 306). By the end of 1970, however, students started to mobilize large demonstrations again as both old and new issues stirred their political convictions. This new protest cycle reached its highest point in 1971 in anticipation of the presidential election that year.

Three key issues drove student mobilization in 1971. First, in the midst of growing labor unrest, highlighted by Chŏn T'aeil's sensational suicide protest, students became concerned with labor conditions and workers' rights. Second, the revised government policy requiring male students to undergo more hours of on-campus military training was correctly seen by students as an attempt to discourage student demonstrations. Third, having reluctantly accepted the possibility of a third presidential term for Park Chung Hee, students were resolved to, at the very least, ensure fair voting procedures in the 1971 presidential election.

Students and the Labor Movement

The global recession in the late 1960s hit South Korea particularly hard and "a severe financial crisis" ensued starting in 1969 (Im 2011: 248). The optimism derived from the economic gains of the first Five-Year Economic Plan (1962–1966) waned during the second Five-Year Economic Plan (1967–1971) as it became increasingly clear that an expanding economy would not lead to the equitable distribution of wealth. Critics of Park's policies argued that his five-year economic plans were merely palliations that did not address the root causes of poverty and inequality. According to a documentary film produced by the Korea Democracy Foundation, "at the end of the 1960s and early 1970s, the public started to lose faith in Park Chung Hee's promise that they will all prosper together because of the growing inequality" (Minjuhwa Undong Kinyŏm Saŏphoe 2006).

During the financial crisis, several large companies were crippled by debt and filed bankruptcies between 1968 and 1972 (Im 2011: 250). The crisis was severe enough to prompt Park Chung Hee to declare the Emergency Decree for Economic Stability and Growth on August 3, 1972, in an attempt to transfer high-interest private curb-market loans to low-interest bank loans (Im 2011: 250). The economic downturn and resultant uncertainties for workers created the conditions for labor unrest, leading to some of "the most volatile years in terms of industrial conflict" (Nam 2009: 187). As discussed in the preceding chapter, labor conflicts accounted for nearly 60 percent of all public protests recorded in the Stanford KDP Events Dataset in 1970.

One event came to embody the growing unrest among workers. The narrative of Korea's modern-day labor movement begins with the life and death of Chŏn T'aeil, a poor garment worker in the textile factories of the Peace Market located near the Great East Gate (Dongdaemun) in Seoul. After years of pleading with employers and the state to uphold the Labor Standards Law (Kŭllo kijunpŏp), Chŏn T'aeil self-immolated on November 13, 1970, as his final protest against a government that sacrificed the well-being of workers for the larger goal of national economic development (Cho 2003). His death galvanized the working class, which was frustrated with the situation but had yet to develop the class consciousness and solidarity necessary to transform itself from "a class in itself" into a "a class for itself" (Marx and Engels 1976: 211; see also Koo 2001).[2]

Chŏn T'aeil's suicide and funeral brought the issues of labor conditions and workers' rights to the forefront of public debate and "more than any other event symbolized growing inequality and despair" (Minjuhwa Undong Kinyŏm Saŏphoe 2006). Hailed as a martyr of the labor movement, Chŏn T'aeil was the "single spark" that ignited widespread protests in 1970 and 1971 (Cho 2003). Several groups joined the fight for workers' rights, including students, who protested in solidarity with laborers. This emerging relationship between students and workers was the beginning of the intellectual-labor alliance that became a critical part of the 1980s democracy movement (Lee 2007).

Students were among the first to react to Chŏn T'aeil's suicide protest. News of his death spread rapidly, and the very next day, November 14, 1970, a group of law students at SNU formed the Student Alliance for the Protection of Civil Rights Preparatory Committee (Minkwŏn Suho Haksaeng Yŏnmaeng Chunbi Wiwŏnhoe) with the purpose of investigating labor conditions (KDF Events Dictionary: 46). Four days later, on November 18, two hundred students from SNU's Business Administration Department held a sit-in rally and declared that they would "promote the linkage between the student movement and labor movement" (KDF Events Dictionary: 47). Students from other universities quickly followed their lead and, on November 20, SNU students were joined by students from Yonsei University, Korea University, and Ewha Womans University in holding a memorial service for Chŏn T'aeil (Yi 2011: 308).

The students demanded better working conditions in the garment factories while declaring solidarity with the workers. On November 23, three hundred Yonsei University Law School students orchestrated a dramaturgical protest in which they burned the effigies of the "five bandits" described in dissident poet Kim Chiha's famous poem of the same name ("Ojŏk"). The five bandits represented society's elite, including high-ranking government officials and business conglomerates, who the students claimed were responsible for Chŏn T'aeil's death (KDF Events Dictionary: 47). Chŏn T'aeil's suicide "woke up" students after a period of quiescence, and there were so many student rallies and demonstrations in the month of November 1970 that the government ordered administrators at several schools to end the fall semester early, hoping that this would put an end to the demonstrations (Yi 2011: 306, 308). The school stoppage did not discourage the students, who continued to stage workers' rights protests into 1971.

Chŏn T'aeil's suicide significantly impacted the student movement in several ways. First, workers' rights was the first issue to capture the students' imagination after the disappointments of the normalization treaty with Japan and the constitutional amendment extending the number of presidential terms. Second, the solidarity that students declared with laborers reflected a significant expansion of the goals of the student movement. Students began to address important social issues related to Park Chung Hee's rapid industrialization programs, which were bringing incredible change to South Korean society. As Yi Chaeo notes, "what is distinct about the student movement in the 1970s was the students' interest in labor conditions, rural issues, and the poor, which was sparked by the Chŏn T'aeil suicide" (2011: 261). As Chŏn T'aeil's death "transformed the labor question into a general social concern" (Choi 2011: 51), students began to realize that political liberties are intimately tied to socio-economic freedoms.

Third, the linking of the student and labor movements was to have a profound effect on the direction of student mobilizing for years to come. Students explored different ways to contribute to the labor movement and in the 1970s conceptualized what became known as the "on-the-job-site movement" (*hyŏnjang undong*). Throughout the Yusin period, students took time off from school or dropped out entirely to seek employment as factory workers. Joined by some progressive Christian groups, their goal was to organize laborers from the "inside" by holding meetings with fellow workers to discuss strategies for forming labor unions. Although the number of students engaged in the "on-the-job-site movement" was relatively small in the 1970s, this tactic became a critical part of the student movement in the 1980s when thousands of students dropped out of universities not simply to organize labor unions but to start a labor revolution (Koo 2001; Lee 2007).

The Antimilitary Training Movement

With the downturn of the economy in the late 1960s, Park Chung Hee's government gave serious consideration to students' growing interest in workers' rights knowing full-well that students possessed the ability to transform labor unrest into massive public demonstrations that potentially could destabilize the entire nation. Wary of the spike in the number of protests in the winter of 1970, and remembering the large student demonstrations in 1965 that subsided only after the declaration of martial law and a garrison decree, the state looked for ways to limit student mobilization. On January 27, 1971, hoping to increase "discipline" among students on campus, the government ordered university administrators to allocate at least 20 percent of class hours to on-campus military training exercises, a significant increase compared to the existing policy established by Syngman Rhee's government (Han 1980: 149). A month later, on February 23, 1971, the government formalized the order by passing the Revised Education Law, which increased the training requirement for all male students from two to three hours a week, with a total of 711 hours needed to graduate (Han 1980: 152). Additionally, after the new law went into effect in the spring semester of 1971, the military reservists who taught the training courses were replaced with active duty officers.

In reaction to the state's direct interference with their curriculum, students began the "antimilitary training movement" (*kyoryŏn pandae undong*). Protests started before the new policy was announced, when students got wind of the government's plan to revise the military training policy. On December 2, 1970, around five hundred Yonsei University students held a demonstration in which mandatory military training was the main grievance. More student demonstrations quickly followed on December 7 and 8 at other universities across the nation, including at Kyungpook National University in Gyeongsang Province (KDF Events Dictionary: 41). Mobilization picked up after the training program was launched in the 1971 spring semester. Although the intent of the revised policy was to enforce discipline and distract students from protesting, it instead became a central issue around which students rallied. The number of demonstrations increased dramatically after the policy went into effect, which accounts for a significant portion of the large protest cycle in 1971.

The month of April brought even more student protests, with Yonsei University leading the charge with a demonstration on April 2. Momentum built from that point on as roughly a thousand students from Sungkyunkwan University, Korea University, and SNU protested at their respective schools on April 8. At one of the several events held that day, students from SNU's Law School burned the military training uniforms they were required to wear, thereby popularizing this dramatic gesture of resistance. The very next day, April 9, about a thousand students gathered at Yonsei University to burn their military training uniforms before marching off campus, where they were confronted by riot police (KDF Events Dictionary: 61).

Dramaturgical or symbolic protests of this sort were popular among student activists, and one event in particular received much public attention. On April 10, as part of a precelebration of Easter Sunday (April 11), Christian students gathered at the Christian Building (Kidokkyo Hoegwan) in central Seoul to begin a march to commemorate the 4.19 student revolution. They carried with them a large cross and chanted antigovernment slogans until they were confronted by the riot police. The police not only physically accosted the students but also destroyed the large cross. The violence against the students and the destruction of the cross shocked the larger progressive community, prompting one organization, the Citizens' Council for the Protection of Democracy (Minju Suho Kungmin Hyŏbŭihoe), to press legal charges against the police (KDF Events Dictionary: 77).

The frequency and size of student demonstrations increased in the month of April: according to the Stanford KDP Events Dataset, forty-eight protest

events were organized by students in that month alone, with an average participation rate of 874 students per event. The April protests culminated on the 15th
in a nationwide day of resistance against the military training policy, with more
than twenty thousand students from many universities staging demonstrations
and rallies (Yi 2011: 314). To meet this prodigious challenge, the state relied on
the same sorts of repression tactics it had used in the 1960s. In addition to deploying riot police to protest sites, the government also closed schools in order
to impede students from gathering on campuses. On April 13, SNU's College of
Liberal Arts and its Law College were shut down, and several other universities
were closed in their entirety after the massive nationwide student demonstrations on the 15th.

The specific tactics that the state used to repress the antimilitary training demonstrations motivated students to revise their protest rhetoric. They
changed the slogan of their movement from "antimilitary training" to "freedom
of the academy" (*hagwŏn chayuhwa*) in order to address the closing of schools,
cancellation of classes, and expulsion of students (Yi 2011: 314). Although state
repression did not completely end the demonstrations, student unrest died
down briefly after April 15, in large part due to the students' decision to stop
protesting temporarily so that they could turn their attention to the upcoming
presidential election (Yi 2011: 314).

The 1971 Presidential Election and the Protection of Democracy

With the 1971 presidential election scheduled for April 27, segments of the
progressive community began to mobilize to address the possibility of electoral fraud. Temporarily halting their movement against military training, students joined these other groups in monitoring voting booths. The 1971 election
proved to be a significant catalyst for the development of social movements in
the 1970s when it motivated the formation of organizations and coalitions that
brought together various movement groups. If the mandatory military training policy concerned primarily students, the 1971 presidential election sparked
the interest of almost all South Korean citizens. Consequently, participation in
election monitoring broadened student networks in the same way that Chŏn
T'aeil's death galvanized their alliance with workers.

The most important organization formed in anticipation of the presidential
election was the Citizens' Council for the Protection of Democracy. Described
in detail in Chapter 7, the Citizens' Council was established on April 19, 1971,
purposely to coincide with the anniversary of the 4.19 student revolution. It

brought together senior social leaders from various occupational backgrounds, including politicians, lawyers, professors, intellectuals and writers, and Christian clergy. Committed to the "protection of democracy" (*minju suho*), the Citizens' Council formalized and concentrated the critical voices that had been raised in 1969 when Park Chung Hee forced the National Assembly to amend the constitution. Although the critics were unsuccessful in blocking the amendment at that time, they created the Citizens' Council to help ensure that the 1971 election would be run in a fair and transparent manner.

Students, for their part, coordinated nationally. More than two hundred of them from several elite schools across the country—SNU as well as Korea, Yonsei, Sogang, Sungkyunkwan, Kyungpook National, and Chonnam National Universities—gathered at the SNU Department of Business Administration library on April 14, 1971, to discuss how best to participate in the protection of democracy movement (KDF Events Dictionary: 78). In conjunction with the leaders of the Citizens' Council, and building on the momentum created by the massive student demonstrations on April 15, students eventually formed the National Alliance of Youth and Students for the Protection of Democracy (Minju Suho Chŏnguk Chŏngnyŏn Haksaeng Chʻongyŏnmaeng), with third-year SNU business major Sim Chaegwŏn as chairperson (*wiwŏnjang*; KDF Events Dictionary: 62–63). The formation of the Students' Alliance (Haksaeng Yŏnmaeng), as it was known, was a significant development in the student movement because it was "the first student alliance of the 1970s" that "set the direction" for formal nationwide student coalitions in the Yusin period (Yi 2011: 314).

Following the lead of the Citizens' Council and the Students' Alliance, two other groups joined the protection of democracy movement. On April 20, Christian students formed the Christian Youth Council for the Protection of Democracy (Minju Suho Kidok Chŏngnyŏn Hyŏbŭihoe). They drew on their own networks, distinct from those of the secular students, including the strong ties they had with Christian churches. Joining these organizations was the Youth Council for the Protection of Democracy (Minju Suho Chŏngnyŏn Hyŏbŭihoe; known as the Youth Council), formed on April 21.

Although the similarities in the names of these four organizations were intended to signal a unified movement for the protection of democracy, each organization mobilized unique constituencies that together constituted a powerful alliance that transcended age, occupational categories, and religious affiliations. The Youth Council was an especially important addition to the network of organizations mobilizing around the presidential election because its members were former students who had participated in the 4.19 student revolution and the antinormalization movement. With the presidential election approaching, a core group of these young adults decided to continue the fight for democracy that they had started in April 1960. They drew on their own personal networks of friends who had participated in social movements in the 1960s and initially formed the Democratic Youth Council (Minju Chŏngnyŏn Hyŏbŭihoe) in February 1971. Although this organization did not last, it became the basis for the Youth Council. Led by founding president Paek Kiwan, the Youth Council represented an important connection between student activists of the 1970s and student activists of the 1960s, with the former looking to their seniors for guidance and support.

On April 24, 1971, these four organizations announced their intention to oversee the upcoming presidential election and registered 312 on-site monitors at various polling locations around the nation (Yi 2011: 296). On April 27, Park Chung Hee won with 6,342,828 votes (53.2 percent) while the opposition candidate, Kim Dae Jung, received 5,395,900 votes (45.3 percent; Nohlen, Grotz, and Hartmann 2001). Although Kim Dae Jung did not win the election, it was significant, and a shock to Park Chung Hee, that Kim Dae Jung secured not only 45 percent of the popular vote, but also the majority of the votes from Seoul.[3] The results were even more impressive given that the government had attempted to sabotage Kim Dae Jung's campaign by engaging in "many illegal and unfair acts" such as limiting access to media and to funding sources (Han 1980: 153). Immediately following the election, the monitors for the Citizens' Council, Students' Alliance, Christian Youth Council, and Youth Council reported irregularities during voting and declared that the election should be voided. The Citizens' Council went further on May 13, 1971, when they not only declared the presidential election invalid but also demanded that the upcoming National Assembly elections on May 25 be cancelled because of the likelihood of further electoral fraud.

After the presidential election, students again took to the streets to stage large demonstrations. This time the issues of labor rights, compulsory military training, and elections were often conflated into a general critique of the legitimacy of Park Chung Hee's regime. Although the government did make attempts to appease students—by reopening schools, replacing Hong Chongchŏl (1967–1971) with the more "moderate" Min Kwansik (1971–1974) as head of the Ministry of Culture and Education (Munhwa Kyoyukpu), and reducing the total number of military training hours needed to graduate from 711 to 180—

student demonstrations only escalated from June to September 1971 (Han 1980: 153).[4] In one sensational event, on May 17, SNU students attacked a motorcade carrying Park Chung Hee by throwing rocks at the vehicles. Park Chung Hee returned the violence in kind by sending seventy policemen from his security duty to SNU, where they beat up students and professors (Yi 2011: 312).

The scope of the student protests and the severity of state repression escalated in tandem. For example, Kim Ch'angsu, a chief election monitor during the National Assembly elections on May 25, 1971, was tortured before his body was found at a train station on June 21. Although he was taken to the hospital, he died from his injuries on June 25 (KDF Events Dictionary: 120). The tense situation was further exacerbated when students expanded the range of their criticism, including deriding Park Chung Hee's Japan policy and the planned visit to South Korea by Japan's Prime Minister Eisaku Satō on June 30. It was becoming clear that student mobilization and state repression were coming to a head as it "now appeared to be an atmosphere of total and emotional confrontation between the students and the government, the issues themselves holding little significance anymore" (Han 1980: 153).

State Repression and the First Fall of the Student Movement

The relentless demonstrations in the summer of 1971 and the mounting criticisms of Park Chung Hee's legitimacy prompted the state to rethink its strategy of engaging students. As discussed in Chapter 1, Park Chung Hee initially argued that his May 1961 coup was a continuation of the 4.19 revolution, even lauding students for acting as catalysts for much-needed political change. But by the mid-1960s, when students challenged his plans to normalize relations with Japan, Park became increasingly patronizing and critical of their methods, as evidenced in a speech he gave on May 2, 1965:

> Dear students! Whenever the politicians wrangle over a big issue in the National Assembly, you, without knowing the real point of the issue, take to the streets or held discussion meetings on the campus with placards saying 'Down with the Government,' or 'Down with the Government Which Conducts Sell-Out Diplomacy.' But I say this to you frankly, that you are the future masters of this nation, but you must train yourself for the job 10 or 20 more years. Then comes the time for your generation, not now. . . . You still have many things to learn; you have to cultivate yourselves, broaden your knowledge and perspective. It is obvious that neither is it your duty nor responsibility to interfere

with the management of state affairs, or political and social affairs. . . . If some students continue to demonstrate on the streets, democracy will not be viable in Korea. . . . Freedom to demonstrate is not democracy. (Park 1970: 201, 203)

Although in 1964 and 1965 such exhortations were accompanied by strong coercion, the 1971 protest cycle increased the stakes in the contest between state and students in several ways. The most significant development was that after the 1971 presidential election, criticisms of government policy were supplemented by challenges to Park Chung Hee's foundational right to rule. In addition, the Students' Alliance, a national network of many student groups, proved to be an effective organization for orchestrating large coordinated demonstrations across the country. This capability was most evident in the antimilitary training demonstrations held on April 15. The emergence of a national network that was able to challenge the very legitimacy of Park's rule required a concerted effort by the state to demobilize students.

The state's resolve in subduing the student movement became evident in the fall of 1971. On October 5, thirty military personnel were sent to Korea University where they violently attacked student activists. This incident was followed by further disciplinary measures: the Minister of Culture and Education and the Minister of National Defense (Kukpangbu Changgwan) jointly announced on October 12 that any student who refused to participate in the compulsory military training exercises would be conscripted into the army (Yi 2011: 318). Alarmed by the deterioration of the situation, university presidents nationwide gathered on October 14 to discuss the student demonstrations and find ways to ease the tensions between students and the state. The possible solutions they came up with at that meeting were moot, however, when on October 15 Park Chung Hee executed the garrison decree that was in effect until November 9.

Following the garrison decree, the military entered and occupied ten key universities, including SNU, Korea University, and Yonsei University. They systematically hunted down movement leaders and arrested 1,889 students, jailing 119 and forcibly conscripting 177 of them into the army (KDF Events Dictionary: 157). Furthermore, a list of 6,322 students who had refused to participate in military training exercises was turned over to the government, which at the same time shut down seventy-four student clubs across seven colleges, suspended fourteen student publications, disbanded seven student governments, and closed eight universities indefinitely (KDF Events Dictionary: 320).[5] To drive the point home, the Ministry of Culture and Education revised university policy so that expelled students were forbidden to transfer to another school or to re-matriculate into their own. In short, the garrison decree in 1971 was the beginning of the total repression of the student movement.

In addition to carrying out mass arrests and school closures, the government also began what amounted to a smear campaign against protesting students. Falling back on the familiar master narrative used against leftist forces in the postliberation period (Cumings 1981, 1990), Park Chung Hee's government accused key leaders in the student movement of being communist agents. In what became known as the Seoul National University Students' Conspiracy to Prepare a Rebellion Incident (Seouldaesaeng naeran yebi ŭmmo sakŏn), four SNU students were taken into custody by the KCIA, tortured, and convicted of mobilizing university students with the intent to overthrow Park Chung Hee's government (NCCK Archive Vol. 1: 201–203).

SNU law student Yi Sinbŏm was the first to be taken. On October 27, 1971, he was brought to the KCIA's "Seobinggo Hotel VIP room," where he was interrogated and tortured. Shortly after, in November, three more students were taken into custody: Cho Yŏngnae (graduate of SNU Law College), Chang Kip'yo (expelled SNU Law College student), and Sim Chaegwŏn (expelled SNU business administration student). During their trial, the four students were accused by state prosecutors of meeting in May or June 1971 at Cho Yŏngnae's house, where they presumably drew up plans to appropriate the massive student demonstrations for the purpose of replacing Park's government with a communist regime. Although several prominent figures in Korean society testified on their behalf—including the "father" of human rights law, Yi Pyŏngnin; Quaker leader Ham Sok Hon; Pastor Kim Chaejun; Chŏn Kwanu, leader of the media freedom movement; and other members of the Citizens' Council—the students were convicted under the National Security Law (NSL) and received ten-year jail sentences on May 1, 1972 (*Kyunghyang Shinmun* 2003; KDF Events Dictionary: 168).[6]

It was not a coincidence that these four students were singled out. Each was an important leader in the Students' Alliance and had a history of engaging in antigovernment activities. Yi Sinbŏm, in 1969, had participated in demonstrations against Park Chung Hee's amendment of the constitution and was arrested under the Anti-Communist Law in 1970, although he was found innocent. He subsequently joined the SNU Social Law Study Group (Sahoepŏp Hakhoe), whose members became the leaders of the student movement in 1971, and was later appointed spokesperson (*taebyŏnin*) for the Students' Alliance.

Cho Yŏngnae, the president of the Social Law Study Group at that time, had been kicked out of high school in 1964 for leading protests against the normalization of relations with Japan, but had still managed to be accepted into SNU's prestigious Law College as one of its top applicants. Inspired by Chŏn T'aeil's self-immolation protest, Cho led the Social Law Study Group in reading critical social theory and discussing how to apply it to the Korean situation. Chang Kip'yo had an unusual background for a student activist in that he had volunteered to fight in the Vietnam War in 1967, in order to "experience the historical situation," before participating in student organizations upon his return (*Kyunghyang Shinmun* 2003).

Of the four convicted students, Sim Chaegwŏn was able to boast the best pedigree in terms of student activism. Both of his brothers were SNU students. The older brother, Sim Chaet'aek, had participated in the 4.19 student revolution in 1960 and in the antinormalization movement in 1964 before becoming a principal member of Dong-A T'uwi, a media freedom movement organization, in the 1970s. The younger brother, Sim Chaesik, was one of the first student activists at SNU's Medical College. With this family background, it is no wonder that Sim Chaegwŏn was immersed in SNU student activist "circles."[7] For example, he teamed up with SNU student Yi Chŏl—principal leader of the National Democratic Youth and Student Alliance in 1974—to organize the Underdeveloped Nations and Society Research Group (Hujin'guk Sahoe Yŏn'guhoe), a mediating organization that brought together various student clubs at SNU. It was this experience of building student networks that allowed Sim Chaegwŏn to play an instrumental role in unifying students nationwide, which earned him the chairperson position with the Students' Alliance in 1971. The arrests of Sim Chaegwŏn (chairperson) and Yi Sinbŏm (spokesperson), along with Cho Yŏngnae and Chang Kip'yo, were clear attempts by Park's government to break the leadership of the Students' Alliance, which was responsible for the massive student demonstrations in the spring and summer of 1971.[8]

The government's concerted effort to repress student protesters and reestablish order, beginning with the October garrison decree, culminated in the Declaration of the State of National Emergency (Kukka pisang sat'ae sŏnŏn) on December 6, 1971. As Hyug Baeg Im puts it, with this declaration, "Park crossed the bridge of no return," because it "formalized the establishment of a 'national security state,' with its six articles defining national security as the first of state priorities" (2011: 247). The declaration of national emergency was likely unnecessary at this point, however, because most of the important student leaders had been either arrested and incarcerated or conscripted into the military. The declaration finalized the state's systematic repression of students, and after its promulgation, as Yi Chaeo bluntly puts it, "the student movement died" (2011: 322). It would be almost two years before students were able to regroup and mount another challenge against the state; this time nothing but the removal of Park from power would do.

THE ANTI-YUSIN STUDENT MOVEMENT (1973–1975)

The student movement was in disarray after the widespread repression in the fall and winter of 1971. Many of the students who had led the protests were in jail, and those who remained on campus refrained from organizing public demonstrations. Other than the circulation of a few important underground publications, 1972 was a quiet year for the student movement.[9] The state continued to monitor antigovernment political activities closely, and several incidents in 1972 reminded students of the constant threat of repression: the April 12 arrest of popular dissident poet Kim Chiha for his article "Piŏ" ("Groundless Rumors"); the April 20 police raid of a Christian student event commemorating the 4.19 student revolution; the KCIA's announcement that it had uncovered a North Korean spy ring, and the subsequent arrest on June 21 of eleven Korea University students; and the August 31 expulsion, for "bad grades," of eighty-three SNU students who had participated in antigovernment demonstrations (KDF Events Dictionary: 180–188).

The most significant impediment to student mobilization, however, was the declaration of martial law in preparation for the promulgation of the new Yusin Constitution in October. With the silencing of opposition party members, the deployment of military into the cities, and state control over the media, October 1972 set the tone for the remainder of that year and most of 1973. In this repressive context, the student movement had to wait for a new cohort of leaders to emerge before resurfacing as a powerful force against Park Chung Hee's Yusin regime.

It took a full year after the Yusin Constitution was announced for students to remobilize. The seminal event occurred at SNU on October 2, 1973, when Liberal Arts College students, led by charismatic senior Na Pyŏngsik, staged a demonstration against the new Yusin government. Gathering at the "4.19 tower," an on-campus memorial to the 1960 student revolution, 250 students chanted antigovernment slogans before marching off campus, where they were met by riot police. Police action was swift and decisive, and when the dust settled, 180 students had been taken into custody; 20 of these were prosecuted under the Law on Public Gatherings and Demonstrations, 9 were indicted but not physically detained, 57 were confined for twenty-five days, and 94 were released (NCCK Archive Vol. 5: 1959).

The government, wary of another round of student protests, did its best to stop the news of the SNU demonstration from spreading by censoring media reports. Despite the resolute repression of the demonstration and the state's attempt to cover it up, the October 2 SNU Liberal Arts College protest proved to be the spark for which students were waiting. It was the first large, "not underground" (Yi 2011: 325) event in the Yusin period and ignited a new protest wave. By November, demonstrations had spread to universities across the nation. As Yi Chaeo, president of the Youth Council at that time, puts it, "The protest that began at Seoul National University on October 2 motivated protests for the whole month of November. The shock of the October 2 protest was that large and it was as if contained water poured out after the dam broke" (2011: 329).

The establishment of the Yusin regime gave students a purpose for mobilizing again and, as in the past, they looked to form a national front. In the fall of 1973, students recommitted to the strategy of establishing a nationwide network that would be able to coordinate diverse student groups across different universities. Orchestrating this national alliance was a new cohort of student leaders that included Na Pyŏngsik, Sŏ Chungsŏk, Yu Int'ae, Yi Chŏl, An Yangno, Chŏng Munhwa, Hwang Insŏng, Chŏng Yun'gwang, Kim Chŏnggil, and Yŏ Chŏngnam (Yu Int'ae and Yi Chŏl, quoted in Minjuhwa Undong Kinyŏm Saŏphoe 2009: 125–126).

These student leaders adopted two organizational structures to create a cohesive nationwide student movement. First, they established vertical networks between different student cohorts by encouraging "senior-junior contact" (sŏn-hubae chŏpch'ok; Minjuhwa Undong Kinyŏm Saŏphoe 2009: 125). As discussed earlier, a core group of the 4.19 and antinormalization protest generations, who were now young adults, were still committed to the democracy movement and involved in their own movement organizations. The student leaders of 1973 attempted to stay in contact with them, as well as with the students who had participated in the 1971 protest cycle, to ensure continuity between different periods of the student movement and to garner additional advice and resources. The second organizational strategy was to create a horizontal network that would include students from regional universities as well as from the elite schools in Seoul. Toward this end, on January 10, 1974, Sŏ Chungsŏk, Yu Int'ae, Yi Chŏl, and Na Pyŏngsik met to design a national network plan. They coined their scheme the "3-3-3" structure because it identified three core groups of students at each of the three important institutional and geographical levels (Yi Chŏl, quoted in Minjuhwa Undong Kinyŏm Saŏphoe 2009: 126).

The 3-3-3 structure, shown in Figure 3.2, reflects SNU's central role in all of the major student movements of the past (in 1960, 1964–1965, and 1971). Student leaders at SNU's Liberal Arts College, Law College, and Department of Business Administration (the "SNU core") would coordinate the national network by first contacting students at other SNU colleges and then contacting central student leaders at Yonsei and Korea Universities. The students at these three schools would make up the core group in Seoul and be responsible for contacting students at other universities in the city. As part of that core, SNU students would also be responsible for contacting students at two key universities in other regions: Chonnam National University in Jeolla Province and Kyungpook National University in Gyeongsang Province. Students at these regional schools would then contact students at other schools in their respective provinces, thus creating a nationwide network of student movement units.

The priority of the national student network was to establish communication channels for the ultimate purpose of coordinating massive nationwide student

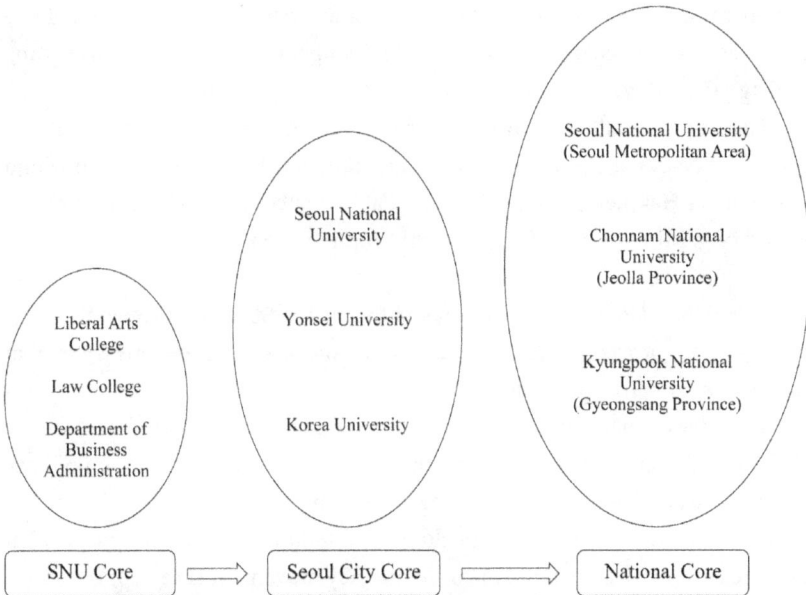

Figure 3.2. Student 3-3-3 national network structure
DATA SOURCE: Minjuhwa Undong Kinyŏm Saŏphoe 2009.

demonstrations against Park Chung Hee's government. Although the number of demonstrations had grown rapidly since the initial SNU protest on October 2, 1973, student leaders wanted to mount a more organized and focused challenge to the Yusin regime. By February 1974, the desired communication channels were established, and in March core student leaders across the nation met several times to select a single day on which to hold student demonstrations across the nation that were modeled on the protests of April 15, 1971, when more than twenty thousand students came together in a nationally coordinated event. Starting on March 5, Hwang Insŏng (SNU), Im Kyuyŏng (Kyungpook National University), and Yun Hanbong (Chonnam National University) held several meetings at different locales across the nation to receive updates and discuss protest tactics (Minjuhwa Undong Kinyŏm Saŏphoe 2009: 129).

Initially, these leaders and the core group at SNU decided that the nationwide coordinated protest would be held on March 11, but the date was changed several times out of fear that information had been leaked to the authorities (Im Kyuyŏng, quoted in Minjuhwa Undong Kinyŏm Saŏphoe 2009: 129). To further ensure that their plans would not be detected by the state, and remembering the government's focused attack on the Students' Alliance in 1971, the student leaders strategically refrained from formally naming their national network during the planning stage. Instead, on March 27—a few days before the national day of protest was to occur—as Yi Chŏl, Kim Pyŏnggon, Chŏng Munhwa, Hwang Insŏng, and others were producing the signs and pamphlets that were to be used in the protest, the students arbitrarily chose a generic name for their movement: the National Democratic Youth and Student Alliance (Chŏn'guk Minju Chŏngnyŏn Haksaeng Ch'ŏngyŏnmaeng; abbreviated Minch'ŏng Hangnyŏn or Minch'ŏng; Minjuhwa Undong Kinyŏm Saŏphoe 2009: 130).

The Minch'ŏng Incident and the Second Fall of the Student Movement

April 3, 1974, proved to be a fateful day for the student movement. On that day, students across the nation held demonstrations and passed out pamphlets under the name of the National Democratic Youth and Student Alliance (NDYSA). At several locations they jointly proclaimed the Declaration of People, Nation, and Democracy (Minjung minjok minju sŏnŏn), one of the earliest articulations of the "three *min* ideology" (*sammin inyŏm*; see Chapter 4) that became a master frame in the 1980s democracy movement (Lee 2007). Because the student leaders had wanted to keep their plans secret, this was the first time the name NDYSA was used publicly.

After months of planning and coordinating across the nation, the students' attempt at staging the largest antigovernment protest since the 4.19 student revolution was immediately met with state repression. On the very day of the protest, from the presidential Blue House, Park Chung Hee promulgated the fourth ED, which went into effect at 10:00 p.m. on April 3. ED 4 contained twelve articles intended permanently to break the power of the student movement. The articles identified the NDYSA as the master organization behind the growing number of student protests and illegalized the specific tactics that students were using in their antigovernment movement. Following are six of the ED's key articles:

> Article 1: Creating or becoming a member of any organization related to the Chŏn'guk Minju Chŏngnyŏn Haksaeng Ch'ongyŏnmaeng (hereafter "organization"), encouraging the activities of the members of the organization, providing resources to aid members who are in hiding, holding meetings, and corresponding, and any direct or indirect participation in the activities of the organization are all banned.

> Article 2: Publishing, creating, possessing, distributing, exhibiting, and selling any texts, documents, books, music albums, and other materials related to the activities of the organization and its members are all banned.

> Article 5: Students' refusal to attend classes and take exams without a just cause; gatherings, demonstrations, rallies, sit-ins, and engaging in any individual or organized activities in and around school outside of normal class; and research activities not supervised by school employees are all banned, with the exception of official apolitical activities.

Having clearly identified the NDYSA as the target of repression and prohibited its activities, ED 4 went on to list the kinds of punishment that students should expect if they continued to mobilize against the government:

> Article 7: The Minister of Culture and Education may expel and suspend students for violating the presidential emergency decree, and disband students' organizations, associations, or other student groups, or close down schools. The criteria for closing down schools will be decided by the Minister of Culture and Education.

> Article 8: Anyone in violation of Articles 1 to 6, anyone in violation of the Minister of Culture and Education's penalty in Article 7, and anyone who criticizes this decree may be sentenced to death, life imprisonment, or a minimum of 5 years of imprisonment. The suspension of qualifications for

up to 15 years may accompany the prison sentence. Anyone who attempts, prepares for, or conspires to engage in the activities in Article 1, Article 2, Article 3, Article 5, and Article 6 will also be punished.

Article 9: Those who violate this decree will be arrested, imprisoned, seized, investigated without a judicial warrant, and tried and punished in the Emergency Martial Court.

The state immediately followed ED 4 with a wide search for students suspected of participating in protests. Within a month of declaring ED 4, the government took into custody 1,024 students; 253 of them were sent to the Emergency Martial Court to be prosecuted, and 180 of these were convicted and sentenced (Yi 2011: 274). After the mass arrests, which became known as the "Minch'ŏng incident," the Yusin regime broadened its search for individuals related to the NDYSA. On April 25, 1974, the director of the KCIA, Sin Chiksu, released a report on the Minch'ŏng incident that purported the following:

> The student leaders of Chŏn'guk Minju Chŏngnyŏn Haksaeng Ch'ongyŏnmaeng planned to organize a national advisory board as a transitional governing body with the objective of establishing a government of laborers and farmers through a four-step revolution. The powers behind Minch'ŏng Hangnyŏn are a complex network of the Inhyŏktang organization [People's Revolutionary Party], a former illegal communist group, the Korean-Japanese pro-North Korean communist party in Japan, and local leftist revolutionaries. (Quoted in Minjuhwa Undong Kinyŏm Saŏphoe 2009: 134)

The report relied on the familiar communist identification frame that was used to eradicate leftist elements in southern Korea in the immediate postliberation period. Central to this narrative was the NDYSA itself: in the same way that the formation of the Students' Alliance provided a tangible target for the repression of student protests in 1971, the naming of the NDYSA, even though the name was chosen arbitrarily by a few student leaders in the last hour, made it easier for the Yusin regime to focus its repression efforts. By calling out the NDYSA specifically in Article 1 of ED 4, Park Chung Hee gave the student movement an identity that could more readily be manipulated by state propaganda. It did not matter that many of the students arrested in April, when asked during interrogations, had never heard of the NDYSA because it had been kept secret until the day of the protest.

The April 25 report imputed a sinister motivation to the anti-Yusin student movement. As part of its justification for putting down their movement once and for all, the state claimed that democracy was not the students' ultimate goal and that the mass arrests successfully obstructed a "communist revolution." A critical part of the application of this communist framing was the identification of the People's Revolutionary Party as "the organization behind the organization."

Fabricating a Repression Narrative: The PRP Case

The government case against the People's Revolutionary Party (PRP; Inmin Hyŏngmyŏngdang or abbreviated Inhyŏktang) has a relatively long history and shows the extent to which the state would go to frame students as communists. The "PRP incident" started a decade before ED 4, when on August 14, 1964, the government accused thirteen individuals of forming a communist organization. The KCIA claimed that these individuals—including To Yejong, Yang Ch'unu, and Pak Hyŏnch'ae—founded the PRP in order to "overthrow the Republic of Korea according to North Korean programs."[10] Furthermore, it purported that in 1964 the PRP, following orders from the North Korean government, had recruited student leaders to orchestrate demonstrations against the normalization of relations between South Korea and Japan (Chinsil/Hwahae rŭl wihan Kwagŏsa Chŏngni Wiwŏnhoe 2010: 166). After a year of interrogations, on August 17, 1965, forty-seven suspects were informally charged with violating the NSL, and the state began the prosecution of the members of the PRP (Chinsil/Hwahae rŭl wihan Kwagŏsa Chŏngni Wiwŏnhoe 2010: 166; NCCK Archive Vol. 1: 448; *Hankyoreh Newspaper,* April 18, 2010).

The PRP case did not go well for the government. After reviewing the evidence procured by the KCIA, prosecutors for the state realized that there were "no grounds for prosecution" (*Hankyoreh Newspaper,* April 18, 2010). When the head of the Seoul District Prosecutors Office, Sŏ Chuyŏn, was informed by the lead prosecutor in the case, Yi Yonghun, about the lack of hard evidence, he conferred with the nation's chief prosecutor,[11] Sin Chiksu. Undeterred by the lack of evidence, Sŏ Chuyŏn then called a meeting with the prosecution team to "persuade" them to find a way to indict and convict the PRP suspects and informed them that failing to do so would result in his and their resignations (*Hankyoreh Newspaper,* April 18, 2010).

The overt pressure backfired when the prosecutors refused to sign the formal indictment against the suspects, and their colleagues in the Ministry of Welfare and Security (Konganbu) threatened to resign en masse in reaction to Sŏ Chuyŏn's coercive tactics. Although only three prosecutors—Yi Yonghun, Kim

Pyŏngni, and Chang Wŏnch'an—actually resigned, it was clear that the KCIA had botched the case against the PRP. Soon enough, knowledge of the irregularities in the judicial process became a scandal for the government. On September 9, members of the National Assembly approached the Minister of Justice, Min Pokki, to address the legitimacy of the PRP case and express their belief that the PRP had been fabricated to retroactively justify the declaration of martial law on June 3, 1964, which had led to the mass arrest of protesters against the normalization treaty with Japan. After the defense lawyer, Pak Hansang, publically declared on September 12 that the suspects were tortured in order to draw out their confessions, some members of the National Assembly suggested that the KCIA should be disbanded altogether (*Hankyoreh Newspaper*, April 18, 2010).

The KCIA was not disbanded in 1965, and during the Yusin period it was imbued with even more punitive power. Nearly a decade after the first PRP case, Sin Chiksu (government chief prosecutor in 1965, now KCIA director), possibly motivated by a personal vendetta,[12] reidentified the PRP as the organizational force behind the student movement in his report of April 25, 1974. With protest against the Yusin government on the rise, the state accused some of the same people of trying to reestablish the so-called communist organization. Twenty-three individuals were rounded up and held in custody for a year before being tried, convicted, and sentenced under the NSL.

During the KCIA's investigation, the state wove together a narrative justifying the prosecution of PRP members within the larger context of the nationwide student movement against the Yusin government. After interrogating student leaders, the KCIA identified key individuals who it said directly linked the NDYSA to the PRP (Minjuhwa Undong Kinyŏm Saŏphoe 2009: 135). According to the KCIA, the central PRP member was To Yejong, who had met with student leaders, including Yŏ Chŏngnam and Yi Chŏl, to provide them with the funds to organize the NDYSA. To Yejong's ultimate goal, the state argued, was to start a violent revolution by appropriating the massive anti-Yusin student demonstrations for that end.

As the state repression narrative unfolded, the net was cast wider and other individuals were arrested for providing resources to students, thus violating Article 1 of ED 4. The students were said to have been supported by international communist agents, as well as by the PRP, which justified the arrests of two Japanese nationals, Kwak Tongŭi (a Korean-Japanese) and Tachikawa Masaki, on May 27, 1974 (Yi 2011: 335). Prominent leaders in the democracy movement were also taken into custody. As detailed in the following chapter, during his interrogation, SNU student Na Pyŏngsik tried to prove that the NDYSA was not a communist organization by informing the KCIA that he had received money from Church Women United Director Yi Ujŏng on behalf of Pastor Pak Hyŏnggyu. The source of that money, it turned out, was former president of South Korea Yun Posŏn, who at the request of Pastor Pak donated 450,000 KRW (about US$400) to the students. Other supporters of the NDYSA included professors Kim Tonggil and Kim Ch'an'guk, dissident poet Kim Chiha, and Catholic Bishop Chi Haksun. These senior leaders in the democracy movement were arrested on July 16, 1974, for their part in advising students.

The arrest of these prominent individuals was a double-edged sword for the government. While it was convenient that, in addition to cracking down on students, the Yusin regime was able to round up some of the most important leaders in the democracy movement, taking into custody prominent Christian and political leaders diluted the power of the communist motive in the state's repression narrative. As Myung-Lim Park puts it, "The arrest of former president Yun Po-sŏn, Bishop Chi Hak-sun, Reverend Pak Hyŏng-gyu, poet Kim Chi-ha, and professors Kim Tong-gil and Kim Ch'an-guk on charges of aiding the students' organization of NDYSA from behind the scenes made the *yushin* regime's legal case seem all the more untenable in the eyes of the general public" (2011: 391–392).

Blatantly ignoring the inconsistencies in their repression narrative and the lack of any "hard evidence" other than the "confessions" of tortured students and dissidents, the state pushed through the PRP trial (Minjuhwa Undong Kinyŏm Saŏphoe 2009: 136). One year after the declaration of ED 4, on April 9, 1975, a martial court convicted the twenty-three "members" of the PRP, giving fifteen-year sentences to all but eight of the defendants, who were given death sentences. In the early hours of the morning following the convictions, the state executed behind closed doors To Yejong, Kim Yongwŏn, Yi Subyŏng, Ha Chaewan, Sŏ Towŏn, Song Sangjin, and U Hongsŏn, along with the student Yŏ Chŏngnam.[13] During their year in prison, they had been tortured to the point that the authorities refused to release some of the bodies to their families after the executions, presumably to hide the scars that the government had inflicted on them (Stentzel 2006).

While the PRP trial was going on, during the fall semester of 1974 and spring semester of 1975, more than half of all the universities in South Korea were closed down and hundreds of student leaders were jailed along with a core group of senior leaders of the dissident community (Park 2011: 393). In short, in reaction to the students' attempt to create a national front and to the diffusion of protests, Park Chung Hee used ED 4 to systematically repress the student movement and root out central leaders of the democracy movement.

STUDENTS DURING THE EMERGENCY DECREE ERA (1975–1979)

The Minch'ŏng incident and the PRP case represented the height of repression during the Yusin period and a critical turning point in the democracy movement. The steady rise in the number of public protests after the promulgation of the Yusin Constitution began to stall in 1974 and dropped precipitously after 1975, as shown in Figure 2.2 in the previous chapter. Much of this drop was the result of the demobilization of the student movement after ED 4. Although Park Chung Hee rescinded ED 4 on August 23, 1974, he quickly replaced it with other political control laws, including ED 7 on April 8, 1975, and the infamous ED 9 on May 13, 1975. However, in addition to achieving the intended goal of subduing the student movement, the EDs also led to several unintended consequences.

The mass arrest of students and the torture inflicted on some of them during the Minch'ŏng incident shocked many segments of Korean society. As described in the following chapters, key social groups—in particular Christians, journalists, and lawyers—began to advocate on behalf of the students, which in turn contributed to their own politicization. As Myung-Lim Park describes it, "student activists still remained the core of resistance after 1970 although, unlike in the 1960s, they were complemented by and fused with protest movements based in other social groups" (2011: 387). Compared to students, these new social movement actors did not organize large numbers of public protests, but nonetheless their entry into the democracy movement represented a significant threat to the Yusin regime. Recognizing this threat, Park Chung Hee enacted ED 9, which was intended as a "permanent instrument of control" (Sohn 1989: 87) to be applied to all who challenged his rule.

Heightened state repression following the EDs negatively impacted the ability of students and other groups to mobilize against the Yusin regime. Still, a few incidents during the ED era inspired dissidents to continue the fight for democracy. One sensational event, described in the opening pages of this chapter, was the death of Kim Sangjin, who committed suicide while addressing hundreds of students just one day after the execution of the eight defendants in the PRP case. His death fueled further anger among students and in the larger dissident community, but ultimately the number of public protests dwindled, reaching its lowest point in 1976. As they did in 1972, however, students attempted to sustain their movement by going underground and spreading "groundless rumors" against the state through a variety of printed materials.

Building on the precedent set in 1972, covert student publications such as *Siron chŏngbo* (*Current Opinion Report*) and *Saebyŏk* (*Dawn*) contributed to the continuation of an organized underground student movement (Yi 2011: 347, 349). This continuity allowed the number of student-run protests to slowly pick up in 1977, beginning with a large student demonstration at Yonsei University on October 26, when four thousand students confronted riot police in a violent exchange (Yi 2011: 362). But even though this demonstration was followed by further attempts to recapture the intensity and breadth of the protests of 1971 and 1974, the student movement never fully recovered after the Minch'ŏng incident. Students remained one of the cornerstones of the dissident community, but after 1975 the responsibility to lead the democracy movement would fall on the shoulders of others. The vacuum left by the students was filled by new social movement groups, including, most importantly, Christians.

4 THE EMERGENCE OF CHRISTIAN ACTIVISM

I saw students shot and killed by guns. . . . From then on I made
up my mind to become a pastor of the true church.

Pak Hyŏnggyu, former pastor of Seoul First Church

The rapid demobilization of students following the Minch'ŏng incident shaped the democracy movement in several important ways. The nature of the repression—including mass arrests, suspension of habeas corpus, and torture—raised the stakes in the contest between dissidents and the state. The Minch'ŏng incident not only infuriated dissident communities but also alarmed the general public given that students, however "radical," represented the future hopes of the Korean nation. The systematic repression of the student movement prompted different sectors of Korean society to criticize the authoritarian nature of the Yusin state, which in turn facilitated the politicization of new movement actors. The conspicuous absence of student street demonstrations in 1975, relative to previous years when student protests had been ubiquitous, allowed other groups to take on a more visible role in the movement. A relatively small but effective group of progressive Christians filled this void, replacing students as the most important actor in the democracy movement during the ED era.

CHRISTIAN SOCIAL ENGAGEMENT

Prior to the politicization of Christians and their participation in antigovernment protests, Christian churches generally, and progressive Christians specifically, were already engaged in various social welfare programs. Christian social engagement in the postliberation period drew from a tradition that dates back to the very beginnings of Christianity in Korea. Catholicism spread in the 1700s and 1800s, in the face of extreme persecution,[1] partly because the lower classes were drawn to its theology of "the essential equality among humans before God" (Kwang 2006: 30). Also, upon their arrival in the late 1800s, Protestant missionaries, most of them from the United States, ingratiated themselves to Koreans by establishing Western educational and medical institutions that serviced all strata of Korean society (Oak 2013).[2] Some Korean Christians, for their part, continued the model established by the missionaries, engaging in a variety of "faith-based social movements" to help revitalize rural Korea during the 1920s and 1930s (Park 2015). These traditions of Christian social engagement were carried through after Korea's liberation from Japanese colonial rule in 1945.

It is important to situate Christian social engagement in the 1960s and 1970s within the larger context of the incredible growth of Korean Christianity. The proliferation of Christian churches was in part a consequence of the urbanization of Korean society that began during the colonial period but accelerated rapidly after liberation (Mason et al. 1980: 80, 385). According to Jang Jip Choi, "nearly 20 percent of the population" migrated from rural areas to urban centers starting in the 1960s and into the mid-1970s (2011: 44). As several scholars of Korean Christianity have noted, the number of churches grew exponentially in the same period in which the state's modernization programs fueled the growth of cities (Clark 1986; Kim 1989; Lee T. 2010).

As millions flocked to urban areas from the countryside in search for greater economic opportunities, South Korean cities witnessed a "population boom" that became the foundations on which industrialization projects were built (Kim and Choe 1997). Once these domestic migrants were in the cities, however, the disjuncture between dreams and reality motivated many of them to turn to Catholic and Protestant organizations to help them deal with the problems of urban poverty, slum dwellings, and atrocious working conditions. As Yi Chŏlsun, a Catholic social worker in the 1970s, remembers:

> People had dreams in the 1970s. I saw a lot of young people in front of Seoul Station. They left their homes with dreams of making money. They believed they could make money once they came to Seoul. They had nothing but dreams. The K'at'ollik Chŏngnyŏnhoe [Catholic Youth Association] opened a house for those young people. They provided rooms for people who left their homes with nothing. (Interview with Yi Chŏlsun, August 20, 2000)

Many of the young men and women who migrated from the countryside to cities like Seoul "became the poor of the city" and found themselves working in difficult conditions and living in makeshift shantytowns (interview with Kwŏn Osŏng, December 24, 2005). Two important events in the early 1970s revealed the growing problems of labor relations and urban poverty. As discussed in Chapter 3, the difficulties facing laborers gained wide exposure when Chŏn T'aeil set himself on fire on November 13, 1970, in protest of the working conditions that young (mostly women) workers faced in Seoul's Dongdaemun garment district. His suicide protest not only motivated students to address labor issues in their demonstrations but also brought workers' concerns to the fore of public debate.

In addition, the underlying problems related to urbanization surfaced on August 10, 1971, when roughly fifty thousand citizens living in shantytowns in Gwangju, Gyeonggi Province, resisted the government's plans to repossess their land because their homes were not up to inspection codes (KDF Events Dictionary: 129). More than eight hundred riot police were sent to put down the demonstrations, which led to violent exchanges with the citizens. The uprising sparked further protest as the government's attempt to clear away makeshift homes in other parts of Seoul, including the Dongdaemun area, resulted in violent exchanges between the urban poor and state authorities (KDF Events Dictionary: 130). Incidents such as the Gwangju shantytown protests and Chŏn T'aeil's self-immolation were stains on the picture of economic growth painted by Park Chung Hee's government. The underside of industrialization and urbanization was becoming increasingly visible to many concerned groups, including Christian clergy, who felt compelled to try to alleviate the suffering of their laity.

Christians organized various social welfare programs in response to the many problems that arose out of Korea's modernization process. They were primarily concerned with the working class poor, and both Protestant and Catholic groups—such as the Methodist Urban Industrial Mission (UIM), the Christian Academy, and the Catholic Jeunesse Ouvrière Chrétienne (JOC or Young Christian Workers)—began programs to educate workers about their rights and to help organize labor unions (Ogle 1990; Kang 1997; Park 2003). Whereas the state would brand Christian activists as political instigators in order to justify their repression, progressive Christians insisted that they were motivated by the call for social justice inherent to their faith. Criticizing the reformation leader Martin Luther's famous credo, Methodist Theological University professor Kim Hong-Ki confesses that it is "not just faith alone (*sola fide*), but Christians also need love and action" (interview with Kim Hong-Ki, August 20, 2004). For some concerned Christians, such as Yi Kwangil, "love and action" was simply a matter of following in Jesus's footsteps:

> As a student and Christian, I tried to define what life really meant based on my understanding of religion. What would I do if Jesus was to come to Seoul and

where should I go to meet him? . . . As I was thinking about these matters, the social problems of our country started to rise. Literally, I followed my belief. (Interview with Yi Kwangil, August 30, 2000)

Other Christians developed a more sophisticated theological justification for their social engagement. The associate director of the Christian Academy in the 1970s, Pak Kyŏngsŏ, points out that

> the role of the church should be seen from two sides. One is that the church should care for the members of the church as Jesus did for all human beings. This is called pastoral care. Another is the prophetic voice. . . . Human beings are created in the image of God. So if there are violations committed against human beings, the church should intervene. This is the prophetic mission of the church. (Interview with Pak Kyŏngsŏ, August 25, 2000)

In the same way that the "prophets in the Bible stood against injustice and corruption in society," Christian activists emphasized "social responsibility" and "social engagement" throughout the 1960s and 1970s (interview with No Ch'angsik, August 20, 2000). These justifications for Christian social engagement mirrored important theological trends in progressive Christian communities worldwide. The social gospel movement that was popular in America in the late nineteenth and early twentieth centuries emphasized the application of Christian ethics to social problems. Representative organizations informed by the social gospel include The Salvation Army and the African Methodist Episcopal Church.

Kim Chaejun, then president of the Korean Theological Seminary (Han'guk Sinhakkyo) and the "father" of liberal theology in South Korea, emphasized the social gospel, and it is not a coincidence that his students and faculty—including Mun Ikhwan, Mun Tonghwan, and Ahn Byung-Mu—became leaders of the democracy movement in the 1970s and 1980s. As a seminary student in the 1970s recalls, "professors at Han'guk Sinhakkyo didn't teach social engagement during class time because we had designated texts for the curriculum, but during chapel time, which was held several times a week, they took turns delivering sermons where they emphasized social engagement. The messages I heard at that time were a great encouragement" (interview with No Ch'angsik, August 20, 2000).

Armed with the social gospel and the belief that it is Christian duty to alleviate the suffering of the oppressed, many Protestants and Catholics began to work on behalf of laborers, farmers, and the urban poor. In the 1960s and 1970s,

Christian "praxis" consisted of various programs, including night schools for workers offered by the Christian Academy, participation in farming activities (*nonghwal*) organized by the Korean Student Christian Federation (KSCF) and the Catholic JOC, and urban poverty missions launched by such groups as the UIM. Some Christians, wanting to follow the example of Christ and other "martyrs," secured employment as factory workers in order to empathize better with those they were seeking to help. Yi Chŏlsun explains:

> I went to the Catholic Church, I saw Jesus on the cross and thought about his sacrifice for human beings. And then I thought about how Chŏn T'aeil sacrificed himself for the love of his people who are living under extreme conditions in the factories. If I follow after Chŏn T'aeil, who sacrificed himself like Jesus, then I can follow the way of Jesus as well. So I quit school and started to work in a factory. . . . I wanted to learn about the life of workers. (Interview with Yi Chŏlsun, August 20, 2000)

The Methodist UIM and the Catholic JOC were leading progressive Christian organizations in the 1960s and 1970s. Their members worked alongside laborers at important industrial locations in cities such as Incheon, Seoul, Chungju, and Busan (Ogle 1990: 87). Their direct experience of factory working conditions solidified their conviction that something had to be done for the rights of workers. Upon securing employment in manufacturing companies, UIM and JOC members organized workers into small, closely knit groups to discuss labor problems. Through these efforts, Christians facilitated the development of "class awareness" and "union consciousness" among the workers (Koo 2001: 75). Some UIM members became important figures in key labor struggles. For example, Reverend Cho Wha Soon worked at the Tongil Textile Company for a short time in 1966 and later helped the women workers there elect the first female labor union president in South Korea's history in 1972 (Sohn 1989: 138; see also Cho, Lee, and Ahn 1988; and Koo 2001).

FROM SOCIAL ENGAGEMENT TO POLITICAL ACTIVISM

Notwithstanding the importance of Christian social welfare and labor programs in the 1960s and 1970s, and the participation of a few Christian leaders in protests against the 1969 constitutional amendment that allowed Park to run for a third presidential term, the progressive Christian community did not directly engage in political matters in large numbers until the 1970s, when Pak Hyŏnggyu's 1973 Easter Sunday protest galvanized Christian political activism (Park 2003: 190).[3]

Indeed, as noted in the Introduction, at the time of Park Chung Hee's coup in 1961, some progressive Christian pastors even supported Park's leadership and his vision of developing South Korea's economy (Hyŏn 1962). But following the 1969 constitutional amendment, it became clear to Christians, and to the larger society, that Park Chung Hee was unwilling to conform to the democratic process. Over time, a group of progressive Christians who ran social welfare programs in the 1960s became political actors proper when they not only joined public protests against the Yusin regime but also led the democracy movement in the ED era.

As discussed later in the chapter, Pastor Pak's 1973 protest and subsequent arrest and trial motivated progressive Christians to reconsider their role in South Korean society. They began to challenge Park Chung Hee's authority directly, while continuing their social work programs with laborers, farmers, and other disenfranchised groups. The transformation of the mission of the UIM is a case in point. Initially, the central goal of the Methodist pastors associated with the UIM was to proselytize Christianity, but as UIM members became entrenched in the life of factory workers, the emphasis on "individual salvation" gave way to the notion of "social salvation," as the pastors realized that the problems that workers faced originated in Park Chung Hee's dictatorship (Park 1996; 24). On the basis of this insight, UIM pastors such as George Ogle and Cho Wha Soon would play critical roles in some of the key contentious events of the 1970s, including the PRP case and the Tongil Textile Company's labor struggle.

We saw in Chapter 2 that the number of protest events fluctuated throughout the 1970s and that this fluctuation was in large part due to the impact of state repression. Until 1974, students maintained their position at the forefront of the democracy movement in terms of the number of protest events, which is why the state implemented EDs 4 and 7 to target their movement directly. As the Minch'ŏng incident unfolded, Christians—"gradually getting upset" (interview with James Sinnott, August 12, 2014)—began to criticize Park Chung Hee's authoritarian government publicly. As Figure 4.1 shows, Christians staged more protest events, as a percentage of the annual counts of protest events, than any other social group from 1975 to 1978, marking a critical turning point, when the leadership of the movement passed from students to Christians. Although several scholars have noted the importance of Christian participation in the democracy movement in the 1970s (Park 2003; Kim 2000; Kang 1997), a more nuanced analysis reveals that Christians were not from the start the main actors in antigovernment protests. Rather, from 1972 to 1975, they became increasingly

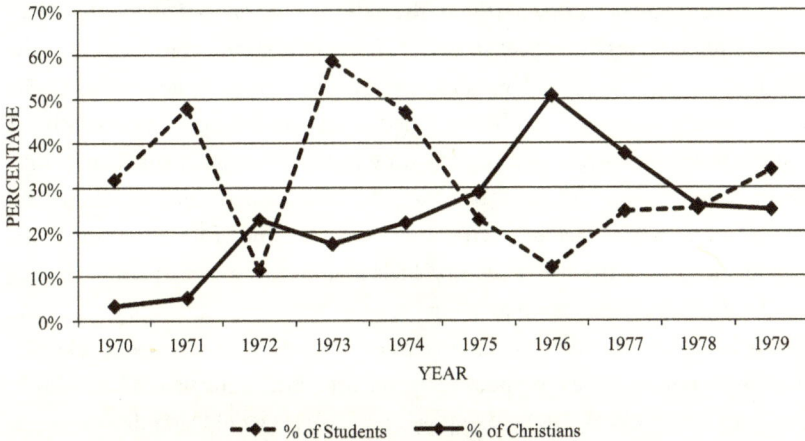

Figure 4.1. Percentage of student and Christian protest events
DATA SOURCE: Stanford KDP Events Dataset (1970–1979).

politicized through a series of specific events that motivated their entry into the democracy movement.

The politicization of Christians began with the Easter Sunday protest led by Pastor Pak Hyŏnggyu in 1973. His role in that seminal event catapulted him to the forefront of the democracy movement, a position that was solidified by his leadership of important social movement organizations in the 1970s and 1980s.[4] Although it was not until the Easter Sunday protest that Pastor Pak became a central figure in the progressive Christian community, his interest in political matters was sparked much earlier. As it was for many who participated in the 1970s democracy movement, the 4.19 student revolution was a transformative moment for Pastor Pak. On April 19, 1960, when he was still a young, freshly ordained pastor, he witnessed the extent of state repression, which facilitated his political awakening:

> Right after becoming a pastor in 1959, 4.19 happened. I was the associate pastor of Gongdeok Presbyterian Church and officiated at somebody's wedding on the day of 4.19. When I was leaving the wedding, I saw students shot and killed by guns. Before that moment I just thought of being an ordinary pastor of a small church, but when I saw that, I repented again. . . . The church was indifferent to all of these things. I cried all day. I walked with the students and [realized] that without a prophetic voice the church is not a church. From then on I made up my mind to become a pastor of the true church. (Interview with Pak Hyŏnggyu: August 23, 2000)

In his quest to become a pastor of "the true church," Pastor Pak moved briefly to the United States, from 1962 to 1963, to attend the famous progressive Union Theological Seminary in New York City. At the seminary, he studied under Professor John Macquarrie, the esteemed Anglican theologian and scholar of Martin Heidegger, while also participating in the larger academic community that boasted the likes of Reinhold Niebuhr. Union Theological Seminary has a rich tradition of social engagement and hosted some of the most important theologians of the twentieth century, including Niebuhr, Dietrich Bonhoeffer, and Paul Tillich.[5] In addition to being exposed to these great theological minds, Pastor Pak also discovered in America role models for Christian political activism: importantly, he was "influenced by Martin Luther King Jr. and Malcolm X" (interview with Pak Hyŏnggyu, August 23, 2000). He would later draw on these models of Christian social and political engagement while on his way to becoming a leader of the Korean democracy movement.

Upon his return to Korea, Pastor Pak was involved in many Christian organizations, and in the period leading up to the proclamation of the Yusin Constitution, he assumed the editorship of the journal *Kidokkyo sasang* (*Christian Thought*), the general manager's position at the KSCF, the directorship of the Christian Broadcasting System (CBS), and the program coordinator position at the Christian Academy. Although much of this work focused on academic or social welfare issues such as urban poverty, Pastor Pak found himself in a unique position to contribute to the democratic process in Korea. In 1971, for example, during the presidential race that pitted Park Chung Hee against Kim Dae Jung in what ended up being a surprisingly close contest, Pastor Pak exercised his discretion as the director of the CBS to organize a radio dialogue between Catholic Cardinal Kim Suhwan, Cho Kwangyun from the Anglican Church, and Kim Dae Jung. Because Park Chung Hee's government limited Kim Dae Jung's access to media outlets during his presidential campaign, broadcasting his dialogue with these Christian leaders was a rare opportunity for the presidential hopeful to address the public. The radio broadcast was to be "religious" in nature and "the rationale was that Kim Dae Jung was a Christian" (interview with Pak Hyŏnggyu, August 23, 2000). Although the state forced the CBS to stop the broadcast after the first hour of a planned two-hour program, Pastor Pak's attempt to give Kim Dae Jung airtime was significant because it involved a Christian organization directly engaging in politics.

Pastor Pak's interest in the 1971 presidential election was somewhat unusual considering that throughout the 1960s and early 1970s the progressive Christian community, for the most part, "avoided political controversies and wanted to focus only on protecting the rights of the urban poor" (interview with Pak Hyŏnggyu, August 23, 2000). But after the promulgation of the Yusin Constitution in 1972, Christians such as Pastor Pak became convinced that the social ills they were trying to ameliorate were part of a much larger problem that originated in dictatorship. The catalyst that motivated Christian leaders to begin to mobilize against the government was their own laity. During the large and violent protest cycle of 1971, many students were jailed or forcibly drafted into the military, and some were even tortured. The state's repressive capacity only increased with the Yusin Constitution, prompting students and parents to seek out Christian leaders for help. As Yi Ujŏng, former professor at Seoul Women's University and chairperson of Church Women United, recalls:

> Mothers of the accused came to my church and told me that their children and husbands were badly tortured by the government. By seeing and hearing all of these things, we thought we needed to do something. Knowing that the Yusin Constitution was wrong, doing nothing was to go against our obligation. . . . People trusted us and thought we were Christians who sacrifice for our suffering neighbors and they knew we also had international support. . . . During the Yusin period the churches were overflowing and there were not enough seats for everybody to sit down. (Interview with Yi Ujŏng, August 17, 2000)

Pastor Pak's First Church (Cheil Kyohoe) also "had lots of students from Seoul National University, Yonsei, Ewha, and Sookmyung Women's University" (interview with Pak Hyŏnggyu, August 23, 2000) who sought his empathy and guidance. Exhorted by students and their parents, Pastor Pak and other Christians realized that Park Chung Hee's turn toward blatant dictatorship demanded a new response from the Christian community, and it was "from then on that we started a political resistance" (interview with Pak Hyŏnggyu, August 23, 2000). Christian "political resistance" began when Pastor Pak and a junior pastor, Kwŏn Hogyŏng, used the opportunity of a large ecumenical gathering of Protestant denominations at Seoul's South Mountain on Easter Sunday, April 22, 1973, to disseminate leaflets that read "Politicians Repent," "The Resurrection of Democracy Is the Liberation of the People," and "Lord, show thy mercy to the ignorant King" (Kang 1997: 102). According to Pastor Pak, the Easter Sunday demonstration "failed" when participants ran away as soldiers monitoring the Christian gathering moved in on the demonstrators (interview with Pak Hyŏnggyu, August 23, 2000). After a government investigation, Pastor Pak was arrested on July 6, 1973, along with other participants in the Easter Sunday protest. Some who were taken into custody were tortured during their incarceration, including Pastor Kwŏn Hogyŏng, and forced to sign "confessions" stating that Pastor Pak's goal was to overthrow and replace Park Chung Hee as president. Armed with these "confessions," the state prosecuted Pastor Pak in what was to become a sensational trial.

Pastor Pak's arrest galvanized the progressive Christian community and the "courts were crowded with people from the Urban-Rural Mission, World Council of Churches (WCC), and Catholic organizations" (interview with Pak Hyŏnggyu, August 23, 2000). Other concerned individuals and groups present at the trial included Quaker Ham Sok Hon, Buddhist monk Pŏpchŏng, human rights lawyer Han Sŭnghŏn, university students, and international journalists. It seemed to Pastor Pak that "the whole world was watching the trial" (interview with Pak Hyŏnggyu, August 23, 2000). The government accused Pastor Pak of "receiving money from the north [North Korea] and trying to turn the south into a communist country," and eventually convicted him under the NSL (interview with Pak Hyŏnggyu, August 23, 2000). Although he received a seven-year prison sentence, it was reduced to two years and he was released even before that, when the US Embassy in South Korea complained that Pastor Pak was obviously not a communist (interview with Pak Hyŏnggyu, August 23, 2000).

If Pastor Pak's Easter Sunday protest and his subsequent arrest and trial rallied the Protestant Christian community to political action, the Korean Catholic community was galvanized by the arrest of Bishop Chi Haksun in 1974. As part of the systematic repression of students during the Minch'ŏng incident, prominent individuals—including Bishop Chi Haksun, Yi Ujŏng, Yun Posŏn, and Kim Chiha—were arrested for providing monetary resources to support the student movement. Chi Haksun was the Catholic Bishop for the district of Wonju and was arrested on July 6, 1974, at the airport upon returning from Europe, for violating EDs 1 and 4 (KDF Events Dictionary: 345; Kang 1997: 104). With state repression escalating, Catholic Christians, like Protestants, asked themselves, "Where does the church stand in all this?" (interview with James Sinnott, August 12, 2014).

Bishop Chi provided a resolute answer to the introspective question in his celebrated Declaration of Conscience, drafted during his confinement. In this document, he explicitly criticized the Yusin Constitution and the EDs, and clarified his *religious* convictions that compelled him to resist an unjust despot. Moreover, he argued that it is the church's duty to stand with the oppressed, and he exhorted others to continue the struggle against injustice (KDF Events Dictionary: 345). Bishop Chi's arrest and impassioned declaration "awoke the Roman Catholic church community in Korea" and facilitated their politicization (Kang 1997: 104). As Catholic social worker Yi Chŏlsun remembers:

> Before 1974, the Catholic Church was fairly conservative. However, after his [Bishop Chi's] arrest, young priests came together and were active in the movement . . . [people like] Han Sŏnju, Kim Sŏnil, [and] Ch'ae Kisik were the center of the [Catholic] movement. The Wonju district was more active. . . . many young people came to church at that time. The number of attendees at Myeongdong Cathedral alone increased by the hundreds in one year. These were students. This was the start of the movement among the laity. (Interview with Yi Chŏlsun, August 20, 2000).

Following Bishop Chi's lead, the progressive Catholic community extended their past commitment to social welfare by participating in the political movement for democracy. Catholic leaders—including the head of the Korean Catholic Church, Cardinal Kim Suhwan—rose to prominence in the democracy movement, and Catholic churches such as Myeongdong Cathedral became spaces in which to both criticize and hide from the government. In addition, Bishop Chi's arrest motivated the founding of the Catholic Priests' Association for Justice (Ch'ŏnjugyo Chŏngŭi Kuhyŏn Sajedan), a central Catholic political organization in the 1970s democracy movement and beyond. Perhaps most troublesome to the Yusin regime was that Bishop Chi's arrest brought international attention to South Korea's democracy movement when Amnesty International began a special campaign for the release of Bishop Chi and thirteen other political prisoners (KDF Events Dictionary: 345). As discussed later, international networks were a critical resource for the Korean church.

The rate of Christian participation in antigovernment protests steadily increased after Pastor Pak's Easter Sunday protest in 1973. After the EDs and the Minch'ŏng incident, however, Christian mobilization accelerated rapidly as clergy and laity "demonstrated on the streets and carried the cross and were hit by tear gas" (interview with Yi Ujŏng, August 17, 2000). As is evident in Figure 4.1, the proportion of Christian antigovernment protests reached an apex in 1976, which was simultaneously the nadir of the student movement during the Yusin period. Although the numbers dropped after ED 9, Christians staged more protests than any other group from 1975 to 1978, reflecting their superior ability, relative to students, to deflect state repression. In the

ED era, as Yi Ujŏng puts it, "we advocated instead of students" (interview with Yi Ujŏng, August 17, 2000).

Christians were responsible for some of the most significant antigovernment events in the 1970s. In particular, the Declaration for the Salvation of the Nation (Minju kuguk sŏnŏnsŏ), delivered on March 1, 1976, by Catholic, Protestant, and oppositional political leaders, was important because of its highly publicized nature. Similar to Bishop Chi's Declaration of Conscience, the Declaration for the Salvation of the Nation—read by Yi Ujŏng on the fifty-seventh anniversary of the March 1, 1919, Declaration of Independence from Japanese colonial rule—was a pivotal moment in the struggle against Park Chung Hee's Yusin regime. Pastor Mun Ikhwan, professor at Korean Theological Seminary, drafted the document in response to the promulgation of ED 9, and it was signed by eleven of the most prominent senior leaders of the 1970s democracy movement, including Ham Sok Hon, Yun Posŏn, and Kim Dae Jung (NCCK Archive, Vol. 2: 687).

Originally, Pastor Yun Kanhong was scheduled to read the declaration, but he was arrested the day before for delivering a sermon that criticized the Yusin government (interview with Yi Ujŏng, August 17, 2000). Instead, the declaration was read by Yi Ujŏng at Myeongdong Cathedral in front of a diverse gathering that included Catholics, Protestants, secular opposition politicians, and students. By staging their event on March 1, the individuals involved in the writing and reading of the declaration were symbolically associating Park Chung Hee's authoritarian regime with the oppression of the Japanese colonial government. The head of the Seoul District Public Prosecutors Office, Sŏ Chŏnggak, promptly accused the signatories of trying to stage a coup d'état. Nineteen persons were then arrested under the NSL and given prison sentences ranging from two to five years. Although the repression was swift, the March 1 declaration, mainly because of the status of the principal participants, was celebrated by dissident communities and became a rallying point for those struggling to mobilize in the highly repressive context under ED 9.

THE CHRISTIAN ADVANTAGE

The entry of Christians into the democracy movement and the surge of Christian protests in the wake of the Minch'ŏng incident were a bane of Park Chung Hee. Christians fared better against state repression compared to other protesting groups for three reasons. First, because of their religious identity, Christians maintained moral distinction in South Korean society (Kang 1997; Park

2003; Lee T. 2010). Not only were they able to capitalize on social perceptions of their moral integrity, but also Christians, as a whole, were known for their strong anticommunist sentiments, making it more difficult for the state to apply the communist frame to them. Second, Christians appropriated their extensive organizational networks to facilitate mobilization and the church became a sanctuary for religious and secular activists. Third, Christians cultivated strong connections with the global community of religious and human rights organizations, hindering the state's ability to repress them without provoking international criticism.

Moral Integrity and Symbolic Power

Christianity has played an influential role in modern Korean history, beginning with the progressive "enlightenment movement" (*kaehwa undong*) in the late 1800s and early 1900s, and the independence movement against Japanese colonialism (Park 2003; Schmid 2002; Lee 2000; Wells 1990; Robinson 1988). Almost immediately upon its arrival in Korea, Protestant Christianity was associated with various social reforms, including the provision of education and modern (Western) health care to previously excluded populations (Oak 2013; Lee T. 2010). In particular, the role of Christian churches and leaders in organizing the March 1, 1919, Independence Movement against Japanese colonial rule solidified Christianity's position in Korean society. In part due to its social reform programs and its active role in the independence movement, Christianity took root in Korea much faster and deeper than it did in neighboring East Asian nations (Lee 2000; Park 2003).

Larger historical developments would further shape the character of Christianity in Korea. The polarization of the Korean political landscape into leftist movements and their conservative counterparts set the stage for the division of the nation in 1948, following Korea's liberation from colonial rule three years prior. During the colonial period, there had been a significant concentration of Christians in the northern part of the peninsula, with Pyongyang boasting one of the first and most important Protestant seminaries. The Presbyterian Theological Seminary in Pyongyang, established in 1901 by American missionary Samuel A. Moffett, produced the first generation of Korean Presbyterian clergy, which contributed to the large number of Christians in northern Korea (Lee T. 2010). Upon Korea's liberation from Japanese colonial rule, the presence of the Soviet Union and the United States above and below the 38th parallel inevitably influenced domestic politics, with Soviet-supported communism taking hold in the north and American-backed "democracy" in the south. As part of his effort to consolidate power, Korean communist leader Kim Il Sung suppressed Christianity while instituting a sweeping land reform in 1946, sparking an exodus of both landowners and Christians from the north to the south (Armstrong 2003). The religious persecution they experienced at the hands of Korean communists fundamentally shaped the political outlook of these "refugee Christians," who established large churches in the south. Henceforth, as Chung-shin Park puts it, "Christianity and the anticommunist political position were practically fused into one" (2003: 176).

As discussed in Chapter 3, Park Chung Hee's government justified the suppression of student protesters by labeling them communists or communist sympathizers, and by utilizing the NSL and ACL to prosecute and incarcerate them. This strategy was more difficult to apply to Christian activists, however, precisely because of the association of Christianity with anticommunism. As Yi Ujŏng explains:

> The reason why we could get together in the name of Jesus was the fact that a Christian cannot be a materialist. Communists are materialists [yumullonja] and Christians are theists [yusinnonja]. A theist cannot be a materialist, so people thought that Christians are not communists who support North Korea. Because of this, the government could not say that we were communists even if we demonstrated. We could act without fear. (Interview with Yi Ujŏng, August 17, 2000)

The association of Korean Christianity with anticommunism did not necessarily stop the Yusin regime from attempting to frame Christian dissidents. Pastor Pak Hyŏnggyu, as discussed, was accused of trying to "turn the south into a communist country" using funds he presumably received from North Korea. During his trial, however, the support he received from Christians, other religious leaders, and the larger public made it evident that Pak was not a communist. According to Pastor Pak, his arrest even solicited criticism from "the ambassador of the United States, [who] complained that Pak Hyŏnggyu was not a communist" (interview with Pak Hyŏnggyu, August 23, 2000). And although some Christian organizations—the UIM and the Christian Academy in particular—were not as able as popular Protestant and Catholic clergy to ward off communist accusations, the Yusin government on the whole had a difficult time accusing Christians of being communists. This additional layer of protection placed them "in a far stronger position to resist ideological persecution than other groups" (Koo 2001: 78).

Drawing on their moral standing in Korean society, Christian leaders enjoyed a symbolic power not afforded to their secular counterparts in the democracy movement. Both Protestant pastors, such as Pak Hyŏnggyu, and Catholic leaders, such as Cardinal Kim Suhwan and Bishop Chi Haksun, used their "symbolic capital" when criticizing Park Chung Hee's government. As Yi Chŏlsun remembers:

> The word of Cardinal Kim Suhwan had power. His criticism of the government had influence. When priests or ministers criticized the government, ordinary people listened to them. Park Chung Hee was maybe afraid of this. Many people believed the words of their priests and ministers. . . . the government was cautious about arresting Christians. (Interview with Yi Chŏlsun, August 20, 2000).

This symbolic power directly translated into the ability of Christians to provide protection to dissidents in the democracy movement, including students. During the 1970s and 1980s, Korean Protestant and Catholic churches—including, most importantly, Myeongdong Cathedral in central Seoul—were "sanctuaries" to which dissidents turned when running from the police. Although not a Christian himself, Park Chung Hee more or less refrained from ordering the police, the military, or the KCIA to infiltrate churches in search of student movement leaders. Whether Park Chung Hee really "believed that they [churches] were sacred ground" (interview with Yi Chŏlsun, August 20, 2000) or was afraid that violating churches would invite criticism from the Korean public and international organizations is less important than the practical protective benefits that churches enjoyed.

Organizational Resources
In addition to providing symbolic capital, Christians contributed to the larger democracy movement in tangible ways. An important asset that Christians possessed was their extensive domestic and international networks of churches and organizations. As Chung-shin Park succinctly puts it, "there was simply no other group comparable in organization and number to the Christian church immediately after the Liberation" (2003: 176). This was true relative to students, who despite their efforts to create a national movement with the Students' Alliance in 1971 and the NDYSA in 1974 did not readily possess the organizational infrastructure that Christians did. Although possibly exaggerating the discrepancy between student and Christian organizational resources, it is worth noting

that Kwŏn Osŏng, a theology student in the 1970s and general secretary of the National Council of Churches in Korea (NCCK) from 2006 to 2010, remembers that "Seoul National University only had their student union, but Christian organizations were everywhere, so Christian organizations became the connection points that [allowed the movement to] spread nationwide" (interview with Kwŏn Osŏng, December 24, 2005).

Churches such as Seoul's First Church, pastored by Pak Hyŏnggyu, opened their doors to students and other important dissidents, who looked to Christian clergy to provide moral leadership in the face of increasing state repression. As Pastor Pak remembers, "students at my church were involved deeply in the Minch'ŏng incident, and the famous dissident poet Kim Chiha also attended my church" (interview with Pak Hyŏnggyu, August 23, 2000). Progressive Christian leaders formed the Galilee Church group, which met at Hanbit Church, which was founded by the father of Pastor Mun Ikhwan, author of the March 1 Declaration for the Salvation of the Nation. Hanbit Church, and the Galilee gathering within it, became main loci for the democracy movement as it brought together Christians and students, as well as providing support for family members of political prisoners. The privileged position of the church in Korean society allowed it to play host to events that could not have occurred elsewhere. Yi Ujŏng explains:

> Pastors Mun Ikhwan and Ahn Byung-Mu were with me and we served together at Galilee Church. . . . Galilee is the land of suffering people and we gathered to pray for the people whose family members were in prison. We prayed for their children and husbands who were arrested and tortured. Many people in need came to the church and shared their hardships with the pastors. Service was held at 11 o'clock at Hanbit Church. After service the prayer started at 3. When incarcerated individuals were released we celebrated it at the church. People could not do that in other places except for the church. Hanbit Church offered us a place to celebrate. The church was truly for people in need. (Interview with Yi Ujŏng, August 17, 2000)

In addition to Protestant and Catholic churches providing shelter and support for dissident groups, Christians also formed several social movement organizations. As movement scholars have pointed out, formal organizations are important vehicles for mobilization because of their role in garnering resources necessary to sustain movements (McCarthy and Zald 1977). Some Christian social movement organizations, such as the Christian Academy, were already active in the 1960s. Founded in 1956, the Christian Academy contributed to the reconstruction of South Korean society in the aftermath of the Korean War by sponsoring various social and education programs. By the 1970s, the Christian Academy had turned its attention to populations negatively affected by Park Chung Hee's industrialization policies. The overarching goal of the Christian Academy was to deepen the "democratic mind" of the Korean people, as Pak Kyŏngsŏ, former associate director of the Christian Academy, recalls:

> We trained laborers, farmers, youth, women, and ministers in the church, believing that through training young people in these five groups we could raise awareness about democracy for all groups in society. The content of the programs included the history of democracy and criticisms about the dictatorship in Korea. We taught that successful development is not possible while oppressing the blue color [workers]. It is not possible, in the long term, to increase the productivity of labor without respecting their rights. This was the same for farmers. We taught that farmers should also have a democratic mind so that they can express their opinions to the government. (Interview with Pak Kyŏngsŏ, August 25, 2000)

Several Christian organizations were founded in the 1970s in direct reaction to heightened state repression (Chang and Kim 2007). Prominent organizations such as the Christian Academy and Church Women United were joined by a host of others that mobilized different constituencies and pursued specific goals. The membership of organizations such as the KSCF and the Ecumenical Youth Council (EYC), for example, consisted primarily of Christian students and youth, although they were advised by senior Christian leaders. The NCCK's Human Rights Mission (Han'guk Kidokkyo Kyohoe Hyŏbŭihoe Inkwŏn Wiwŏnhoe) was a champion of human rights and became one of the most active groups following the promulgation of ED 9. Some Christian organizations, on the basis of their industry-specific resources, made unique contributions to the movement. The CBS, for example, publicized workers' issues by broadcasting news about the self-immolation protest of Chŏn T'aeil. Other groups, such as the Association of Family Members of Prisoners of Conscience (Yangsimbŏm Kajok Hyŏbŭihoe) and the Thursday Prayer Meeting, though not formal social movement organizations, mobilized families that shared the experience of state repression.

Many of these organizations, including the EYC and the Human Rights Mission, were founded in direct response to state repression. The EYC was formed to coordinate the antigovernment activities of students and youth outside of their university settings to avoid restrictions set by ED 4. The Human Rights Mission was founded as the public became increasingly aware of the appalling treatment of political prisoners. The NCCK officially formed the Human Rights Mission on April 11, 1974, and this organization quickly became the central node in the Christian network that linked together a variety of other groups, thereby expanding the organizational infrastructure of Christian activism. At times the very form of Christian organizations was influenced by state repression. Although the Thursday Prayer Meeting was not technically a formal organization, the meetings provided a consistent space for Christian activism in the ED era because of their informal structure and overt religious agenda. The Human Rights Mission, for instance, distributed its newsletter at these prayer meetings as released political prisoners shared their testimonies. It was in large part due to the efforts of the Thursday Prayer Meeting, the Human Rights Mission, and other Christian organizations, such as the Association of Family Members of Prisoners of Conscience, that Christians were able to publicize the stories of political prisoners and state torture to the larger public.

The efficacy of these organizations, and the participation of prominent Christian leaders in them, did not go unnoticed by the government. Some individuals were targeted by the state because of their positions in these social movement organizations, as Yi Ujŏng recalls:

> I became the chairperson for Church Women United and we filed petitions and made statements against the government to save students who were arrested. . . . The government hated us. Because I was the chairperson of Church Women United I had to resign [from my university professorship] when Kim Chiha and other people were arrested. They forced me to resign. The Dean of Seoul Women's University told me to resign. She told me that the Minister of Education called her and said that she needed to fire me. (Interview with Yi Ujŏng, August 17, 2000)

The government had good reason to target Christian leaders. Both pastors and lay leaders, such as Pak Hyŏnggyu and Yi Ujŏng, not only provided symbolic power and leadership to the larger dissident community but also supported the student movement with monetary resources. Describing a sensational case, Pastor Pak recalls a fascinating account of the complex relationships between students, church leaders, and oppositional politicians during the Minch'ŏng incident. Pastor Pak's attempt to aid students led not only to his re-arrest but also to the arrests of several other prominent figures, including former president of South Korea Yun Posŏn, Yi Ujŏng, Bishop Chi Haksun, and poet Kim Chiha:

> A student at my church, Na Pyŏngsik [a central student leader and one of the main architects of the 1974 national student network], was organizing a demonstration. Yi Chŏl [another student leader] was involved although he did not attend my church. . . . Na Pyŏngsik was looking for someone to fund their activities but couldn't find anyone so he came to me. I gave him some money at Kŭmjandi [Golden Lawn] Café, where we met. I also went to Yun Posŏn's home at 4 a.m. and left a memo concealed in a newspaper. I wrote that I needed money to do an important thing. I asked him for 1,000,000 KRW. He gave me 450,000 KRW [about US$400] and I gave that to Yi Ujŏng who gave it to Na Pyŏngsik. The money was used to support Minch'ŏng Hangnyŏn [NDYSA]. Kim Chiha was with Chi Haksun at the time. Later, Na Pyŏngsik and Yi Chŏl were arrested and tortured and Na Pyŏngsik learned that the government fabricated a confession, claiming that Minch'ŏng Hangnyŏn was related to the Inhyŏktang [PRP] and that students received money from the north [North Korea]. Na Pyŏngsik thought that if they confessed as the government wanted them to, everybody involved would be considered a communist. So he came to think of me and told them that he received the money from me. So I was arrested. . . . I told them I received the money from Yun Posŏn. They were so embarrassed because that meant they could not accuse us of being communists. They went to Yun Posŏn and asked if he gave the money to me. He said yes, so he was also arrested. . . . I was also sorry to Yi Ujŏng. She was a peaceful teacher, but because she was connected to me she was taken by the KCIA and interrogated for a week. But really she didn't know anything. She just delivered the money for me. She didn't know where the money came from and how it was used. I didn't tell her. She was just doing me a favor. (Interview with Pak Hyŏnggyu, August 23, 2000)

This insightful account reveals the several tangible ways that Christians contributed to the democracy movement. Although the monetary resources that Pak Hyŏnggyu provided via Yi Ujŏng to NDYSA student leaders was not insubstantial, the more important assistance was Christians' ability to challenge the identification of antigovernment protests with a communist movement. Government officials were in a conundrum when they traced the source of the money used to organize student protests to the former president of South Korea, Yun Posŏn. After accusing students of receiving money from

North Korea, they now found themselves in the absurd situation of having to take the former president into custody for questioning. Finding that the money came from Yun Posŏn did not, ultimately, stop the government from prosecuting student leaders and other individuals related to the Minch'ŏng incident and the PRP case, but the application of the communist frame to student protesters was made that much more untenable. In this and other ways, Christians and their organizations provided unique resources to the larger democracy movement.

International Networks

Christian churches and organizations not only had strong networks within Korea but also maintained direct ties to international Christian and secular human rights groups. International networks were a significant advantage that Christians possessed compared to other protesting groups because "Park Chung Hee was aware of the voices outside of Korea" (interview with Yi Chŏlsun, August 20, 2000). Comparing the Christian and student movements, No Ch'angsik argues:

> The power of the student movement was weak. Compared to them, Christians had advantages. The government had difficulty arresting Christians since the church had links to other organizations like the WCC. The government was afraid of letting others outside of Korea know about the oppression. They controlled the Korean press but they couldn't control presses outside of Korea. (Interview with No Ch'angsik, August 20, 2000)

Several ecclesiastical organizations, both Protestant and Catholic, are formally affiliated with international religious bodies. For example, the NCCK is the Korean chapter of the WCC, and the KSCF is the Korean chapter of the World Student Christian Federation. All Korean Catholic priests and nuns, including Bishop Chi Haksun, are technically speaking employees of the Roman Catholic Church and it is noteworthy that the Vatican made pleas for Bishop Chi's release when he was arrested for violating EDs 1 and 4 in 1974. In addition to ecclesial networks, Christian social movement organizations are also integrated globally: Church Women United, for example, maintains chapters in several countries, including South Korea.

The organization outside of Korea that probably made the largest contribution to the democracy movement was the North American Coalition for Human Rights in Korea (later known as the Korea Church Coalition for Peace, Justification, and Reunification). Originally based in Washington D.C., its activities in the 1970s and 1980s included monitoring and archiving daily developments in South Korea, providing monetary assistance to various Korean organizations and individuals, playing liaison between Korean dissidents and international supporters, and lobbying the U.S. government to help protect human rights in Korea. The efforts of the North American Coalition produced the largest archive of English-language materials related to South Korea's democracy movement: the UCLA Archival Collection on Democracy and Unification in Korea.

International support for the democracy movement was also found within Korea as sympathetic missionaries in the country began to help Korean dissidents. The efficacy of the missionaries was in part a function of their foreigner status. Police refrained from engaging foreigners in the same way in which they accosted Koreans. This allowed a certain amount of leeway and emboldened the foreign supporters of Korea's democracy movement. Catholic priest James Sinnott, for example, recalls:

> I knew from previous demonstrations they [the police] had orders, "don't touch the foreigners," particularly me. And I knew that and I would push policemen around and take off their helmets, knowing they couldn't [retaliate] or [were] told not to. So I was spoiled in that sense and so I was wild, I could do these things and they wouldn't hit me back. (Interview with James Sinnott, August 12, 2014)

The role of foreign missionaries in Korea's democracy movement crystalized with the founding of the "Monday Night Group" (Stentzel 2006). Formed to consolidate resources and develop strategies to aid Korean dissidents, the Monday Night Group brought together a small number of determined missionaries and lay leaders, including Pastor George Ogle, Friar James Sinnott, and Faye Moon. In a fascinating volume that chronicles the experiences of the Monday Night Group, Jim Stentzel, a key member, describes the advantages that foreigners enjoyed:

> The Monday Night Group had several layers of protection. They were foreigners, mostly North Americans. They were Christians. And they were missionaries, which meant they had quick and easy access to world-wide ecclesiastical structures and media networks. The Park Chung Hee government, which otherwise tended to throw caution to the wind, wanted to avoid charges in foreign media that it was persecuting Americans, Christians, and/or missionaries. (Stentzel 2006: 26)

Although Park Chung Hee may have wanted to avert perceptions that he was "persecuting Americans, Christians, and/or missionaries," his government took the foreigners seriously enough to enact a law on March 19, 1975, that made it illegal to defame the Korean nation and government to foreigners in and outside of Korea (Yi Chaeo 2011: 342–343). In many cases, the "layers of protection" did not prevent the foreign missionaries from being harassed, or worse: both George Ogle and James Sinnott were forcibly deported in December 1974 and April 1975, respectively, for criticizing the government's PRP case (Ogle 1977; interview with James Sinnott, August 12, 2014).

Part of the reason the government monitored foreigners in Korea so closely was that they provided unique resources to the democracy movement. For instance, Faye Moon—wife of dissident Christian leader Mun Tonghwan and sister-in-law of Mun Ikhwan—recalls working at a U.S. Army base in Korea and using the U.S. Army APO mail system to send communications about what was happening in Korea to concerned groups, including the North American Coalition (Moon 2006). She also used the Army APO to receive foreign news about the Korean situation, including transcripts of U.S. congressional hearings on Korea's human rights situation led by Representative Donald Fraser of Minnesota (see Chapter 6). As Faye Moon remembers, "this kind of information was vital to the movement leaders in Korea and to the student leaders. They could learn the direction the U.S. government was taking in relation to Korea" (2006: 183).

The connections that Korean Christians had to international supporters translated into substantial resources for the democracy movement. The KSCF received invaluable guidance from famous U.S. community organizer Saul Alinsky, who visited Korea in the fall of 1971, shortly before he passed away in June 1972, to help KSCF develop their Student Social Development Corps (Zoh 2004: 117). Moreover, several Christian social welfare programs were funded by external donations: international NGO Bread for the World, for example, supported the Seoul Metropolitan Community Organization, donating a total of US$80,000 to this Christian group. Another example was the Christian Academy. During his time as program coordinator at the Christian Academy, Pastor Pak Hyŏnggyu met George Todd, who came to Korea in his capacity as director of the WCC Office for Urban and Industrial Missions. Pastor Pak was able to secure US$100,000 from George Todd, half of which went to the Urban Problems Research Center (Tosi Munje Yŏn'guso) at Yonsei University and half to various Catholic and Protestant urban poverty relief efforts (interview with Pak

Hyŏnggyu, August 23, 2000). More international aid for the Christian Academy came from the progressive church in Germany. Pak Kyŏngsŏ remembers that "the German church provided about 70 percent of the budget [for the Christian Academy in 1979]. The rest of the funds were raised in Korea and members of the academy paid fees for training. The German church wanted us to engage in democratic movements as they did in their country" (interview with Pak Kyŏngsŏ, August 25, 2000).

In addition to providing monetary assistance, international supporters also showed their solidarity with Korean Christian dissidents by physically coming to Korea in times of need. The status of some of the foreign visitors confirmed the perception that Korean Christians had powerful allies, which provided a certain amount of protection from state repression. In one important case, when the police arrested NCCK Director Kim Kwansŏk and two staff pastors for the "illegal" use of 203,000 Deutsche Marks (about US$133,500) donated by the German branch of Bread for the World, several prominent foreigners—including Pastor Wolfgang Schmidt of Bread for the World; Japanese lawyer Kenkichi Nakadaira; four delegates from the WCC, including Central Committee member Kurt Scharf; and future president of Germany Richard von Weiszäcker—flew to Korea to witness the trials (NCCK Archive, Vol. 2: 586–641). International groups petitioned for the release of these and other political prisoners, and at times were effective in liberating Korean dissidents. Yi Ujŏng recalls the reasons she was released early after her arrest following her reading of the sensational Declaration for the Salvation of the Nation on March 1, 1976:

I called a missionary whom I was supposed to meet the next day after reading the statement and told him that I could not see him. He understood the situation and reported it to the press. News about the event was released in the U.S. on the 1st of March.[6] The church in the U.S. said that Yi Ujŏng is not a socialist but a Christian. There were only two women arrested at that time. People from all over the world wrote letters of petition to save us. The prosecutor was so embarrassed . . . he asked me how this can happen and I said I did not know. Anyway, the church in the U.S. acted for us. . . . I think our church was so blessed and this was so special. We united globally and we were supported by our global network. . . . the national [domestic] network helped us a lot but those in the U.S. helped us much more. Because of all of this, the Korean government could not treat us badly. (Interview with Yi Ujŏng, August 17, 2000)

In sum, Christians enjoyed symbolic and material advantages that allowed them to take the lead in public demonstrations against Park Chung Hee's Yusin government at a critical time, when the student movement was in disarray following ED 4 and the Minch'ŏng incident. From 1975 on, Christians staged more protest events than any other group. The relative strength of the Christian community was a function of their moral power, organizational resources, and international networks. Indeed, Christians, more than any other group in the democracy movement, engaged in solidarity work with international organizations and, as Pak Kyŏngsŏ puts it, "the democratic movement in the 1970s was not performed only by Koreans. . . . All the churches in the world, including those of Germany, the U.S., Canada, and Australia, supported the churches in Korea" (interview with Pak Kyŏngsŏ, August 25, 2000).

These advantages allowed Christians to effectivly support others in the larger democracy movement as well. In regard to the labor movement, for example, Hagen Koo notes that "unlike the intellectuals, who were highly sympathetic to workers' problems but organizationally weak, the church organizations were in a stronger position to render support to the workers because of their international networks and internal organizational structure" (2001: 78). For Park Chung Hee, repressing Christians "became a highly costly political option. Any arrest of Christian activists instantly triggered diplomatic protests and especially eroded support for Park in America" (Park 2011: 390). Their unique resources thus allowed Christians to carry the movement through its darkest hours.

FROM LIBERAL THEOLOGY TO LIBERATION THEOLOGY

An important contribution that Christians made in addition to providing moral leadership, organizational resources, and international networks was their articulation of the *minjung*. In the 1980s, the "three *min* ideology"—*minju* (democracy), *minjung* (people), and *minjok* (nation)—became the discursive foundation of the democracy movement such that some simply refer to it as the "*minjung* movement" (Lee 2007; Wells 1995a). For their part, Christians added an ontological layer to what Nancy Abelmann (1996) has called the "*minjung* imaginary" by constructing a Korean liberation theology. Minjung Theology did not so much motivate Christian participation in political activism in the 1970s as it justified it. If Christian social engagement in the 1960s and early 1970s initially centered around social welfare programs, it was only with time that this *liberal* theological emphasis on the social gospel evolved into an out-

right *liberation* theology that legitimated Christian participation in antigovernment protests.

Before the development of a systematic Korean theology of liberation, the
discourse surrounding Christian social engagement was already saturated with
theological justifications. The president of the progressive Korean Theological
Seminary and "father" of liberal theology in Korea, Kim Chaejun, had emphasized the social gospel and the importance of Christian engagement in social
activism. It is not difficult to see how the labor reforms—factory regulations,
shorter workweek, abolition of child labor, and so on—that were advocated
by the original social gospel movement in the United States were pertinent to
the Korean situation in the 1970s. Amid rapid industrialization and rampant
labor exploitation, the work of Protestant and Catholic organizations such as
the UIM and the Catholic JOC can be construed as Christians' attempt to carry
out the social gospel in the Korean context.

Initially applied to American labor conditions in the early part of the twentieth century, the "social gospel theology," best articulated in Walter Rauschenbusch's classic *A Theology for the Social Gospel* (1918), paved the way for more
radical political theologies. American pastors engaged in political activism,
such as Martin Luther King Jr., found in the social gospel not only a theological
justification for addressing the oppression of the poor and downtrodden, but
also a Christian rationale for challenging the political structures that undergird
that oppression. In the 1960s, theologians published a string of critical texts—
Harvey Cox's *The Secular City* (1965), Jürgen Moltmann's *The Theology of Hope*
(1964), and Richard Shaull's *The Theology of Revolution* (1966)—that collectively
argued that a "discussion of God was at the same time a political discussion"
(Park 2003: 191).

Ecclesiastical support for social and political activism also gained a significant boost from the Roman Catholic Church when in 1962 Pope John XXIII
called the Second Vatican Council to reassess the Church's relationship to
the modern world. Vatican II recommitted the Church to aiding the poor
and oppressed and motivated Catholic theologians, especially in Latin America, to develop liberation theology, beginning with the publication of Gustavo Gutiérrez's foundational work, *A Theology of Liberation: History, Politics,
and Salvation* (1973). Although the Yusin government tried to limit access
to these "subversive" publications by banning them in Korea, the "growing
theological radicalism in the world church community at the time influenced
Korean liberal Christians" (Park 2003: 191). Some Christians in Korea, includ-

ing Yi Chŏlsun, were able to get their hands on translated copies of liberation theology texts:

> I also read books about liberation theology between 1976 and 1978. The books were banned so I hid those books in a rice pot. You could be punished by the National Security Law when you read those books. Those books helped me a lot. And also Paulo Freire's *Pedagogy of the Oppressed*—I tried to practice the methods in that book. (Interview with Yi Chŏlsun, August 20, 2000)

The fundamental axiom in liberation theology—namely the "preferential option for the poor"—found currency in progressive Korean Christian circles in the 1970s. Pak Kyŏngsŏ remembers:

> I was influenced by my pastors such as Pak Wŏlryong, Pak Hyŏnggyu, and Kim Kwansŏk. The idea that churches should not stand by the rich and sustain the powerful influenced me. I thought churches should care for the poor and protect their rights. Churches should be the voice for those who do not have a voice. This was a common belief among students at Seoul National University and not only among the theology students. (Interview with Pak Kyŏngsŏ, August 25, 2000)

The theological connection between social engagement and political activism was especially important in 1970s Korea because only a small group of progressive Christians challenged Park Chung Hee's government while the great majority of Korean Christians either accepted or actively supported the Yusin regime. According to Pak Kyŏngsŏ, "Conservative Christians criticized their [progressive Christians'] participation [in the democracy movement] and said that it was not because of religion but for politics" (interview with Pak Kyŏngsŏ, August 25, 2000). But for Christians participating in the democracy movement, social engagement and political activism could not be separated, as Pastor Pak Hyŏnggyu explains: "If we do not have freedom, there is no love. God's absolute command, 'Love your neighbor as yourself,' can only be realized when we have political liberty. Without this we cannot love our neighbors as ourselves" (interview with Pak Hyŏnggyu, August 23, 2000). Other Christians looked to Jesus's example to justify their participation in political movements, claiming "that Jesus was in fact a political prisoner, so it is not consistent with the Bible that religion should be separate from politics" (interview with No Ch'angsik, August 20, 2000).

Christians defended their participation in antigovernment protests in these ways and, ironically, state repression gave them ample opportunity to clarify both their purpose and their identity. Pak Hyŏnggyu's arrest after the Easter Sunday protest in 1973 not only galvanized Christian participation in the democracy movement but also contributed to the evolution of the cultural contest between the state and Christian dissidents. The accusation of political opportunism by both the state and conservative Christian groups vexed Christian activists, but more important, it prompted them to carefully and consciously articulate the reasons for their protest. It was this need to respond to government accusations that provided the motive for developing a theological understanding of Christian political activism. Throughout the 1970s, Christians made several important declarations that outlined the religious reasons for their participation in antigovernment protests.

The 1973 Theological Declaration of Korean Christians, declared shortly after Pak Hyŏnggyu's arrest, was the first public statement by Christian dissidents that defined their position specifically from a religious standpoint. The declaration challenged Park Chung Hee's justifications for the Yusin Constitution, specifically national security and economic development, before redefining Christian political action as a religious act. This "framing contest"—the state's accusation of political opportunism versus Christians' insistence on the religious basis for political action—was manifest in a number of important events in the 1970s.

The UIM's work with labor groups centered on improving the material conditions in factories, but it also sparked a discursive debate that revolved around the identity of Christian dissidents. The government's sponsorship of Hong Chiyŏng's tendentious pamphlet "What Is the UIM Aiming at?" in 1978 was one attempt to frame members of the UIM as communists (UCLA Archival Collection: Box 09-1, Folder 09-1-04; Ogle 1990: 90). UIM activities, Hong argued, challenged the capitalist foundations of South Korean society because they "imply companies belong to workers not to employers" (UCLA Archival Collection: Box 09-1, Folder 09-1-06). This pamphlet was cited by the government as a justification for the violent repression of the UIM. In response, members of the UIM and other Christian dissidents declared that their actions were the natural manifestations of their Christian faith. Several Christian organizations, including the Catholic Justice and Peace Committee, the Human Rights Mission, and denominations affiliated with the NCCK, publicly decried Hong's pamphlet (UCLA Archival Collection: Box 09-1, Folder 09-1-06). Further justifying Christian activism, the Human Rights Mission organized a conference held October 19–21, 1978, titled "Consultation on Ideology," which provided a forum for a more thorough investigation of how the government had historically used anticommunist ideology to suppress civil rights and basic political freedoms (UCLA Archival Collection: Box 09-1, Folder 09-1-05).

The repression of the Christian Academy was another important occasion for clarifying the rationale for Christian political action. As discussed, by the 1970s the Christian Academy was involved in educating laborers and farmers about their particular roles in Park Chung Hee's industrialization programs. These efforts, interpreted by the state as subversive to social stability, led to the arrests on May 28, 1979, of Professor Chŏng Changyol, six staff persons, and "about four hundred to five hundred trainees in our programs" (interview with Pak Kyŏngsŏ, August 25, 2000). Having accused the members of the Christian Academy of violating the NSL and the ACL, a judge presiding over the case asked one of the defendants, Yi Uje, to define "socialism" (UCLA Archival Collection: Box 09-1, Folder 09-1-05). In his reply, Yi focused on his duties as a Christian to help alleviate the suffering of the Korean people, and he argued that his actions had nothing to do with the secular political ideology of socialism or communism (Chang 2006: 216). The magnitude of the case, based on the large number of people arrested, ensured a prodigious audience for the debate both inside and outside of the courtroom, and thus helped publicize Christian justifications for political activism.

The justifications for political participation, in addition to responding to the state, were also targeted at conservative evangelical Christians, who criticized their progressive counterparts for "meddling" in politics. While progressive Christian leaders were being arrested and interrogated by the Yusin regime, the much larger conservative Christian community was enjoying tremendous growth. In the 1970s, evangelical Christians staged some of the largest religious revivals in Korean history, including the Fifty Million to Christ crusade led by Billy Graham in May and June, 1973; the Explo 1974 revival; and the 1977 Holy Assembly for the Evangelization of the Nation (Lee T. 2010: 94–101). Some evangelical leaders not only criticized protesting Christians but also went further by overtly supporting the Yusin government. The Annual National Prayer Breakfast Committee, for example, organized breakfast meetings for Park Chung Hee. At these meetings, pastors such as Kim Chun'gon and Yi Sangno claimed that "when church and government are harmonious through assistance and cooperation, the church will be holy and the state will prosper" (Yi Sangno, quoted in Park 2003: 184–185).

Recognizing the need to respond to their critics, as well as driven by the desire to understand their own actions and sacrifices, a small handful of progressive theologians began to systematically explore the theological justifications for political engagement in the form of a Korean liberation theology. The collective signifier, *minjung*, a populist term denoting the masses or "common people" (Lee 2007: 1), which enjoyed wide circulation among leftist groups during the first half of the twentieth century (Em 1999), first entered the Christian theological imagination in the mid-1970s. In December 1974, Sŏ Namdong, professor of theology at Yonsei University and a founding member of the Galilee Church group, delivered a lecture at a faculty retreat, laying out the theological propositions that would become the foundations of Minjung Theology (Song 1984). He spent that winter revising the lecture and published it in the February 1975 issue of the journal *Kidokkyo sasang* with the title "Jesus, Church History, the Korean Church" ("Yesu, kyohoesa, Han'guk kyohoe"; Sŏ 1975a).

The April issue of *Kidokkyo sasang* acted as the vehicle for the public debut of a Korean liberation theology when the journal published the first collection of articles on Minjung Theology. Included in this seminal statement were articles penned by Sŏ Namdong and Ahn Byung-Mu, professor of New Testament studies at Korean Theological Seminary, titled "Minjung's Theology" ("Minjung ŭi sinhak"; Sŏ 1975b) and "Nation, Minjung, Church" ("Minjok, minjung, kyohoe"; Ahn 1975).[7] Professors Ahn and Sŏ had been forcibly dismissed from their respective universities in November 1974 because of their antigovernment activism, but along with other progressive theologians they were able to develop Minjung Theology further in various periodicals, including *Kidokkyo sasang* and *Sinhak sasang* (*Theological Thought*; Kim 2006). In the spring of 1979, the Korea Theological Study Institute, founded by Ahn Byung-Mu in 1973, published a special edition of *Sinhak sasang* under the thematic title "Theory of 'Minjung.'" This issue brought together the first generation of *minjung* theologians—including Kim Chŏngjun, Kim Yongbok, Sŏ Namdong, and Ahn Byung-Mu—who attempted to develop more fully a uniquely Korean version of liberation theology.

Building on the special issue of *Sinhak sasang*, the Christian Conference of Asia and the NCCK held a conference in Seoul in October 1979. The title of that conference, "The People of God and the Mission of the Church" ("Hananim ŭi paeksŏng kwa kyohoe ŭi sŏn'gyo"), was chosen intentionally in order not to attract the attention of government authorities: the term *minjung*, which at that time already carried subversive political connotations, was replaced with the apolitical term *paeksŏng* (people). The conference was held from October 22 to 24, just a few days before President Park Chung Hee was assassinated, on October 26, 1979. The conference produced an English-language volume titled

Minjung Theology: People as the Subjects of History (CTC-CCA 1981), which is the first systematic presentation of Minjung Theology and the culmination of the process of "theologizing" the Christian struggle against the Yusin regime. Justified by the belief that "the function and task of theology is to test, criticize and revise the language which the Church uses about God" (Thomas 1983: 2), Minjung Theology was born after nearly a decade of protests, arrests, incarceration, and torture.

THE SIGNIFICANCE OF CHRISTIAN ACTIVISM

Although several scholars have recognized the important role that Christians played in the 1970s democracy movement (Park 2011; Park 2003; Clark 2002; Kim 2000; Kang 1997), this chapter has offered a more nuanced analysis by situating the emergence of Christian activism within the larger context of the state repression strategy that first targeted students. By focusing on differential participation rates, I have shown that the timing of Christian entry into the movement was a function of the demobilization of the student movement. Nineteen seventy-five proved to be a turning point in the democracy movement as Christians stepped in to fill the void left by incarcerated students after the Minch'ŏng incident. Thus a "changing of the guard" took effect as Christians emerged to lead the movement during the dark ED period.

Christianity's contributions to the democracy movement in the 1970s were many. First, Christians helped develop the movement's ideology in the form of a Korean liberation theology. Second, they utilized existing church networks and formed new organizations to mobilize groups that lacked organizational infrastructure. Organizations such as the NCCK's Human Rights Mission and the UIM conducted the important work of building bridges between different social groups in the democracy movement. Other Christian gatherings, such as the Thursday Prayer Meeting, the Galilee Church group, and the Monday Night Group, became spaces for subversive activities when other outlets were closed to dissidents. Finally, Christians drew on their international relationships to publicize the Korean situation to the outside world while receiving considerable amounts of symbolic and material resources. These advantages were de facto "weapons that the government could not control completely and that other antigovernment groups lacked" (Park 2003: 195).

Chung-shin Park is right to point out that the "majority of Christians went the easy way of supporting the regime," and only a small minority of Christians participated in antigovernment protests: roughly 5 percent of churches,

5 percent of Protestant pastors, and 4 percent of the laity (2003: 183–184). Their relatively small numbers belied, however, their significance for the democracy movement. Park's claim that progressive Christians "remained voices in the wilderness which elicited little or no echo not only in the Protestant community under conservative control, but even in the liberal denomination to which they belonged" (2003: 172) fails to consider the consequences of Christian activism for communities outside of the church. Theirs was not a movement directed toward other Korean Christians, whether liberals or conservatives, but rather was motivated by the desire to aid dissident groups that were struggling against a despot. The contributions that progressive Christians made to Korean society and to the democracy movement far surpassed their minority status *within* the Korean church. At a time when most Christian leaders either passively or actively supported Park Chung Hee's regime, a small group of concerned Christians made a large impact by carrying the torch in the darkest hours of the democracy movement (Chang 2006).

The emergence of Christian activism in the wake of the Minch'ŏng incident motivated Park Chung Hee to rethink his repression strategy. After targeting students with EDs 4 and 7, the state worded ED 9 generally enough so as to be applied to any and all antigovernment protest activities. ED 9 was, in short, a direct response to the diversification of social actors participating in the democracy movement and, justified by the new measure, the state began targeting Christians as well. As No Ch'angsik puts it, "Park Chung Hee hated all the activities of the church. If there were movements from other parts of society, he would not so much care about the Christians. But as he severely oppressed [other] social movements, there were no other movements except the church in larger society. So he could not help but take them very seriously" (interview with No Ch'angsik, August 20, 2000). Still, as I have argued, Christians were able to fare better relative to other groups because their religious identity and connections to international religious and human rights organizations provided unique layers of protection.

It is critical to understand the evolution of South Korea's democracy movement before and after the EDs. The shift in momentum from student to Christian mobilization transformed the character of the movement in significant ways. As detailed in Chapter 6, the diversification of the movement motivated new understandings of democracy as Christians and other groups brought to light issues and grievances particular to their communities. Furthermore, whereas students tended to rely on disruptive demonstrations, there was a shift toward nondisruptive protest tactics when Christians came to lead the movement in the latter half of the 1970s. In short, the evolution of the discursive character and tactical repertoire of the movement were fueled by new dissident groups, which included journalists and human rights lawyers, who joined Christians as salient actors in the movement in the ED era.

5 THE POLITICIZATION OF
JOURNALISTS AND LAWYERS

Freedom of thought and speech must be guaranteed by law, and so must
be the right to make constructive criticism of Government measures.

Park Chung Hee, *Our Nation's Path*

Symbolizing the independence and integrity of the Korean media, the National
Press Club building stands tall in Gwanghwamun, the heart of Seoul city. On
a brisk October day in 2009, more than fifty former journalists gather on the
twentieth floor of the Press Club to commemorate the thirty-fifth anniversary
of the Declaration of Action for a Free Press, first proclaimed on October 24,
1974. Organized by the Dong-A Committee for the Struggle to Protect a Free
Press (abbreviated Dong-A T'uwi), the memorial event begins with the ceremonial reading of this foundational declaration that marked the beginning of
the free press movement.

It is a remarkable group that has gathered at the Press Club, a short block
from the original *Dong-A Ilbo* headquarters. The joyous handshakes and hugs
that are exchanged prior to the start of the memorial event belie the common
bond that brings the participants together.[1] Members of Dong-A T'uwi gather
every October to remember events that are long passed but have shaped their individual lives, as well as the possibility of the freedom of speech in South Korea.
Started by a group of journalists who were fired in 1975 for taking a stand against
state censorship, Dong-A T'uwi continues to advocate for press freedom forty
years after its founding. Although when asked about their "political" movement
in the 1970s members of Dong-A T'uwi claim that they were simply trying to do
their jobs, the politicization of journalists and their participation in antigovernment protests represented a significant contribution to the democracy movement precisely at the time of heightened state repression.

The story of Dong-A T'uwi and the entry of journalists into the democracy movement is a representative case of the politicization of diverse sectors

of Korean society in the 1970s. Although students and a small group of dissident intellectuals could boast a long history of political engagement, hundreds of journalists and a handful of lawyers emerged as important movement actors in the wake of the EDs that led to the arrest of more than a thousand students and the murder of eight defendants in the PRP case. Diversification was an unintended consequence of state repression that reflected the ability of the movement to continue to grow and adapt even as public protests were stifled in the ED era.

This chapter explores why and how journalists and lawyers joined the larger movement for democracy in the 1970s. I draw on various quantitative and qualitative data sources to show that, similar to Christians, these new movement actors were politicized in large part because of the specific repression strategies that Park Chung Hee's government employed to quell growing antigovernment protests. The data speak to the importance of state repression in motivating the differential participation rates for social movement actors and, consequently, the diversification of the 1970s democracy movement.

THE STATE AND MEDIA

The emergence of the free press movement (*chayu ŏllon undong*) was an important development in the 1970s. Scholars have noted the critical role the media can play in the diffusion of social movements (Snow, Vliegenthart, and Corrigall-Brown 2007; Strang and Soule 1998). Consequently, dictators are motivated to constrain the press as part of a larger strategy to limit the spread of antigovernment movements (Dobson 2013). If it is true that "the heart of democracy is the freedom of speech" (interview with Chŏng Tongik, October 16, 2009), it follows that "censoring the media is the first step in controlling society" (interview with Yun Sŏkpong, November 16, 2009).

Several characteristics associated with the vocation of journalism lend themselves to effective political mobilization. First, it is the job of journalists to be aware of and to communicate newsworthy material. They are thus, by trade, privy to political and economic developments. In the 1970s in South Korea, journalists gathered information on political protests and on problems associated with the state's economic policies, and attempted to disseminate that information through various media channels. A second attribute is their ready access to forms of mass communication. Through newspapers, magazines, television, and radio, media groups possess the capability to spread the word about political demonstrations to a wide audience. Third, journalists, like Christians, have connections to foreign media organizations; the international relationships that Korean journalists maintained in the 1970s were an important resource for the democracy movement and a bane for Park Chung Hee, who did not want stories of social unrest and state repression to leak out to the international community.

The modern media industry in Korea was relatively young and underdeveloped when Park Chung Hee came to power in 1961. Korea's "first modern vernacular newspaper," the *Tongnip Sinmun* (the *Independent*), was started by Sŏ Chaep'il, a reform-minded political and intellectual leader, on April 7, 1896, but publication was discontinued just a few years later (Eckert et al. 1990: 234). Reviving the novelty of publishing a newspaper in the Korean vernacular, the *Chosun Ilbo* and *Dong-A Ilbo* were founded in 1920 after the Japanese colonial government relaxed some of its censorship policies in the wake of the March 1, 1919, independence movement.[2] Throughout the remainder of the colonial period, however, these Korean-language newspapers were strictly monitored and "the concept of freedom of the press was too alien for Koreans" (Youm 1996: 37).

According to Kyu Ho Youm (1996), it was only after the liberation of Korea from Japanese colonial rule that the concept of a free press was "introduced" to Koreans by the Americans, who governed southern Korea from 1945 to 1948. Lieutenant General John R. Hodge, commander of the United States Army Military Government in Korea (USAMGIK), declared on September 11, 1945, "Since the U.S. troops entered Korea, there now exists in Korea complete freedom of the press" (quoted in Youm 1996: 38).[3] Even as a free press was the official policy of the USAMGIK, the reality of the political situation—especially the communist threat—motivated U.S. military authorities to promulgate several regulatory laws that restricted news content. In particular, the USAMGIK issued Ordinance No. 88 in May 1946 in order to revoke the licenses of most leftist newspapers and other publications that the United States considered subversive. Still, the reach of modern media grew prodigiously after liberation, and "from 1945 to 1960 the circulation of leading newspapers went from 17,000 to 400,000—mostly in the capital city of Seoul" (Cole and Lyman 1971: 24).

Notwithstanding the growth of the media industry, the discrepancy between the policy of a free press versus the reality of censorship continued during Syngman Rhee's presidency. Although the Constitution of the Republic of Korea, promulgated July 17, 1948, stipulated that "citizens shall not be subjected to any restrictions on the freedom of speech, press, assembly and association except as specified by law," the communist purges by Rhee's First Republic all but silenced leftist organizations and their publications in the period leading up to the Korean War in 1950 (Cumings 1990). Press freedom remained an elusive ideal after the war as strict censorship and state interference in the production of news continued on the basis of "security laws," including the National Security Act (passed in 1948, revised in 1958). After the 1960 student revolution, however, and during Chang Myŏn's ephemeral parliamentary government, journalists enjoyed the kind of freedom that had been denied to them in the 1950s. Capitalizing on this newfound freedom, the press became a vocal critic of Chang's government and, as one observer noted, "Almost no newspapers had any thoughtful regard or sympathy for the problems which the Chang regime was struggling to solve in a democratic framework" (Lee 1968: 180; quoted in Cole and Lyman 1971: 32).

Park Chung Hee and the Media
Because of the potential of mass media to fuel civil unrest, Park Chung Hee placed restrictions on the media industry immediately after his coup d'état in May 1961. As part of the new restrictions, the 5.16 Military Administration revoked registrations and forced 91 percent of the smaller media companies to close down following its 11th decree, which stipulated building standards for offices that housed news production facilities. The severity with which Park Chung Hee dealt with the media during this period was evident when the 5.16 Military Administration's Revolutionary Court meted out death sentences for three executives of the newspaper *Minjok Ilbo* for "advocating political and ideological doctrines similar to those of North Korea" (Youm 1996: 51). The execution of one of the senior staff, Cho Yongsu, on December 20, 1961—the other two were eventually given life imprisonment instead—sent a clear signal that although the new regime promised to "fully guarantee freedom of thought and speech as one of the basic human rights," it would not tolerate media that "threaten to harm the interest of the entire nation" (Park 1962: 39, 40).

The control of the media industry continued with the promulgation in June 1962 of the 5.16 Military Administration's Media Policy (Ŏllon chŏngch'aek). The content of the policy was then codified in the Media Law (Ŏllonpŏp) passed on December 16, 1963, the same month that Park was inaugurated as president of the Third Republic. The 1963 Media Law detailed further regulations, including architectural standards for buildings that house media companies, employee benefits, and publication schedules. Overall, the Media Law gave the government the authority to monitor and censor media publications as well as televised and radio news.

The following year, in the context of the brewing controversy over Park's attempt to normalize relations with Japan, the government passed the Media Ethics Committee Law (Ŏllon yulli wiwŏnhoepŏp), which further compromised the autonomy of the press. When some newspapers, including *Dong-A Ilbo* and *Kyunghyang Shinmun*, balked at the new regulations, Park Chung Hee's government "took a number of retaliatory measures," including restricting government and private organizations from advertising in those papers (Youm 1996: 53). Limiting the funding sources of newspapers was, we will see, an important precedent for how Park's government disciplined media companies in the Yusin period. In addition, the state used a combination of carrot-and-stick incentives to keep the media in line, including selectively raising wages, controlling promotions, and placing security agents in editing rooms to oversee the production of news.

State censorship increased in the late 1960s as a preemptive strategy in preparation for Park Chung Hee's bid to amend the constitution to allow a third presidential term. Government officials, for instance, would "request cooperation" (*hyŏpcho yochŏng*) from the media, which translated into the state shaping the content of some news articles while censoring others altogether (Dong-A T'uwi 2005: 69). Government regulators often forced newspapers to use euphemisms for sensitive issues: "inflation" became price "readjustment" (*chaejojŏng*), "corruption" became "social irregularities" (*sahoe pujori*), and student "demonstrations" became the "school situation" (*hagwŏn sat'ae;* interview with Sŏng Yubo, September 23, 2009; interview with Yun Sŏkpong, November 16, 2009; Dong-A T'uwi 2005: 128).

"Requests" were also coupled with direct coercion. Two editors and several journalists, for example, were taken into custody by the KCIA in 1968 after *Dong-A Ilbo* printed a story that questioned the government's policies on distributing business loans. In return for releasing its employees, *Dong-A Ilbo* agreed to meet all government demands, including firing three senior editors. In another example, when *Dong-A Ilbo* published a series of stories critical of the government's crackdown on student demonstrations during the 1964–1965 antinormalization protest cycle, Park Chung Hee ordered paratroopers to break into the newspaper's offices to "threaten reporters and editors" (Kim J. H. 2011: 172). These cases are representative of the state's attempt at controlling the media at a time when criticism of Park Chung Hee's refusal to step down as president after his second term was on the rise.

EMERGENCE OF THE FREE PRESS MOVEMENT

Despite government restrictions on the media industry, journalism was still an attractive occupational choice. Throughout the 1960s and 1970s, journalists enjoyed high status and many of them came from the upper echelons of Korean society. Some of the media personnel who participated in the free press movement in the mid-1970s were graduates of elite universities in Seoul, such as Chŏng Tongik and Sŏng Yubo (from SNU), Hong Myŏngjin (from Ewha Womans University and SNU), and Han Hyŏnsu (from Korea University). Partly because good jobs were hard to come by in the late 1960s, positions at the top media companies were highly coveted and carried a certain level of prestige. As former photographer for *Dong-A Ilbo* Yun Sŏkpong reminisces, "Back then, people used to say 'Do you want to be a judge or do you want to be a *Dong-A Ilbo* journalist?' and many preferred to be a journalist" (interview with Yun Sŏkpong, November 16, 2009).

Of the major media companies, *Dong-A Ilbo* and Dong-A Pangsongguk (Dong-A Broadcasting Company) maintained especially strong reputations because many believed they were "real media" that put on "quality shows." Former Dong-A Pangsongguk radio announcer Hong Myŏngjin remembers that "Dong-A was more independent [from the government] than other media companies, including TVC and KBS, and we dealt with many political issues and also tried to tell the story of the underprivileged in the changing economic situation. . . . We employees were very proud of this" (interview with Hong Myŏngjin, November 19, 2009). Hong's colleague at the time, Han Hyŏnsu, also points out that other media companies only had programs "about nature conservation, birds, animals and such, and people asked journalists whether a person had less value than animals" (interview with Han Hyŏnsu, November 19, 2009).

Possibly because of its reputation as an independent newspaper, *Dong-A Ilbo* attracted many young journalists with progressive political values. Indeed, a significant factor that contributed to *Dong-A Ilbo*'s central place in the free press movement in the 1970s was the influx of a new cohort of journalists in the late 1960s. Many who joined the newspaper company between 1965 and 1971 had directly participated in or "were inspired by the 4.19 revolution" during their student years and brought to the newspaper personal commitments to democracy and the freedom of speech (interview with Sŏng Yubo, September 23, 2009). It is not surprising then that *Dong-A Ilbo* reporters considered the large student demonstrations against Park Chung Hee's government newsworthy. For some reporters, these students were their *hubae* (juniors) both academically and as political activists.

Partly due to *Dong-A Ilbo*'s elevated status among media companies, its employees considered the newspaper to be the "watchdog" of society and politics (interview with Han Hyŏnsu, November 19, 2009). The ability of reporters to "deliver the truth and tell the story objectively" was significantly compromised, however, by security agents who were present in the production rooms to literally "look over the shoulders of *Dong-A Ilbo* editors" (interview with Yun Sŏkpong, November 16, 2009). Hong Myŏngjin still remembers the face of the KCIA agent in the recording studios at Dong-A Pangsongguk who would "cut the news even five minutes before going on air" (interview with Hong Myŏngjin: November 19, 2009). In this highly constrained situation, some editors found creative ways to publish sensitive news, as Chŏng Tongik recalls:

> Before I was fired, I worked in the editorial department at *Dong-A Ilbo*. It was my job to edit articles and stories from our reporters and then decide what would be printed as the main story. We were the "chefs" of our company. But we did not have full authority because of the intervention of the KCIA. Then we came up with the idea to publish articles about the student movement just below the famous comic strip section of our paper. This was one way we could get these stories out. (Interview with Chŏng Tongik, October 16, 2009)

Newspapers challenged state censoring only in relatively small ways in the late 1960s and it was not until the 1970s that journalists organized an overt movement for a free press. Censorship became a much more salient issue as journalists attempted to report on the massive student demonstrations in 1971. As described in Chapter 3, the death of Chŏn T'aeil, Park Chung Hee's third presidential election, and the revised campus military training policy enraged students and motivated them to demonstrate against the government in large numbers. And while "journalists tried their best to deliver true stories of the oppression and arrests of students fighting against the government," the various censoring strategies used by the state were more or less effective in silencing the media (interview with Chŏng Tongik, October 16, 2009).

During a year when public protests were so widespread and socially crippling that it took nothing less than a garrison decree and the entry of the military into Seoul to reestablish social order, the conspicuous silence of newspapers about the student demonstrations made it painfully obvious that a free press in Korea was only an ideal. Students, desperate to spread news of state violence against them, became vocal about media censorship and exhorted journalists to do their job. On March 24, 1971, students at SNU staged a dramaturgical protest in which they set fire to media paraphernalia to symbolize the "death" of the press and to criticize journalists who succumbed to government censorship. Two days later, these same students held a protest in front of the *Dong-A Ilbo* building, where they questioned the integrity of the newspaper. Some of the students asked journalists, "Why do you even bother writing and interviewing if you're not going to publish the story?" while others "claimed that the press was propping up Park's political rule" (Dong-A T'uwi 2005: 70; Park 2011: 384).

Students' suspicions of reporters who were present at their protest events further strained their relationships with them. Reporters wore armbands that designated their media affiliation, but government agents sometimes wore the same bands to disguise themselves in order to get close to student protesters. Students especially distrusted newspaper photographers, as Yun Sŏkpong recalls:

> Students were cautious of us because policemen deliberately put on the armband of the media and pretended to be *Dong-A Ilbo* photographers, and they couldn't identify who they really were. The police would take part in the protest and take pictures of the students' faces, and then later would arrest students based on the shots they took. The protesting students never lowered their guards around us. They thought we were either the police and would use the pictures to arrest them afterwards, or even if we were able to prove who we were, they did not trust us because they thought we would sell the photos to someone else. (Interview with Yun Sŏkpong, November 16, 2009)

Even with the reservations that students harbored against journalists, their need for media coverage and reporters' desire to "deliver the truth" were the foundations for the alliance that eventually developed between them. Journalists were in no small way "ashamed that the rest of society—students, laborers, and Christians—were fighting for democracy and yet journalists were not even writing about it" (Dong-A T'uwi 2005: 84). Partly because they were ashamed and partly because they wanted simply to be "responsible to their vocation," young journalists at *Dong-A Ilbo* began the fight for freedom of the press (interview with Yun Sŏkpong, November 16, 2009). On April 15, 1971, the same day that students staged massive nationwide demonstrations, thirty reporters proclaimed the first of a series of declarations for media freedom. The Declaration to Protect the Freedom of the Press (Ŏllon chayu suho sŏnŏn) set an important precedent for the free press movement. Following suit, pockets of reporters at several other newspaper companies made similar declarations in the weeks after the *Dong-A Ilbo* declaration.

Though they were an important initial step, these declarations were not enough to overcome media censorship, especially after the installation of the Yusin Constitution in 1972. Leading up to Yusin, the National Assembly passed a censorship law on December 27, 1971, that prohibited publications that "threatened the security of the nation." The independence of the press was further compromised with the revision of the Media Law in 1973, which essentially gave Park Chung Hee ultimate control over the production and dissemination of news. The revised law imbued Park with the power to censor undesirable materials before or after their publication, as well as to dictate the content of radio and television broadcasting. In addition, to further consolidate its power over media companies, the government forced the mergers of several newspapers before pressuring the Korean Newspaper Association (Han'guk Sinmun Hyŏphoe), the professional organization of newspaper publishers and executives, to stop young journalists from interfering in politics (KDF Events Dictionary: 256).

Journalists responded to this heightened censorship by ramping up their movement for a free press. Frustrated that their articles on rising inflation and antigovernment protests were not being published, fifty *Dong-A Ilbo* reporters gathered on October 7, 1973, to stage an overnight sit-in rally. Because they vowed to hold a rally every time a newsworthy article was censored, the newspaper's board of directors forbade collective action of any kind at the *Dong-A Ilbo* building (KDF Events Dictionary: 257). In response, the same young journalists issued their second Declaration of Media Freedom on November 20, 1973. Following their lead, media personnel from several other companies also made declarations and held rallies for press freedom: *Hankook Ilbo* on November 22, *Chosun Ilbo* on November 27, Munhwa Pangsongguk on November 28, *Korea JoongAng Daily* on November 30, Tongyang Pangsongguk on November 30, and Han'guk Sinmun P'yŏnjip Wiwŏnhoe on December 5 (KDF Events Dictionary: 256).

Wary of the budding movement for a free press, government officials met with top executives of several newspaper companies on multiple occasions in the winter of 1973 to apprise them that unless they were able to control their employees, the state would repress the journalists directly (KDF

Events Dictionary: 256). After being forced to sign a document stating that their companies would neither interfere with national security nor criticize the Yusin Constitution, publishers and media executives warned, threatened, and pleaded with the journalists to stop causing trouble. In defiance of both their employer and the state, *Dong-A Ilbo* reporters made their third Declaration of Media Freedom on December 3, 1973 (Dong-A T'uwi 2005: 81). Furthermore, they attempted to increase the organizational strength of their emerging movement by establishing a labor union. Ignoring threats from their employer, *Dong-A Ilbo* journalists formally registered their labor union on March 7, 1974, prompting the company to fire thirteen founding members the very next day (Dong-A T'uwi 2005: 89). Although several others faced further disciplinary measures imposed by senior management, the establishment of the *Dong-A Ilbo* labor union was an important moment that gave young progressive journalists an organizational identity and additional motivation to continue the fight for media freedom.

Building on the momentum created by the establishment of the labor union, and encouraged by the increasing participation of journalists from other newspaper companies, *Dong-A Ilbo* journalists organized the single most important event of the free press movement in the 1970s: the Declaration of Action for a Free Press (Chayu ŏllon silch'ŏn sŏnŏn). The declaration was delivered on October 24, 1974, in the *Dong-A Ilbo* building at 9:15 in the morning, specifically because that day was a holiday (United Nations Day) and security agents were absent. Also, because it was a holiday, reporters who were usually off-site were at the *Dong-A Ilbo* headquarters, where more than 180 were present when the declaration was read (Dong-A T'uwi 2005: 115). The Declaration of Action stipulated three main points of contention:

1. We stand together to eliminate external interference of any form with newspapers, broadcasting, and magazines.
2. We vehemently reject the entrance of government officials [*kigwanwŏn*] into our buildings.
3. We reject media personnel being unlawfully taken into custody [*pulpŏp yŏnhaeng*] by authorities. If someone is unlawfully taken, we will not leave the office until he or she is released.

Although the bulk of the content of the Declaration of Action did not differ significantly from the three *Dong-A Ilbo* declarations of media freedom that preceded it, it was a defining moment in the free press movement because it

facilitated the diffusion of the censorship issue to other groups in the larger democracy movement and gained the attention of the international press. Media
groups around the world—including the *Washington Post*, the *New York Times*,
the *Asahi Shimbun*, the Associated Press, AFP, Reuters, the *Mainichi Shimbun*,
the Japan Broadcasting Corporation, and the *Baltimore Sun*—carried stories
about the Declaration of Action, giving the Korean free press movement unprecedented international coverage (Dong-A T'uwi 2005: 120). Also, leading
organizations in the democracy movement, such as the NCCK and the Free Action Literary People Association (Chayu Silchŏn Munin Hyŏbŭihoe), as well as
prominent dissident leaders—Hong Sŏn'gu, a human rights lawyer; Pastor Pak
Hyŏnggyu; Yi Ujŏng, director of Korea Church Women United; former president Yun Posŏn and his wife, Kong Tŏkkwi; James Sinnott, Roman Catholic
priest; Paek Kiwan, student leader; and Kim Dae Jung, oppositional politician
and future president—pledged their support for journalists fighting for media
freedom. In short, the Declaration of Action facilitated solidarity between journalists and several dissident groups, and marked the moment when the free
press movement became part of the larger democracy movement.

In the period immediately following the Declaration of Action, journalists
enjoyed the kind of freedom that had eluded them in the past. The day after the
declaration, journalists posted a conspicuous sign on the door of the *Dong-A
Ilbo* building stating that government officials, who had been regulars at the
newspaper company before the declaration, were now banned from the premises. They were surprisingly successful in keeping KCIA agents from entering
the building for the next 144 days. Consequently, *Dong-A Ilbo* began to publish stories about antigovernment protests and state repression (Dong-A T'uwi
2005: 118; interview with Chŏng Tongik, October 16, 2009).

This opening was short-lived, however, as the government reformulated
its repression strategy and turned to tactics that in the past had successfully
brought newspapers in line. In retaliation against the defiant journalists, the
Yusin government, on December 24, 1974, made an announcement prohibiting
all businesses from advertising in *Dong-A Ilbo* and on Dong-A Pangsongguk.
This "advertisement repression" (*kwanggo t'anap*), which began on Christmas
Day, had a significant impact on both Dong-A companies because roughly
50 percent of their revenues came from advertisements (interview with Yun
Sŏkpong, November 16, 2009). As we saw earlier, cutting off funding sources
was a tested tactic that Park Chung Hee first used in 1964 when newspaper
companies criticized the state's increasing regulation of the media industry.

By February 1975, Dong-A Pangsongguk had lost 98 percent of the revenue generated from advertisements, and the magazine division had lost 90 percent (Dong-A T'uwi 2005: 146). As Sŏng Yubo remembers it, "one day the ads completely disappeared" (interview with Sŏng Yubo, September 23, 2009). The government's advertisement repression campaign was thus an effective strategy that significantly limited the media company's resources and created great pressure to conform to government demands.

To the chagrin of the government, however, this tailored repression tactic led to unintended consequences when both domestic and international groups critized the advertisement ban. Just a few days after the ban, on December 27, 1974, several foreign media companies and international NGOs, including the *Asahi Shimbun*, the *New York Times*, the *Mainichi Shimbun*, *Nikkei*, the *Sankei Shimbun*, and Freedom House, released statements condemning the state's blatant interference in the daily operations of the Dong-A media companies (Dong-A T'uwi 2005: 155). Possibly more damaging, however, was that this show of international solidarity sparked a response from the American government. On January 6, 1975, Robert Anderson, spokesman and special assistant for press relations at the U.S. State Department, publicly announced that "while it is not the place of the United States government to release a statement about *Dong-A Ilbo*, the principle of a free press must be protected" (quoted in Dong-A T'uwi 2005: 156).

Throughout January 1975, international awareness of media censorship in Korea grew as the advertisement repression incident was reported in several foreign newspapers: the Japan Broadcasting Corporation, the *Times* of London, *Le Monde* and the *International Herald Tribune* in France, the BBC, the *Tages-Anzeiger* of Switzerland, and *Newsweek* and the *Washington Post* in the United States. Some international media organizations, including the International Press Institute and the International Federation of Journalists, sent letters directly to Park Chung Hee demanding that he retract the ban on advertising and respect the freedom of the press (Dong-A T'uwi 2005: 156, 158). *Dong-A Ilbo* journalists also received domestic support from several sectors of the democracy movement, including multiple Christian organizations (NCCK, Church Women United, and Catholic organizations), the Free Action Literary People Association, and the Citizens' Conference for the Recovery of Democracy. The incident also motivated solidarity within the media industry as journalists from other newspaper companies, including the *Korea JoongAng Daily* and *Chosun Ilbo*, declared their commitment to the free press movement. In brief, as Han

Hyŏnsu remarks, "It is ironic that as the dictator suppressed us further, more people came to our aid" (interview with Han Hyŏnsu, November 19, 2009).

To the state's dismay, the advertisement repression also prompted a strong reaction from the larger public. One creative and direct response was to use the advertisement pages in the newspaper as platforms for protest. The first ad to support the cause of press freedom was purchased on December 30, 1974. After this, *Dong-A Ilbo* was flooded with people who wanted to purchase ads in order to show their solidarity with the journalists. The contents of these "solidarity ads" were simple: most encouraged the journalists and criticized the government, others were left purposely blank (*paekchi kwanggo*) to symbolize the silencing of the press. Some challenged the government by appropriating the state narrative of economic progress: "You keep saying export, export, but now you are even exporting human rights and the freedom of the press.—Hijung from Choch'iwŏn," read one ad. Others declared their resolve: "The great tiger, although starving, will still not eat grass," quoting a freshman from Korea University's Department of Political Science. Foreign support of *Dong-A Ilbo* journalists was also recorded in these ads. One ad purchased by "a German" read, "Of course as a foreigner I am not trying to intervene, nor can I, but I want to express my gratitude and great praise, and send encouragement to *Dong-A Ilbo*." Another dramatically declared, "Let's die together and let's live together, hurray hurray!—the 9 Canadians who love Korea."[4]

These small acts of resistance caught fire and through January and February of 1975 it was common to see long lines of people waiting outside the doors of *Dong-A Ilbo* to purchase advertisement space (Stentzel 2006). Supporters came from all walks of life, including one woman who had been jailed for three days in 1965 for opposing the Korea-Japan normalization treaty. Upon making her way into the *Dong-A Ilbo* building, she pulled out all the money that was in her bag and told the reporters how precious freedom was and encouraged them to keep up the fight (Dong-A T'uwi 2005: 162). Other sentimental stories arising from this period include one about two sisters, one five years old and the other six, who broke their piggy banks in order to purchase an ad, presumably with the permission of their parents. Another example was fifteen paperboys who pooled their money together to donate to the journalists' cause (Dong-A T'uwi 2005: 160). As Chŏng Tongik interprets it, "placing an ad in *Dong-A Ilbo* was an act of protest by individuals" (interview with Chŏng Tongik, October 16, 2009); and Sŏng Yubo remembers that the citizens' willingness to advertise in *Dong-A Ilbo* "gave us hope" (interview with Sŏng Yubo, September 23, 2009).

Support for *Dong-A Ilbo* journalists was so forthcoming in the wake of the advertisement repression that by February 1975 more than one thousand ads were sold—nearly 10 percent of them purchased by international groups (Dong-A T'uwi 2005: 166). It was clear to both the dissident community and the Yusin government that media censoring was quickly becoming the most salient sociopolitical issue in the spring of 1975. To curb the growing popularity of the free press movement, the state pressured *Dong-A Ilbo*'s board of directors to install new management, and in his inaugural speech on March 3, 1975, freshly appointed Editor-in-Chief Yi Tonguk warned employees that rallies and other disturbances would no longer be tolerated. Making good on his threat, Yi Tonguk began immediately to "downsize the company" by ordering a series of layoffs at *Dong-A Ilbo* and Dong-A Pangsongguk. Between March 8 and May 1, he fired forty-nine journalists, and another eighty-four were forced to go on indefinite unpaid leave (Dong-A T'uwi 2005: 179). Although "business restructuring" and "profit sustainability" were cited as reasons for the layoffs, it was evident to everybody that this policy targeted the "troublemakers" (*nandong punja*) in the company (interview with Hong Myŏngjin, November 19, 2009).

The mass firing of employees proved to be the spark that ignited the transformation of journalists into social movement actors. No longer able to gather at their offices, journalists began to participate in street protests. Until the spring of 1975, reporters had relied on relatively nondisruptive tactics, such as declarations and refusing to work for short periods of time. After the layoffs, however, they were literally put out on the streets and were given no other recourse other than staging public protests. As Chŏng Tongik explains, "We didn't need to protest before getting fired. But as soon as we were fired, we formed Dong-A T'uwi and started to protest" (interview with Chŏng Tongik, October 16, 2009). Journalists joined the ranks of other protesting groups, including students, intellectuals, and Christians, thus contributing to the diversification and solidarity of the democracy movement in the 1970s.

It is important to acknowledge that the politicization of journalists during this period was not a simple process, nor an exhaustive one. Not all journalists joined the free press movement, and Hong Myŏngjin recalls that "there were some who worked for Dong-A after we were kicked out and there was hatred between us and them. . . . it was sad" (interview with Hong Myŏngjin, November 19, 2009).[5] The core group that joined the movement consisted of younger journalists who were inspired by the 4.19 student revolution and entered the newspaper company in the late 1960s. Following the lead of senior mentors like Chŏn Kwanu, an outspoken director at *Dong-A Ilbo* and a leader in the progressive intellectual community, this unique cohort rose to become the vanguard of South Korea's free press movement. Interestingly, some of the journalists who participated in antigovernment protests were not consciously trying to join a "democracy movement," but rather found themselves on the streets as a consequence of their participation in what they initially considered to be an internal struggle to carry out the duties of their vocation. As Hong Myŏngjin remembers:

> This is what I thought then regarding when and why we joined the democracy movement.... Rather than thinking that we should join the democracy movement, our company, *Dong-A Ilbo*, was in this situation and they [company executives] were in line with the government. And critical groups started to form. The older people didn't think that way and the movement was formed by the younger generation of journalists. . . . We weren't trying to join the democracy movement but in fact we agreed with the leaders of the movement and we followed them. (Interview with Hong Myŏngjin, November 19, 2009)

Through the spring of 1975, *Dong-A Ilbo* reporters, Dong-A Pangsongguk announcers and producers, reporters from other newspaper companies, and dissidents in the larger democracy movement organized a series of public protests advocating a free press. On March 17, 165 media personnel and their allies staged a protest march in central Seoul, from the *Dong-A Ilbo* building through Gwanghwamun. The march culminated the next day in the founding of the first Korean social movement organization to mobilize around the issue of media censorship. The Dong-A Committee for the Struggle to Protect a Free Press (Dong-A Chayu Ŏllon Suho T'ujaeng Wiwŏnhoe, abbreviated Dong-A T'uwi) was established on March 18, 1975, and became the central organization that brought together journalists and other media personnel outside the confines of the company itself. With the founding of Dong-A T'uwi, and other organizations modeled after it (such as Chosun T'uwi), journalists became an integral part of the larger democracy movement.

No longer able to work at their companies, and no longer bound by managerial and state oversight, fired journalists and media personnel came to rely on extra-institutional tactics to express their grievances. The number of public protests staged by journalists steadily increased from 1973, when the first media freedom declaration was made, and reached a zenith in 1975 after the mass

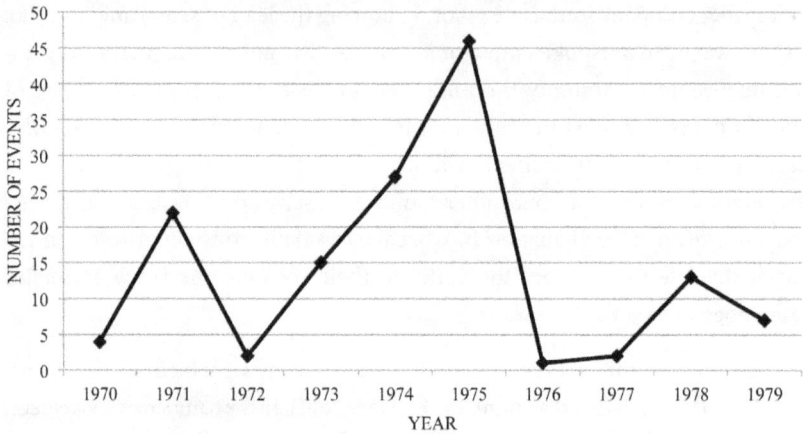

Figure 5.1. Annual counts of protest events by journalists
DATA SOURCE: Stanford KDP Events Dataset (1970–1979).

firing of journalists. As indicated in Figure 5.1, the spike in journalists' protests in 1975 occurred in the same year that the number of student demonstrations rapidly declined, reflecting the rise of new social movement actors discussed in the previous chapter. After effectively stopping students from protesting, however, the state turned its attention to other dissident groups and was able to subdue the free press movement primarily through the arrest of several Dong-A T'uwi leaders. Sŏng Yubo and other members of Dong-A T'uwi were swept up in the "communist purging" campaigns that followed ED 9, and public protests organized by journalists all but vanished in the ED era.[6]

Although members of Dong-A T'uwi found it difficult to stage public protests after ED 9, they continued to engage in clandestine activities, such as holding meetings with other dissident groups, including Christians, laborers, intellectuals, and opposition politicians (interview with Chŏng Tongik, October 16, 2009). In the ED era, Dong-A T'uwi members focused on important solidarity work and supported some of the most significant events in the late 1970s, including the Y. H. Trading Company incident on August 9, 1979 (discussed in Chapter 7), and the human rights rally in front of the Amnesty International building on June 29, 1979 (discussed in Chapter 6). Furthermore, the decline in public acts of defiance did not stop the free press movement from continuing to gain the attention of international media as Dong-A T'uwi members spread news of the Korean situation to their counterparts abroad. In these ways, Dong-A T'uwi was able to contribute to the antigovernment movement by facilitating alliances with domestic and international advocates of Korean democracy.

Understandably, the media industry played a critical role in Korean society because it wielded the power to shape the public image of both Park Chung Hee's government and the movement against it. The regulations that Park imposed on media companies almost immediately after assuming power in 1961 continued throughout his rule, in the form of revised media laws, to further limit the content and reach of news that did not conform to the state narratives of economic progress and political stability. This, however, led to unintended consequences, including the politicization of journalists and the greater exposure of state repression in international media. Initiated by the restrictions placed on the reporting of student demonstrations, the issue of censorship snowballed into a larger free press movement that challenged the dictatorship itself. The entry of journalists into the democracy movement reflected a larger process of movement diversification, and joining them at this time was the first generation of human rights lawyers.

THE STATE AND JUDICIARY

On July 28, 1971, two judges and a court clerk were accused by the Seoul District Public Prosecutors Office (Seoul Chigŏm Konganbu) of diverting public funds for personal use. The case involving Judge Yi Pŏmyŏl, Judge Ch'oe Kongung, and Clerk Yi Namyŏng was dismissed, however, on the same day by a lower district court because of insufficient evidence. The Seoul District Public Prosecutors Office in turn re-accused the three members of the judiciary the following day, evidently adamant about seeing this case through. Word of the case spread quickly, and immediately after the second accusation, thirty-nine judges from the Seoul District Criminal Court (Seoul Hyŏngsa Chibang Pŏbwŏn) released a statement criticizing what they believed to be the politically motivated framing of the two judges and the clerk.

One week before the 1971 general elections scheduled for May 25, 1971, twenty-seven SNU students affiliated with the National Alliance of Youth and Students for the Protection of Democracy had held a rally inside the opposition New Democratic Party building to protest for fair elections. Ten students were arrested for staging that rally but were subsequently found innocent of criminal charges by Judges Yi and Ch'oe. The thirty-nine judges from the Seoul District Criminal Court believed that Judges Yi and Ch'oe, and Clerk Yi, were being accused of embezzlement as punishment for not convicting the students, and in a dramatic show of solidarity, they resigned en masse after publicly listing several complaints against the state prosecutors (KDF Events Dictionary: 121):

1. When judges oversee cases involving antigovernment "criminals" and they do not have the same opinion as the public prosecutors, judges are treated as supporters of communism and our backgrounds are investigated.

2. Public prosecutors threaten that the careers of judges who disagree with the state will be tarnished or jeopardized.

3. When we deny search warrants (*yŏngchang*) to police who are investigating suspects, or when we find innocent somebody who the prosecutors say is guilty, we are accused of corruption by public prosecutors.

4. State agents stalk judges, following them around, and investigate bank accounts and other personal information in order to trap and frame judges.

5. Prosecutors do not follow proper procedure when obtaining arrest warrants: instead of first going to the Court Window (*pŏbwŏn ch'anggu*) to present evidence and documents for processing before the judge signs the warrant, prosecutors go straight to the judge to obtain the signature without the proper documents.

6. When judges disagree with the state's opinion on suspects, public prosecutors swear, threaten, and insult the judges.

7. All of these points occurred in the case against Judges Yi and Ch'oe and Clerk Yi, and this threatens the rights of judges.

The statement and resignations of the thirty-nine judges of the Seoul District Criminal Court reflected the long-held frustrations of some members of the judiciary, who for the most part enjoyed high social status and prided themselves on their moral integrity when carrying out the duties of their office. During the 1960s, Park Chung Hee periodically forced the hand of judges when they disobeyed the government's wishes. In 1965, for example, when judges refused to issue arrest warrants for students participating in the antinormalization movement, "twelve armed members of the airborne unit under the Capital Garrison Command broke into the court and forced the judges to issue the warrants" (Kim J. H. 2011: 172).

The 1971 incident was another example of the state's attempt to control the judiciary, but this time judges across the country responded to it in an impressive and unprecedented fashion. The very next day, July 30, forty-four judges from the Seoul District Civil Court (Seoul Minsa Chibang Pŏbwŏn) resigned in support of their colleagues. The day after that, July 31, two judges from the Court of Family Affairs, fifteen judges from Daegu District Civil and Criminal Courts, and six judges from the Cheongju District Court resigned. In total, one hundred six judges gave up their judicial seats in the three days following the initial accusation against Judges Yi and Ch'oe and Clerk Yi, constituting "the first judicial defiance of its kind since the establishment of the Republic in 1948" (KDF Events Dictionary: 121; Park 2011: 389). Judges possessed significant legal and symbolic power, and this unprecedented show of solidarity was an important challenge to Park Chung Hee because it signaled resistance to his rule from within the government itself.

Although ad-hoc repression measures were applied to individual judges, prosecutors, and lawyers throughout the 1960s and 1970s, the Yusin Constitution represented a more systematic strategy to secure executive control over the justice system. The most important change was to do away with the semi-independent Council on the Nomination of Justices and place the power to appoint the chief justice of the Supreme Court in the hands of the president. This simple move gave Park Chung Hee incredible influence over the judiciary, because the chief justice, with the approval of the president, appointed all other Supreme Court and lower court justices. In addition, as discussed in Chapter 2, under ED 2 the state transferred judicial jurisdiction for cases involving antigovernment protesters to the General Emergency Martial Court in order to process more efficiently the large number of people arrested under the EDs. These measures led many to believe that judges were nothing more than a rubber stamp for state prosecutors during the Yusin period (interview with Kang Sinok, February 18, 2010). Park Chung Hee's power over the judicial system was indeed an essential component of his authoritarian control, but it also led to the politicization of some judges, prosecutors, and lawyers.

EMERGENCE OF HUMAN RIGHTS LAWYERS

Although Yi Pyŏngnin is recognized as the "father" of human rights law in South Korea—his activities in the 1960s were critical to maintaining the independence of the Korean Bar Association vis-à-vis the government—and lawyers such as Pak Hansang played an important role in the first PRP case in 1964, it was only in the 1970s that the designation "human rights lawyer" (inkwŏn pyŏnhosa) gained circulation in the dissident community (interview with Kim Hyŏngt'ae, December 8, 2009). The term was applied to the first generation of lawyers who not only were willing to represent defendants charged with antigovernment activities but also joined the democracy movement themselves (Goedde 2011: 225). And although the number of lawyers willing to take on cases involving "political criminals" was very small in the 1970s—"only about 20 lawyers" (Cohen and Baker 1991: 212; quoted in Goedde 2011: 226)—their participation in the democracy movement inspired future generations of human rights lawyers. Their legacy is reflected in lawyers such as Kim Hyŏngt'ae, Yi Sŏkt'ae, and Pak Wŏnsun, who in the late 1980s facilitated the institutionalization of human rights by forming the Lawyers for a Democratic Society (Minju Sahoe rŭl wihan Pyŏnhosa Moim, abbreviated Minbyŏn), an organization that oversees a large network of progressive lawyers dedicated to protecting human rights (interview with Kim Hyŏngt'ae, December 8, 2009; see also Goedde 2011).

Kang Sinok is a representative member of the first generation of human rights lawyers in Korea. Inspired after reading Dale Carnegie's (1932) biography of Abraham Lincoln, *Lincoln the Unknown*, Kang graduated from SNU's prestigious College of Law and was appointed a judge in 1962, the year after Park Chung Hee's coup d'état.[7] After working a little over a year at the Seoul District Court, however, Kang and another colleague, Yi Saejung, were reassigned to a court far from Seoul in the city of Gyeongju. Kang learned later that his displacement from the central judicial administration in Seoul and his reassignment to provincial Gyeongju were punishment for having made critical statements toward the government in an informal setting (interview with Kang Sinok, February 18, 2010). Dissatisfied with his marginalization, Kang resigned his position as judge and, following the suggestion of a mentor, decided to move to the United States to continue his legal education. In America, Kang took courses at Yale Law School and George Washington University Law School, on topics ranging from human rights law to social ethics. Upon returning to Korea, he went on to participate as legal counsel in some of the most important human rights cases in the late 1960s and 1970s, including the Reunification Revolutionary Party case (1968), the PRP case (1974), and several cases related to the Minch'ŏng incident (1974–1975).

If Kang Sinok's participation in the democracy movement was predicated on a direct experience of state repression, Im Kwanggyu's motivation to take on human rights cases in the 1970s stemmed from his growing disillusionment with Park Chung Hee's blatant manipulation of the law in order to secure political power. Im, like Kang, graduated from the College of Law at SNU and served his country in the Vietnam War before being appointed a public prosecutor in

1966. Im was not critical of President Park at the start of his career and even welcomed Park Chung Hee's coup in 1961 because he believed that South Korea needed a strong leader to avert the possibility of a communist takeover (interview with Im Kwanggyu: March 13, 2010). Moreover, appreciative of Korea's desperate need for economic development and foreign capital, Im accepted Park Chung Hee's plan to normalize relations with Japan when other university students staged large-scale protests against it. Im's relatively favorable opinion of Park Chung Hee started to change, however, during the three years he served as a public prosecutor. The catalyst for the change in attitude was the increasing number of North Korean spy cases he was ordered to investigate and prosecute.

Im worked as a prosecutor for the Seoul District Prosecutors Office (Seoul Chibang Kŏmch'alch'ŏng) from 1966 to 1968 and for the Jeonju District Prosecutors Office (Jeonju Chibang Kŏmch'alch'ŏng) in 1968. During that time, he was inundated with cases involving individuals accused of being North Korean spies. Im and his colleagues were ordered to investigate these cases and make the contents of their investigations available to the media. While he was carrying out the investigations, it became increasingly clear to Im that there was no strong evidence to support most of these accusations. He realized that his office was being manipulated by the government to frame individuals as North Korean spies in order to heighten citizens' fear of a communist takeover, which would then justify the constitutional amendment that would allow Park to run for a third presidential term in 1971. As Im explains, "The government wanted people to believe that there was a big increase in the number of spies. And what's the next step then? People would demand that Park Chung Hee stay in power. I believe that the government induced people to support Park Chung Hee's third presidential term in fear of a North Korean takeover" (interview with Im Kwanggyu, March 13, 2010). Im's disillusionment with the legal process during that time led him to resign his post as government prosecutor. He went on, as a private lawyer, to represent important participants in the democracy movement, including Bishop Chi Haksun and students who were arrested during the Minch'ŏng incident.

Kang Sinok and Im Kwanggyu were part of a small group that made up the first generation of human rights lawyers in South Korea. Lawyers such as Han Sŭnghŏn, along with the so-called gang of four human rights lawyers (4-inbang inkwŏn pyŏnhosa)—Yi Tonmyŏng, Hong Sŏn'gu, Cho Chunhŭi, and Hwang Inch'ŏl—were inspired by the example set by Yi Pyŏngnin in the 1960s and, against the advice of their more trepid colleagues, represented dissidents arrested under the various political control laws. The decision to defend antigovernment protesters was not an easy one, particularly because of the likelihood of government repercussion. Government officials warned lawyers to stay clear of "political" cases and punished those who did not obey. Im Kwanggyu, for example, worked as an in-house lawyer for the Asset Management Corporation in 1974 after giving up his public prosecutor appointment, but he was forced to quit the position when he signed on to defend students arrested during the Minch'ŏng incident (interview with Im Kwanggyu, March 13, 2010). The real possibility of repression discouraged most lawyers from representing dissidents, and simply taking on an antigovernment case was enough to get one labeled a human rights lawyer. Im Kwanggyu explains:

> I am not sure what a so-called human rights lawyer is. The responsibility of a lawyer is to protect people's rights, freedom, and honor. However, despite their responsibility, lawyers at that time avoided cases involving antigovernment protesters. There were many disadvantages of taking these cases. Many lawyers at that time thought it was a risk to take antigovernment cases. This is why people made the term "human rights lawyer." However, my opinion is that protecting human rights is the job of all lawyers. This is why I took the cases, not because I thought I was a human rights lawyer. (Interview with Im Kwanggyu, March 13, 2010)

Even if "protecting human rights is the job of all lawyers," because of state pressure, dissidents found it difficult to find legal representation when formally charged with violating security laws and the EDs. Lawyers such as Kang Sinok were rare, and it was his experiences studying human rights law and ethics in the United States that prompted Sin Yŏngbok's father to seek Kang out in 1968 to represent his son in what became known as the Reunification Revolutionary Party (T'ongil Hyŏngmyŏngdang) case. Members of this "communist organization" were accused of accepting money directly from North Korea and engaging in several pro-North Korean activities, including supporting student organizations and publishing North Korean propaganda in the south. Sin Yŏngbok, who had taught economics at the South Korea Military Academy, was identified with this group and arrested for spying for North Korea. Kang agreed to take on Sin Yŏngbok's case because he saw it as another instance of Park Chung Hee manipulating the justice system. Although Sin Yŏngbok was found guilty for espionage, Kang's simple willingness to take the case established his reputation as a legal advocate for dissidents.[8] After the Reunification Revolutionary Party case, Kang was sought after by the progressive community to represent others arrested for antigovernment activities. He was asked by the NCCK to defend students involved in the Minch'ŏng incident, and he represented the famous dissident poet Kim Chiha as a favor to leading progressive intellectual Paek Nakchŏng (interview with Kang Sinok, February 18, 2010).

Other lawyers were motivated by their personal convictions. As a Catholic, Im Kwanggyu was shocked when in 1974 the government arrested Chi Haksun, the Catholic Bishop of his diocese in the city of Wonju. The state accused Bishop Chi of jeopardizing national security by funding antigovernment movements when he allegedly gave money to poet Kim Chiha to support dissident students. Having served as a public prosecutor, Im was well aware that the government often trumped up charges in order to frame participants in the democracy movement. Convinced that the arrest of Bishop Chi was a violation of the freedom of religious expression, Im readily agreed to represent him. As Im puts it, "I took the case because I was a Catholic and because I believe that secular political authority should be separate from religious authority" (interview with Im Kwanggyu, March 13, 2010). Im's experience as Bishop Chi's counsel reinforced his belief that the judicial system under Park Chung Hee was neither independent nor objective, which further motivated him to represent several students involved in the Minch'ŏng incident.

The willingness of lawyers to take on antigovernment cases did not necessarily mean they were able to defend their clients effectively. Human rights lawyers were restricted by state organs, and the police and KCIA would harass, investigate, and monitor them. They were also limited in what they could do by the military courts, which often rejected procedural requests, including refusing witnesses, quashing possible absolving evidence, and shortening the length of defendants' arguments (interview with Im Kwanggyu, March 13, 2010). In the aforementioned Reunification Revolution Party case, for instance, Kang Sinok was not even allowed to visit Sin Yŏngbok in jail (interview with Kang Sinok, February 18, 2010). As Patricia Goedde notes, in most instances, "lawyers for the defendants were present at their trials more as statements of principle than as advocates able to free their clients" (2011: 226).

Probably the most audacious interference with a lawyer's ability to represent clients occurred during the case of Yŏ Chŏngnam, who was accused of being the student liaison connecting the Minch'ŏng student network to the PRP. At the request of the NCCK, a small team of lawyers, including Kang Sinok, Im Kwanggyu, Hwang Inchŏl, Hong Sŏng'u, and Yi Sejŏng, represented Yŏ and other individuals in the PRP case. Throughout the entirety of the trial, lawyers were not able to consult with the defendants, who were incarcerated at the infamous Great West Gate Prison (Seodaemun Hyŏngmuso).[9] In the courtroom, the lawyers were indeed there merely as "statements of principle" rather than as effective counsel. But as the PRP case was closing and death sentences were being meted out for Yŏ and the other seven "members" of the PRP, Kang Sinok seized the opportunity to address the court. In his closing remarks, Kang lamented having become a lawyer in a society where the law is used to rationalize and serve power rather than defend justice. Making comparisons to Nazi Germany and predicting history's harsh judgment of the military court, he declared that citizens have the right to disobey "bad laws" (akpŏp) and that the death sentences were essentially "legalized murder" (pŏpchŏk sarin). For these closing remarks, Kang Sinok was promptly arrested and sentenced to fifteen years in prison (interview with Kang Sinok, February 18, 2010). Although he served only a fraction of his sentence before being released, Kang's arrest reflected the resolve of the state not only to prosecute dissidents but also to persecute lawyers who defended them.

The relative impotence of lawyers in protecting their clients from state prosecution should not detract from the significance of the emergence of the first generation of human rights lawyers in the 1970s. The participation of lawyers in the most important legal cases connected to the democracy movement in the Yusin period signaled a new possibility for human rights law in South Korea. The first generation of human rights lawyers was born during the zenith of state repression, and although small in numbers, their contributions to the movement were distinct. For example, as a constitutional lawyer, Im Kwanggyu was able to question the legality of the Yusin Constitution while in the courtroom defending Bishop Chi Haksun (interview with Im Kwanggyu, March 13, 2010). And although he was arrested for his "outburst," Kang Sinok's closing remarks in the PRP case were a rare opportunity to address state prosecutors and the military tribunal directly. Some lawyers transcended their immediate occupational community and became important leaders in the democracy movement. Yi Pyŏngnin, for example, headed Amnesty International's Korean Committee, and Hong Sŏng'u participated in the free press and labor movements (Dong-A T'uwi 2005).

REPRESSION AND MOVEMENT DIVERSIFICATION

The sustainability and potential success of large-scale social movements are often dependent on the participation of multiple sectors of society. Though this seems to be the empirical reality, many studies conceptualize protest-repression dynamics as a "two-actor world populated by a state and a dissident group" (Moore 2000: 108). Recognizing that "opposition groups are not monolithic" (Lichbach 1987: 273), scholars argue for the need to disaggregate social movements based on the unique configurations of specific networks in a movement (Davenport 2005: xxi). The criteria used to define "social groups" are admittedly fluid because individuals have multiple identities and can act according to any one of them depending on context (Barvosa-Carter 2001; Tajfel and Turner 1986). In the 1970s democracy movement, boundaries between social groups were grounded in *socio-vocational* identities (Kim and Lee 2011; Kim 2009). The justification for this criterion follows the inductive logic of how actors self-identified.

In South Korea, protest events were staged by groups of actors who shared similar socio-vocational identities and often times made their claims based on them. Christian clergy, for example, assumed that the job of caring for the souls and well-being of their laity applied to the political and humanitarian spheres as well as to the religious. Also, journalists who organized "freedom of speech" protest events were motivated by the belief that it was their responsibility to communicate domestic (and international) news. Likewise, lawyers, relying on their unique training, criticized the legal foundations of the Yusin system. We will see in Chapter 7 that the diversification of social groups participating in antigovernment protests led to coalitional strategies that facilitated solidarity within the movement. Some groups, such as Christians, were especially adept at organizing intergroup protest events in the 1970s. Still, for the most part, each socio-vocational group maintained its own distinct identity, which compromised the state's ability to dismiss the democracy movement as only a collection of radical students and intellectuals.

In Table 5.1, we can see the rich diversity of social groups participating in protest events. The largest numbers of protests were staged by students, laborers, Christians, journalists, intellectuals, Christian students, and politicians. But there were other groups in the movement as well. For example, family members of political prisoners were a strong supporting social network who were usually found rallying outside of prisons. Foreigners, although small in number, played a significant role as mediators between dissidents and the international community, as we saw with the American Christian missionaries in Chapter 4 (Stentzel 2006).

In her study of high-risk activism in Latin America, Mara Loveman has shown that "state repression may stimulate collective organization and op-

Table 5.1. Social groups participating in protest events

Social Group	Frequency	Percentage
Students/youth	690	31.71
Laborers/workers	370	17.00
Christians (Protestant and Catholic)	359	16.50
Journalists/media personnel	139	6.39
Christian students	137	6.30
Intellectuals	118	5.42
Politicians (and staff)	96	4.41
Professionals	37	1.70
Family of prisoners	37	1.70
General activists/civil groups	33	1.52
Prisoners	27	1.24
Foreigners (including Diaspora)	18	0.83
Educators/school officials	15	0.69
Other religious	12	0.55
Christian farmers	11	0.51
Citizens (general)	7	0.32
Urban poor	6	0.28
Farmers	5	0.23
Student prisoners	4	0.18
Others	3	0.14
Judges/judicial system staff	2	0.09
Merchants	2	0.09
Other religiously identified students	2	0.09
Christian prisoners	2	0.09
Military personnel	1	0.05
(MISSING)	43	1.98
TOTAL	2176	100

SOURCE: Chang 2008. Reprinted with permission of Oxford University Press.
DATA SOURCE: Stanford KDP Events Dataset (1970–1979).

position from certain sectors of society as a direct result of the severity and cruelty of its attempts to stifle it in others" (1998: 517). That is, as certain movement groups are heavily repressed, others come to the fore to take their place. "Cohort replacement," then, is one way that social movements are able to survive in the face of extreme repression. Nancy Whittier, for instance, notes that in America's New Left movement, activists who "were the most immediate targets of repression . . . brought new actors into the resistance movement, further broadening its scope" (1997: 90). Diversification of movement actors, in short, is often a function of state repression.

It is clear from Figure 5.2 that the diversity of actors participating in South Korea's democracy movement increased over time.[10] The dips in the graph point to the influence that repression had on the total number of protest events and consequently on the number of actors staging them. We can see, for example, the tangible impact of ED 9 reflected in the drop in the diversity index score in 1976. But this was only a short-term effect. Although the Yusin regime maintained its draconian repression campaign after 1976, and this resulted in lower numbers of protests compared to before the EDs, it was during this same time, in 1978 and 1979, that diversity scores reached their highest points. That is, there might not have been as many protests in the ED era, but there were more groups organizing them as key movement actors received their "political baptism" through the crucible of state repression after the EDs (Jennings 1987: 379).

The entry of new actors into the movement not only contributed to the overall strength of antigovernment mobilization in the 1970s, but would also have implications for the long-term development of South Korean civil society. If the seeds of human rights lawyering were first planted by a small group in the 1970s, their efforts bore abundant fruit, as evident in the important role that lawyers play in contemporary civil society. The creation of the aforementioned lawyers group, Minbyŏn,[11] was an indicative moment in the institutionalization of social movements: NGOs and other "citizens' organizations" (*simin tanch'e*) are in-

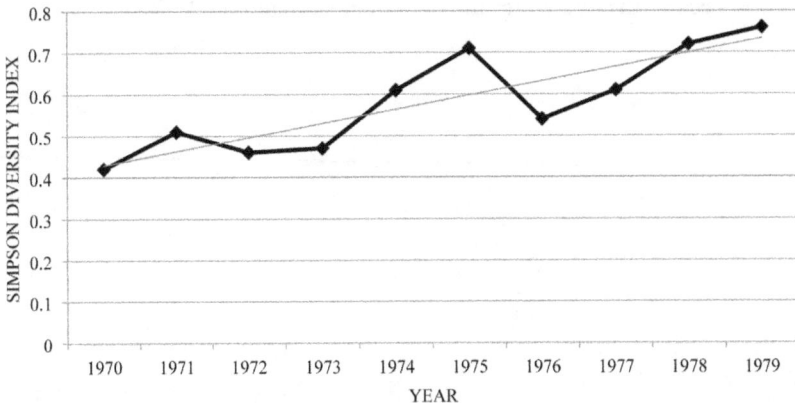

Figure 5.2. Diversity of social groups participating in protest events
DATA SOURCE: Stanford KDP Events Dataset (1970–1979).

creasingly relying on the rule of law as a strategy for mobilization (Goedde 2011; see also Hong 2011).

Today there are several law firms in South Korea that champion human rights. Many lawyers at firms such as Duksu Law Offices, Han'gyŏl Law Firm, and Chip'yŏng Chisŏng Law Firm provide pro bono services on cases involving the violation of civil and human rights.[12] This legal community traces its history to the lawyers of the 1970s who set the precedent for human rights law in South Korea. And some who started out as human rights lawyers (inkwŏn pyŏnhosa ch'ulsin) have gone on to influential positions in South Korean politics and society, including former president Roh Moo Hyun and Pak Wŏnsun, who was elected mayor of Seoul in 2011.

But before influencing South Korea's contemporary civil society, the politicization of new movement actors had an immediate impact on antigovernment mobilization in the ED era. The shift in participants—from students to Christians, journalists, lawyers, and others—reshaped the overall character of the democracy movement. In the next two chapters I explore how movement diversification led to the introduction of new goals and tactics. Chapter 6 looks at the development of the movement's tactical repertoire and tracks the shift from more violent to less disruptive forms of protest after the decline of the student movement. In that chapter I also examine the rise of the human rights discourse, arguably one of the most important legacies of the movement against the Yusin regime. The diversification of the movement also created the possibility of alliances and coalitions, which I discuss in Chapter 7. In short, the emergence of the democracy movement, as represented by the politicization of diverse social groups, became the catalyst for the movement's evolution.

Park Chung Hee campaigning for the 1971 presidential election with his wife, Yuk Yŏngsu, at his side. Photo printed with the permission of the Korea Democracy Foundation.

Korea University students demonstrating against the constitutional amendment that allowed Park Chung Hee to run for a third presidential term in 1971. The banner reads, "We absolutely oppose the constitutional amendment" (kaehŏn kyŏlsa pandae). Photo printed with the permission of the Korea Democracy Foundation.

Riot police confronting Seoul National University students on October 2, 1973. The banner in the background reads, "Seoul National University Liberal Arts College." This protest sparked the re-emergence of the student movement in the Yusin period. Photo printed with the permission of *Kyunghyang Shinmun*.

Pastor Pak Hyŏnggyu speaking at a Thursday Prayer Meeting (no date). Banner reads, "Together with those who suffer, Thursday service: National Council of Churches in Korea." Photo printed with the permission of the Korea Democracy Foundation.

Dong-A Ilbo journalists declaring the freedom of the media on October 24, 1974. The banner reads, "Declaration of Action for a Free Press" (Chayu ŏllon silchʻŏn sŏnŏn). Photo printed with the permission of Kim Sunkyŏng.

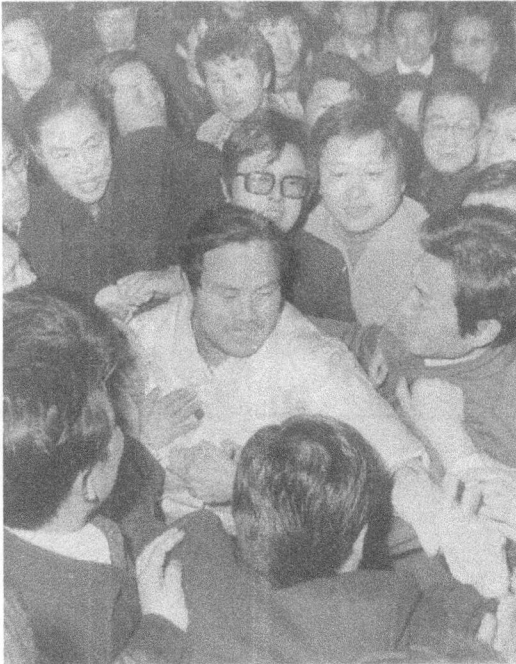

Defense lawyer Kang Sinok being arrested for declaring that the death sentences given to defendants in the People's Revolutionary Party case are "legalized murder" (pŏpchŏk sarin). Photo printed with the permission of the Korea Democracy Foundation.

Chaeya leaders meeting at the Seoul YMCA on November 5, 1973, to discuss the "state of affairs." Sitting around the table from left to right: unknown, novelist Lee Ho-Chul, Bishop Chi Haksun, Quaker leader Ham Sok Hon (*standing*), Pastor Kim Chaejun (*middle standing*), Dong-A Ilbo director Chŏn Kwanu (*eyes closed*), Buddhist monk Pŏpchŏng, Sasangge Monthly editor Kye Hunje, and poet Kim Chiha (*back turned*). Banner in the background reads, "We can no longer be patient" (*ije tŏ nŭn mot ch'amketta*). Photo printed with the permission of *Dong-A Ilbo*.

Women workers from Y. H. Trading Company being dragged out of the New Democratic Party building, August 11, 1979. Photo printed with the permission of the Korea Democracy Foundation.

MOVEMENT EVOLUTION

Part 3

6 TACTICAL ADAPTATION
AND THE RISE OF HUMAN RIGHTS

Violent movements have limitations, but peaceful ones are effective.

Pak Kyŏngsŏ, former associate director of the Christian Academy

As student protests grew into a nationwide movement against Park Chung Hee's government, the Yusin regime responded with repression strategies intended to quell student mobilization for good. The harsh repression of students motivated the emergence of new movement actors who took it upon themselves to continue the struggle in the darkest hours when presidential EDs limited the ability of dissidents to mobilize against the state. The politicization of Christians, journalists, lawyers, and other groups marked a critical juncture in the movement, reflecting growing discontent across a wider sector of society. Movement diversification in turn led to secondary consequences, as dissidents adapted to an authoritarian state that reached the pinnacle of its repressive power in the ED era. Different social groups pursued particular mobilizing strategies and raised unique concerns relevant to their stations in society, which reshaped the overall character of the democracy movement.

Very different images come to mind when newspapers report that movement participants organized a violent rally or a protest prayer meeting. The choice of tactics defines in fundamental ways the empirical experience of participants. Also, to observing bystanders, the tactics used by activists are quite possibly the most salient aspect of a social movement. Dissidents have an assortment of tactics at their disposal that together comprise a movement's "tactical repertoire" (McAdam 1983; Tilly 1978; Ennis 1987). Protest repertoires, as defined by Charles Tilly, constitute "the ways that people act together in pursuit of shared interests" (Tilly 1995: 41; quoted in Tarrow 1998: 30). Building on Tilly's definition, Sidney Tarrow reminds us that "repertoires of contention" are "culturally inscribed and socially communicated . . . [because they] are part of a society's public culture" (Tarrow 1998: 20). Protesters are able to draw on existing tactics inherited from earlier social movements, as well as to develop new forms of expressing grievances as they adapt to changing conditions. Adaptation is especially relevant in authoritarian settings, where "tactical choice reflects activists optimizing strategic opportunities" in the context of diminished avenues for political participation (Meyer 2004: 128).

The character of a social movement is also defined by the issues and goals that dissidents pursue. Raising new issues and claims-making in general are part of the process of developing a movement "frame" (Benford and Snow 2000; Snow et al. 1986). Invoked by activists in a variety of settings, movement frames are the discursive structures that articulate the motivations and justifications for engaging in extra-institutional political action. In closed-door meetings, dissident leaders deliberate about what they see are the main problems plaguing society. Through various literary forms—from dissident poetry to flyers handed out at marches—potential participants learn about social problems and are encouraged to join the movement to ameliorate them. At protest events, activists reinforce the movement's frame by articulating their demands through speeches and declarations, singing the potent lyrics of movement songs, and reading the literature disseminated at large gatherings. Through these different venues and mediums, the pertinent issues are diffused to movement participants and the public at large.

While the fight for democracy centered on real material goals, part of the struggle was to define and narrate the ideal of what South Korea should be. Park Chung Hee propounded "Korean-style" democracy along with his vision for economic development, and dissident groups challenged state rhetoric in several ways. As Italian neo-Marxist theorist Antonio Gramsci pondered in his prison notebooks, power is secured by monopolizing the culture and worldview of the people in a polity (Hoare and Smith 1971). Cultural hegemony is as fundamental to maintaining power as material might. So it follows that social movements that challenge authoritarian states wage a discursive battle against governments' rhetoric of self-legitimization. Raising an alternative discourse over and against the state's own legitimizing rhetoric is a critical task of a social movement because it contributes to the "cognitive liberation" of the oppressed (McAdam 1982).

The diversification of actors participating in South Korea's democracy movement led to tactical innovations and the articulation of new issues and goals. In the ED era, dissidents were limited in the types of public protests they were able to organize, and they adapted accordingly. In addition, with greater state repression, human rights became an increasingly important focus of antigovernment mobilization. In this chapter I draw on the Stanford KDP Events Dataset, archival sources, and interviews to assess how movement diversification facilitated tactical adaptation and the rise of the human rights discourse. The chapter further explicates the dialectical relationship between state and society by identifying the specific mechanisms through which the Yusin regime's repression policies motivated the evolution of the democracy movement.

TACTICAL DIVERSITY AND ADAPTATION

Susan Olzak and S. C. Noah Uhrig define tactics as "recognized patterns of activities that express the claims and demands of protesters" (2001: 700). Throughout the 1970s, participants in South Korea's democracy movement pursued a variety of protest tactics. Some were quite dramatic, such as self-immolation, while others, such as prayer protests, were less disruptive. Still others were universal to settings outside of Korea, such as the sit-in rally that was a mainstay in the American civil rights and peace movements in the 1960s (Andrews and Biggs 2006; Biggs and Andrews 2010). Table 6.1 lists the wide range of tactics used by activists in the 1970s as recorded in the Stanford KDP Events Dataset. The public demonstration (commonly referred to in Korea in shorthand as the *temo*) was the most frequently used protest tactic by democracy movement participants: nearly one in every five protests took the form of a demonstration. Demonstrations were ubiquitous in antigovernment movements of the postliberation period and variations of this quintessential protest tactic are still popular today. In addition, protesters often made declarations (*sŏnŏn*), which were opportunities to criticize the dictatorial regime in formalized public statements.

In addition to demonstrations and declarations, movement tactics often took the form of infrastructure building. Meetings and other forms of movement organizing were coded as "events" when they involved the determination to fight the authoritarian state. Though they were not intended to be public actions, organizational meetings were an important part of antigovernment mobilization and consequently were repressed by state authorities, who stormed buildings and rooms to disrupt them. Similarly, the founding of a formal social movement organization was an important event that marked the increasing organizational capacity of the democracy movement. The formation of organizations within a dissident community (such as student net-

Table 6.1. Tactics used in protest events

Tactic	Frequency	Percentage
Demonstration	455	18.83
Declaration/proclamation	453	18.74
Resolution meeting	206	8.52
Request/petition	196	8.11
Propaganda	176	7.28
Sit-in rally	146	6.04
Creating organization	131	5.42
Prayer/religious ceremony	130	5.38
Fasting	78	3.23
Boycott	70	2.90
Strike	67	2.77
Symbolic protest/dramaturgy	43	1.78
Legal/formal channels	42	1.74
Memorial event	41	1.70
Spoken criticism	36	1.49
Consciousness raising	18	0.74
Press conference	18	0.74
Parade/march	15	0.62
Silent rally	13	0.54
Resignation/quit job	13	0.54
Fundraising	13	0.54
Self-harm/suicide	11	0.46
Riot/vandalism	6	0.25
Violence	6	0.25
Monitoring elections	5	0.21
Spontaneous disruption	4	0.16
Picketing	4	0.17
Investigation	3	0.12
Not trying hard at work	3	0.12
Naked protest	1	0.04
Take hostage	1	0.04
Other	1	0.04
(MISSING)	12	0.50
TOTAL	2417	100

DATA SOURCE: Stanford KDP Events Dataset (1970–1979).

works) and between them (such as coalitions) were strategies to garner the material and human resources necessary to sustain the movement in the face of severe state repression.

Complementing this standard repertoire are unique protest tactics that reflect the rich imagination of dissidents in the 1970s. More often than other groups, student activists staged symbolic and dramaturgical enactments that expressed their grievances in creative ways. Culture was appropriated for political purposes in street theater, such as the *madanggŭk*, which "synthesized and amalgamated Korean traditional folk drama with elements of Western drama" (Lee 2007: 187). Examples of these "cultural protests" include the event mentioned in the previous chapter in which SNU students set fire to media paraphernalia to symbolize the death of free speech in Korea. Another example occurred on November 7, 1973, when students from SNU and Hansin University held a joint "mock court" in which they put Park Chung Hee's government "on trial" for its dependence on Japanese capital to fuel South Korea's economic development (KDF Events Dictionary: 659). These examples of dramaturgical protest popularized the appropriation of cultural traditions by activists in the 1970s. As Namhee Lee notes, "intellectuals and students gradually transformed the maskdance drama of the 1960s into a 'theater of resistance' during the Yusin era of the 1970s" (2007: 203).

Other tactical forms in the 1970s were less dramatic and simply small gestures of resistance against the Yusin regime. Discussed in the previous chapter, purchasing ads in support of *Dong-A Ilbo* journalists after the government restricted companies from advertising in the newspaper was this sort of small gesture. Some tactics required individualized initiative and creativity as Yi Ujŏng recalls:

> I carried an umbrella on Sejong Road. Inside of the umbrella it was written "We want democracy, not the Yusin Constitution." When the umbrella is closed you cannot see the phrase. Sometimes the police took me to the police station [with the umbrella]. . . . it was fun and kind of a thrill. (Interview with Yi Ujŏng, August 17, 2000)

Although less confrontational, these small acts of dissent—what James C. Scott (1985) calls "everyday forms of resistance"—were part of the larger tactical repertoire that defined the character of the democracy movement in the 1970s. Some tactics were standard ways of expressing grievances and part of an established repertoire; other strategies were not so much tactics as improvised action to evade repression. Again, Yi Ujŏng remembers a clever trick she used to escape from the KCIA agents who often followed her:

> I'll tell you one more episode. Detectives kept a close watch on me and one day one of them followed me onto a bus. It was crowded in the bus but I could walk among the people as I am small. I was wearing a coat that was a different color on the inside than the outside. I turned my coast inside-out so that the detective could not find me in the bus. By doing this, I was finally able to escape from him. (Interview with Yi Ujŏng, August 17, 2000)

Participants in the 1970s democracy movement relied on a hodgepodge of tactics to challenge the authoritarian regime. While large demonstrations, usually orchestrated by students, and public declarations—usually made by Christians, intellectuals, opposition politicians, and journalists—were the two most frequently used tactics in the democracy movement, there were many other ways of expressing grievances. The rich diversity of the tactical repertoire used against Park Chung Hee's government reflects the creative strategies that protesters employed in response to the Yusin regime's attempts to silence dissent.

Actor-Tactic Symmetry

The variety of tactics that dissidents used in antigovernment protests speaks to the dynamic nature of the democracy movement in the 1970s. The use of specific tactics, however, was not uniform across the different social groups participating in protests. Because tactical repertoires are "culturally inscribed," protesters often choose tactics that resonate with their particular community. Following a cyclical logic, "movement cultures" influence tactical choices which in turn define the overarching character of a social movement (Johnston and Klandermans 1995). If, as Susan Olzak and S. C. Noah Uhrig (2001) define them, tactics reflect "recognized patterns of activities," then it is important to consider the unique cultures of distinct communities that influence patterns of political action.

Simple bivariate analysis reveals the associations between popular tactics and the different social groups participating in Korea's democracy movement. Table 6.2 reports the percentile distribution of tactics employed by the seven most active protesting groups in the 1970s. It is fairly clear from the table that the choice of tactics varied depending on who organized the protest. Although demonstrations constituted the most common protest form, it was a tactic used primarily by secular and Christian students. Secular students employed dem-

Table 6.2. Actor-tactic symmetry[1]

	Demon-stration	Declara-tion	Resolu-tion Meeting	Request, Petition	Propa-ganda	Sit-In Rally	Create Organi-zation	Prayer Protest
Students	48.99	22.17	12.32	5.36	14.78	2.90	2.61	2.32
Laborers	7.03	3.78	5.14	21.08	3.78	27.84	14.59	1.08
Christians	8.08	40.11	11.14	13.09	5.57	1.11	9.47	22.01
Journalists	5.76	43.88	20.14	4.32	9.35	2.88	9.35	0.72
Christian Students	36.50	29.93	8.03	2.92	13.14	6.57	5.11	27.74
Intellectuals	4.24	44.07	17.80	14.41	7.63	0	6.78	7.63
Politicians	6.25	53.13	5.21	10.42	5.21	1.04	11.46	7.29

[1] Percentages reflect the total number of a specific tactic used by a single social group, divided by the total number of protest events by that social group. Total row percentages can exceed 100 percent in cases where multiple tactics were used in a single protest event.
DATA SOURCE: Stanford KDP Events Dataset (1970–1979).

onstrations in 49 percent of all the protest events they organized, while Christian students used demonstrations in 37 percent of their events. Combining multiple tactical forms in a single event was not unusual, and a student demonstration usually included the reading of a formal declaration and the dissemination of antigovernment propaganda: declarations were read in more than 22 percent of all student protest events, and propaganda literature was dispersed in nearly 15 percent of student organized events.

Demonstrations were usually disruptive and invited greater repression relative to other protest forms (Chang and Vitale 2013). Students would begin preparations for a *temo* inside the university campus by making posters and placards featuring democracy-related slogans. They sang movement songs to raise their spirits before marching toward the front gate of the university, where more often than not police in riot gear awaited them. Shouting slogans and singing songs, the students confronted the police and sometimes engaged them in hand-to-hand combat. The police in turn resorted to tear-gassing, clubbing, and other forms of physical violence to turn back or arrest the student demonstrators. The *temo* is now such a common form of protest in contemporary South Korean social movements that it is not too much of an exaggeration to say it has become routinized, with both demonstrators and repressive forces following an expected set of scripts (Kwon 2011).

Unlike students, workers relied primarily on the sit-in rally (*nongsŏng*), utilizing the tactic in 28 percent of their protest events. Sit-in rallies almost always occurred in the local place of business. Disturbance of the normal work routine was an effective way in which employees made their concerns known to both their employers and the government. In addition to sit-ins, laborers also took advantage of regulatory processes designed to sublimate workers' concerns through institutional means. The state-sanctioned Federation of Korean Trade Unions (FKTU) monitored and regulated labor unions across industries, and workers frequently filed legal petitions with their particular FKTU chapter: requests and petitions constituted more than 21 percent of their events. Also, because at the time many registered unions were "company unions" dictated by employers' interests, workers organized "democratic unions," although those unions were not recognized by their employers (Koo 2001). The establishment of pro-labor organizations constituted nearly 15 percent of all workers' events in the 1970s.

Christians opted for less disruptive tactics and primarily made formal declarations that criticized Park Chung Hee's government. More than 40 percent of all the protest events that Christians staged during the 1970s were formal declarations. Public declarations hark back to the practice of protesting through "memorials" (Kim 2007: 54) during the Chosŏn Dynasty, when aggrieved Confucian scholars and government officials used formal statements to express their concerns to the king (Koo 2007). Although declarations might seem to be a relatively innocuous and nonthreatening protest tactic, they had great symbolic power, especially if delivered by individuals and groups who enjoyed high moral status in Korean society. Indeed, the significant role of declarations in the 1970s democracy movement is clear: two of the most publicized events that occurred in the 1970s were the Declaration for the Salvation of the Nation, delivered by Christian and political leaders on March 1, 1976, and Bishop Chi Haksun's Declaration of Conscience, drafted after his arrest in 1974.

One tactic unique to Christians and Christian students was the prayer protest. Religious ritual and ceremonies oftentimes became platforms from which Christians criticized the government. Twenty-two percent of all Christian protests in the 1970s were prayer meetings, with the Thursday Prayer Meeting, discussed in Chapter 4, being the most significant example. Also, consistent with their nonviolent inclinations, Christians relied on formal petitions in more than 13 percent of their protest events. Finally, as part of their role as supporters of other social groups in the democracy movement, Christians often held meetings to articulate their resolve (*kyŏrŭimun*) to fight for democracy and foster solidarity in the movement.

The association between a group's identity and its choice of tactics is clearer in the case of Christian students, a distinct group relative to Christians and secular students. Christian students consciously (and proudly) straddled the boundary between their two identities. Although they were university students, and thus part of the larger student movement, they specifically drew on their Christian networks when mobilizing. Christian students developed their own organizations, such as the Korean Student Christian Federation and the Ecumenical Youth Council, which received support from the NCCK and other large Christian organizations while maintaining a degree of independence from them. Christian students organized joint protest events with both secular students and Christian pastors, but they claimed a unique identity throughout the 1970s in their organizational founding statements and protest paraphernalia. Reflecting these multiple identities, Christian students readily utilized the demonstration in their antigovernment protests, using this standard student tactic 37 percent of the time in their events. Also similar to secular students, Christian students spread literature during their demonstrations: antigovernment literature was dispersed in more than 13 percent of their protest events. But because they were also influenced by their Christian identity, Christian students used declarations 30 percent of the time, and prayer protests accounted for more than 27 percent of their events. It is apparent that the tactical forms that Christian students used in protests were consistent with their dual-identity as both students and Christians.

Journalists, like Christians, eschewed disruptive demonstrations in favor of the relatively more peaceful declaration. In nearly 44 percent of their protest events, journalists made declarations in order to voice their concern for media freedom, including the pivotal Declaration of Action for a Free Press in October 1974. In addition to declarations, they also made resolutions in one-fifth of all of their protest events. These resolutions consisted of agreeing to fight for media freedom and continue their reporting of the protest events of other social groups.

Similarly, because the majority of the intellectuals and politicians identified in the Stanford KDP Events Dataset were older social and political leaders, they did not participate in rowdy and confrontational protests but rather relied on nondisruptive tactics such as declarations, resolution meetings, petitions, and the creation of organizations. Intellectuals made declarations in more than 44 percent of the events they organized, while resolution meetings accounted for nearly 18 percent of them. Certain intellectuals, such as university professors, also regularly registered formal petitions with government authorities in order to complain about state intrusion in academic affairs. Politicians also used the declaration tactic in 53 percent of their events—more than any other group. Importantly, because pro-democracy politicians were marginalized in the National Assembly and in institutional politics generally, they created their own extra-institutional political organizations, accounting for more than 11 percent of their events.

In sum, the diversification of protesting actors led to the diversification of the movement's tactical repertoire. Each of the main social groups participating in protests used tactical forms that were consistent with their group's identity and culture. If protest tactics are the most visible attribute of a social movement, then temporal shifts in the tactical repertoire are an easy indicator of movement evolution. We saw in Chapter 3 that the systematic repression of students during the Minch'ŏng incident resulted in their demobilization, which in turn prompted other groups to rally in their stead. When the number of student protests declined between 1974 and 1976, the rate of protest events by Christians, journalists, intellectuals, and politicians increased in the same period. Because students tended toward disruptive protests, the proportion of events using less disruptive tactics grew in the ED era. Figure 6.1 shows the percentage of protest events that used nondisruptive tactics[1] juxtaposed to the total number of events in the 1970s.

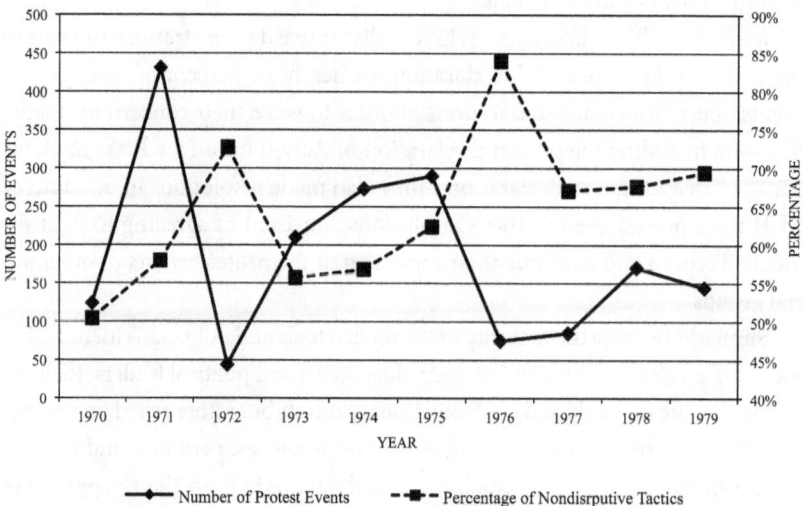

Figure 6.1. Percentage of nondisruptive tactics used in protest events

DATA SOURCE: Stanford KDP Events Dataset (1970–1979).

According to Figure 6.1, the proportion of nondisruptive tactics was inversely correlated with annual counts of protest events. That is, it was in the very years when heightened repression resulted in smaller numbers of protests that dissidents fell back on nondisruptive strategies. The garrison decree in the fall/winter of 1971 discouraged political mobilization in 1972, effectively reducing the number of public protests. Adapting to this repressive context, dissidents relied on nondisruptive means to express their grievances: more than 70 percent of protests in 1972 used nondisruptive tactics. Similarly, in 1976, following the EDs in 1974 and 1975, the number of protests dropped precipitously. The combination of increasing repression and entry of new social movement actors, such as Christians and journalists, resulted in dissidents using nondisruptive tactics in nearly 85 percent of their protest events in 1976. It was not until the end of the decade, when students began to regain some momentum, that the percentage of nondisruptive tactics tapered off. Clearly, state repression had a profound impact on the character of antigovernment mobilization as dissidents in the ED era shifted their tactical strategies toward nondisruptive forms.

DIVERSIFICATION OF ISSUES

The issues that protesters pursue are also a critical component of social movements. Along with the ultimate goal of recovering democracy, dissidents raised new concerns about the monumental transformations that were taking place in Korean society during the Yusin period. The range of issues covered in the 1970s democracy movement reflects both the large number of grievances harbored by dissident communities and the richness of their discursive challenge against the state. Table 6.3 presents a list of specific issues that were mentioned in protest events as recorded in the Stanford KDP Events Dataset.

Predictably, past acts of repression were the most frequently cited issue in protest events. As discussed in previous chapters, repression was a central motivation for key social groups to begin to mobilize against the state. Other popular topics for protest included workers' rights, media censorship, the Yusin Constitution, freedom of the academy, political reforms and antidictatorship (*pan tokchae*), military training, and movement solidarity. These and less frequently cited issues—corruption, reunification with North Korea, foreign relations, urban slums, and sexual tourism—show that for antigovernment dissidents, the recovery of democracy meant the total transformation of Korean society and not simply the institutionalization of a democratic constitution.

Table 6.3. Issues raised in protest events

Issues	Frequency	Percent
Specific acts of repression	857	29.12
Workers' rights	411	13.97
Media censorship	191	6.49
Yusin Constitution	184	6.25
Freedom of the academy	156	5.30
Political reforms	144	4.89
Dictatorship	118	4.01
Mandatory military training	94	3.19
Movement solidarity	94	3.19
Election corruption	70	2.38
Human rights	65	2.21
Political control laws	55	1.87
Corruption	53	1.80
Critique of individual politicians	47	1.60
Japan policy	45	1.53
Reinstatement of students	44	1.50
Freedom of religion	31	1.05
National referendums	28	0.95
North Korea/reunification	23	0.78
Memorialization of deceased activists	20	0.68
KCIA	17	0.58
Torture	13	0.44
Rural/farmers' issues	13	0.44
Foreign relations	12	0.41
Economic dependence on foreign nations	11	0.37
Prisoners' rights	11	0.37
Urban slums	8	0.27
Sexual tourism	5	0.17
Taxes	4	0.14
President Jimmy Carter's visit	2	0.07
OTHER	71	2.73
MISSING	46	1.77
TOTAL	2943	100

DATA SOURCE: Stanford KDP Events Dataset (1970–1979).

Actor-Issue Symmetry

Not every issue was equally important to the different social groups participating in the democracy movement. Table 6.4 presents percentage statistics for the distribution of popular issues attributed to the seven most active movement groups. State repression was a salient issue for all of the groups. Students, for example, mentioned past acts of state repression in 45 percent of the protest events they organized; and Christians, acting as the conduit for the moral consciousness of the movement, criticized state repression in more than 60 percent of their events. Students also mentioned media censorship in nearly 13 percent of their protests—more than any other group besides journalists. As discussed in the previous chapter, students and journalists formed a mutually dependent relationship and supported each other's causes. Also, addressing their specific situation, students highlighted freedom of the academy in more than 16 percent of their protest events in order to criticize the closing of schools, the expulsion of student demonstrators, and the presence of the military on university campuses.

The relationship between group identity and grievances is most clear in the case of laborers. Unlike most other groups, who were concerned with multiple issues, laborers focused almost exclusively on workers' rights. In 94 percent of the protest events they organized, workers raised issues pertaining to working conditions, wage increases, and fair labor policies. Aside from a few labor

Table 6.4. Actor-issue symmetry[1]

	Specific Acts of Repression	Workers' Rights	Media Censorship	Yusin Constitution	Freedom of the Academy	Political Reforms and Dictatorship
Students	44.93	4.35	12.75	15.22	16.52	9.71
Laborers	23.78	93.78	0	0.27	0	1.62
Christians	61.28	11.42	5.01	10.31	3.34	5.85
Journalists	51.80	0.72	50.36	0.72	2.16	0.72
Christian Students	54.01	6.57	12.41	18.25	7.30	7.30
Intellectuals	58.47	5.93	5.93	5.93	16.10	5.93
Politicians	35.42	7.29	4.17	18.75	4.17	13.54

[1] Percentages reflect the total number of a specific issue raised by a single social group, divided by the total number of protest events by that social group. Total row percentages can exceed 100% in cases where multiple issues were raised in a single protest event.

DATA SOURCE: Stanford KDP Events Dataset (1970–1979).

disputes discussed in the next chapter, and despite efforts by Christian groups such as the Methodist UIM and the Christian Academy to raise workers' political consciousness, it is clear from the data that in the 1970s the labor movement had yet to develop the broad political framework that guided it in the late 1980s and 1990s (Koo 2001).[2]

Compared to laborers, Christians pursued a broader discursive agenda intended to foster solidarity with diverse groups participating in the democracy movement. This intention is evident in the high percentage of protest events that addressed state repression. As discussed in Chapter 4, their biggest concern was the repression of students and workers. Along with the support they provided to students during the Minch'ŏng incident, Christians' concern for laborers was evident in more than 11 percent of their protest events. Journalists, like Christians, criticized specific acts of state repression, but predictably were primarily concerned with media censorship, raising this issue in more than 50 percent of their protest events.

It is also clear from Table 6.4 that intellectuals and politicians raised issues relevant to their positions in society. University professors and administrators comprised a significant portion of the intellectual community and, troubled by the fate of their students, they addressed the issue of state repression in more than 58 percent of the protests they organized. They also were concerned with the state's interference in university affairs and raised the issue of academic freedom in more than 16 percent of their protest events. Politicians, on the other hand, were less concerned with labor issues, freedom of the press, and academic freedom and instead focused their attention on political governance. Consistent with their vocation, politicians more than any other group demanded political reforms while criticizing the Yusin Constitution and dictatorship.

In short, different dissident communities raised issues that mirrored their unique group identities. This is important to keep in mind when considering the secondary impact of state repression on movement diversification. As repression motivated the entry of new movement actors into the democracy movement, it also indirectly led to dissidents diversifying their criticisms of state and society under Park Chung Hee's rule. The repression of the democracy movement might have limited the total number of public protest events, but this same repression led to several unintended consequences, including the diversification of movement actors, tactics, and issues. Of the several new issues adopted by participants in the 1970s democracy movement human rights would become a foundational concern, leading some to label antigovernment mobilization in the ED era as a human rights movement (Han 2002; Lee 2001).

FROM DEMOCRACY TO HUMAN RIGHTS

The homage paid to human rights is ubiquitous in contemporary Korean civil society. Not only is it invoked in struggles as different as the foreign workers' movement and the gay and lesbian movement (Piper 2004; Kim and Cho 2011), but human rights have also been reified in government-supported organizations, including most importantly the National Human Rights Commission of Korea, founded in 2001. Some studies trace the development of human rights in South Korea to historical resources, such as the proto-human rights ideals in Confucian traditions (de Bary and Weiming 1998; Shaw 1991). Others point to the impact of the modern "global human rights regime" on the worldwide diffusion of human rights (Cole and Ramirez 2013; Koo 2011; Koo and Ramirez 2009; Wotipka and Tsutsui 2008).

Notwithstanding the importance of domestic cultural resources and contemporary international organizations, it is curious that the role of collective action and social movements has been neglected in explanations of human rights in Korea. As I show in this section, human rights became part of South Korean civil society for the first time when antigovernment dissidents made it an integral part of the larger democracy movement in the 1970s. The integration of human rights into protests during the ED era signified a marked departure from the human rights organizations that were embedded in government bureaucracies in the 1950s and 1960s. Before the 1970s, human rights institutions in South Korea were for the most part products of top-down calculations by the South Korean state, whose attempts to mimic a democratic polity belied postliberation realities.

Following liberation from colonial rule, important institutional foundations for human rights were laid with the establishment of an independent South Korean state in 1948. For the first time in Korea's history, human rights were codified in the national constitution, including protections for basic political freedoms and social and economic equality. With an eye toward winning international recognition by joining the United Nations, the newly formed South Korean government directed much media attention to the United Nations Universal Declaration of Human Rights. In 1948 the South Korean media broadcast shows describing the process of drafting the UN Declaration, making an extra effort to explain what human rights are to a citizenry who for the most part were not privy to the notion of individual-based and legally protected rights (Lee 2009: 132).

The formal adoption of the Universal Declaration of Human Rights by the UN was commemorated by Syngman Rhee's government in 1950 when Rhee designated December 10 as the Memorial Day of Human Rights in line with the international day of human rights (Lee 2009: 142). A year later, in 1951, in the throes of the Korean War, the annual commemoration of human rights on December 10 was followed by a full Human Rights Week sponsored by the Ministry of Justice.[3] More significantly, human rights became part of government institutions in the form of human rights consulting centers (*inkwŏn sangdamso*) housed within the Ministry of Justice, the Supreme Prosecutor's Office, the Labor Bureau, and the FKTU (Lee 2009: 146).

The fanfare paid to the UN Universal Declaration of Human Rights, and the institutionalization of human rights vis-à-vis the state constitution and government human rights centers, belied the sociopolitical realities of Korea in the immediate postliberation period. National division in the context of the burgeoning international Cold War contributed to gross violations of the rights of individuals (Lee 2009; Henderson 1991). The violent purges of leftist groups that began under the watch of the United States Army Military Government in Korea (1945–1948) continued after the establishment of the Republic of Korea in 1948. One of the most egregious incidents took place on Jeju Island in 1948–1949 when Syngman Rhee ordered the massacre of Korean citizens who had criticized the division of the Korean nation and challenged the legitimacy of his government (Cumings 1990).

In this political environment, the government's human rights consulting centers were essentially a symbolic homage paid to the ideal of what modern liberal democratic nation-states were supposed to "look like" rather than actual effective organizations able to protect individuals' rights (Lee 2009). In turn, the onset of the Korean War (1950–1953), and the need to rebuild society and nation in the aftermath of its devastation, all but put a halt to the development of human rights in South Korea. In short, even with constitutional protection and government human rights consulting centers, the concept of human rights did not permeate civil society during Syngman Rhee's presidency (1948–1960; Lee 2001).

Although human rights was not an unknown concept to dissidents in the early 1970s, the focus of the democracy movement centered on political concerns. Notwithstanding the founding of Amnesty International's Korean Committee in 1972, and a few sensational "human rights cases" (such as the arrest of poet Kim Chiha in 1970), human rights received relatively little attention in public protests before 1974. As Figure 6.2 indicates, less than three percent of protests in the years before 1974 raised the issue of human rights. But after the EDs, human rights became more important. It is significant that the saliency of human rights increased during the nadir of the movement in 1976: the proportion of protests that raised the issue of human rights grew as the total number of protests shrank. Less attention was given to human rights in 1977 and 1978, but it became a popular issue again in 1979, when 12 percent of all protest events explicitly mentioned human rights.

The incorporation of human rights into the discursive framework of the democracy movement began when Amnesty International approved the establishment of the Amnesty Korean Committee (AKC) in 1972. Spearheaded by leaders in the progressive community, including founding chairman Pastor Kim Chaejun, the AKC worked to make human rights an important part of the anti-Yusin movement (KDF Events Dictionary: 177). It was not a coincidence that a Christian pastor from the progressive wing of the Korean church was named AKC's first chairman. As shown in Table 6.4, Christians more than other movement groups criticized state repression. The large prayer meeting in October 1973 that was organized by the Gwangju Christian Association to protest the hundreds of students arrested that month is a representative case

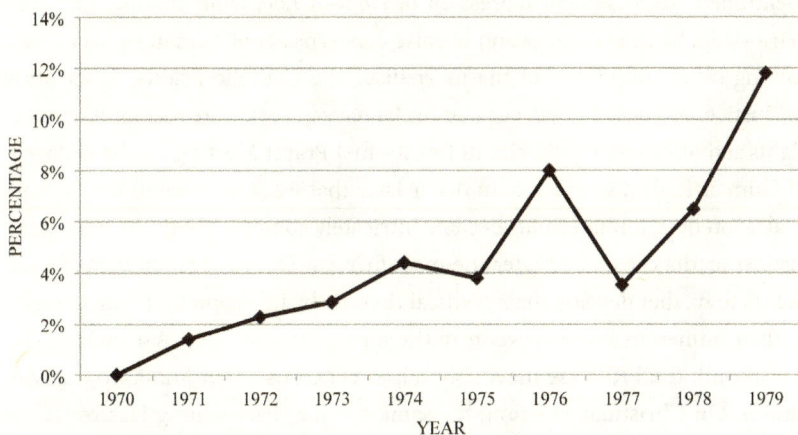

Figure 6.2. Saliency of human rights issues in protest events
DATA SOURCE: Stanford KDP Events Dataset (1970–1979).

of Christians criticizing the state for violating the rights of university students (KDF Events Dictionary: 279).

Repression continued to trigger the issue of human rights throughout the 1970s. During the Minch'ŏng incident, the state accused prominent leaders in the democracy movement of fomenting student rebellion, including dissident poet Kim Chiha and Bishop Chi Haksun. While confined to St. Mary's Hospital in Myeongdong, central Seoul, Bishop Chi made his celebrated Declaration of Conscience, discussed in Chapter 4, on July 23, 1974. In the declaration, Bishop Chi explicitly raised the issue of human rights, arguing that the Yusin regime "crushed people's basic human rights and basic human dignity by the will of a single person in power" (KDF Events Dictionary: 345).

The content of Bishop Chi's declaration circulated widely among the dissident community and helped popularize the inclusion of human rights in protest events. For example, on November 14, 1974, Christian students from Hansin University promulgated their own Human Rights Declaration in support of Bishop Chi and to commemorate the self-immolation protest of Chŏn T'aeil (KDF Events Dictionary: 357). The very next day, fifty-four politicians from the New Democratic Party staged a protest in which they combined political and human rights concerns (KDF Events Dictionary: 373). These events reflected the increasing importance of human rights in the democracy movement while Park Chung Hee was consolidating his authoritarian system through the EDs.

Three events were especially important in galvanizing the issue of human rights following the demobilization of the student movement. First, the aforementioned advertisement repression of *Dong-A Ilbo*, while highlighting state censorship, became an occasion to raise concerns about human rights as well. Joining other supporters of the journalists, the Catholic Priests' Association for Justice purchased a full-page ad on January 4, 1975, to report on its human rights activities and to publicize its twenty-first Prayer Meeting for the Recovery of Human Rights, which was to occur later that week at Myeongdong Cathedral. Moreover, human rights became intricately combined with the movement against media censorship after the mass firing at *Dong-A Ilbo* motivated journalists to further develop their political rhetoric by incorporating human rights in their numerous protests events in the spring of 1975 (Dong-A T'uwi 2005).

Second, the PRP case inevitably raised concerns about human rights violations. On Christmas Eve 1974, the same day that Park Chung Hee restricted companies from advertising in *Dong-A Ilbo*, the NCCK's Human Rights Mission made a public declaration condemning the government for deporting foreign missionary George Ogle (KDF Events Dictionary: 392). After more than twenty years serving workers and the urban poor in and around Incheon and Seoul, Pastor Ogle was forced to leave the country on December 14, 1974 (Ogle 1977). Not knowing where to turn, the wives of the PRP defendants solicited the help of Pastor Ogle, who, after "look(ing) into the matter," became convinced that the government had fabricated the PRP in order to "inject a new wave of anticommunist fear into the people of South Korea so that it could tighten its control over the nation" (Ogle 2006: 89).

During their campaign to free the accused, Pastor Ogle, Father James Sinnott, and the NCCK Human Rights Mission strongly criticized Park Chung Hee's government in international news outlets. Because he was a foreign missionary with connections to Christian churches and organizations in the United States, Pastor Ogle's outspoken criticism of the PRP case pressured the Korean government to silence him. Their shortsighted solution was to deport George Ogle in 1974, then James Sinnott in April 1975.[4] Though ultimately these foreign clergymen failed in their efforts to free and save the lives of the defendants, their public protests and deportations helped spread the news of Korea's human rights situation both inside and outside the country. As James Sinnott recalls, "I left here and went to the States and spent years talking about this stuff. . . . I spent two years in Washington going here and there . . . and all the people who were, you know, human rights oriented and I would go and tell them my story" (interview with James Sinnott, August 12, 2014).

A third event that brought human rights to the fore was the Declaration for the Salvation of the Nation, discussed in Chapter 4. Proclaimed on March 1, 1976, the declaration brought together the most prominent leaders in the progressive community, whose presence lent credibility to the democracy movement. The declaration was made when the number of protests plummeted in 1976, thus providing a much-needed spark to antigovernment forces (NCCK Archive Vol. 2: 684). Human rights became a salient theme after the event, when the state, before meting out long prison sentences, accused the signatories of the declaration of trying to carry out a coup d'état (KDF Events Dictionary: 490). On March 18, 1976, families of the 3.1 (March 1) prisoners made a public declaration reflecting on the importance of the UN Universal Declaration of Human Rights and the need for human rights protection in Korea (KDF Events Dictionary: 486). A month later (April 12), on behalf of the 3.1 prisoners, the NCCK Human Rights Mission held the largest prayer protest meeting conducted in the wake of ED 9 (NCCK Archive Vol. 2: 821). At the gathering, members of the mission demanded that the state release the prisoners and publicly listed the government's human rights abuses (KDF Events Dictionary: 486).

International Pressures

More protests in the highly repressive ED era incorporated human rights, such as when former president Yun Posŏn, on January 6, 1978, addressed an audience of five hundred people to criticize Park Chung Hee's human rights violations (KDF Events Dictionary: 487). Emboldening these domestic actors was the modern global human rights regime that emerged after the UN Universal Declaration of Human Rights (Cole and Ramirez 2013). With the goal of enacting the ideals articulated in the UN declaration, various international meetings, treaties, and organizations disseminate universal norms intended to curb human rights violations in different political and geographical settings. According to Daniel C. Thomas, for example, the 1975 Helsinki Final Act contributed to the "demise of Communist rule" as opposition forces in the communist Eastern bloc were able to rally around the "formal commitment to respect human rights" articulated in this agreement signed by thirty-five nations (2001: 4). Margaret E. Keck and Kathryn Sikkink (1998) have also shown that "transnational advocacy networks" help to spread the ideal of human rights globally. Transnational advocacy networks support local social movements by providing an assortment of material and discursive resources (Meyer 2003). Based on "'rights' claims [as] the prototypical language of advocacy networks," international organizations like Freedom House challenge governments that violate the "principled ideas or values" that makeup global human rights norms (Keck and Sikkink 1999: 93, 89; see also Cole 2005).

In South Korea, organizations such as Amnesty International played a significant role in publicizing the Yusin regime's human rights record to the international community. External support also came in the form of the growing interest of the U.S. government in human rights issues abroad, a concern that was reflected in its revised Foreign Assistance Act of 1973 (Forsythe and Welch 1986). The 1973 act, seen as a renewal of America's commitment to freedom and liberty, stipulated that "the President should deny any economic or military assistance to the government of any foreign country which practices the internment or imprisonment of that country's citizens for political purposes."[5] Following the 1973 act, human rights became one of the central issues in U.S.–South Korea relations, a policy consideration that culminated in President Jimmy Carter's visit to Korea in 1979.

Lobbied by organizations such as the "North American Coalition for Human Rights in Korea, Asia Watch, Amnesty International, and the International Human Rights Law group" (Kim Y. J. 2011: 461), a subcommittee of the United States Congress Committee on International Relations, chaired by Congressman Donald M. Fraser (D-MN), opened hearings on South Korea's human rights situation (United States House of Representatives, Committee on International Relations 1975). In 1974 and 1975, individuals who had directly experienced repression by the Yusin regime, including Pastor George Ogle and Father James Sinnott, testified before Fraser's subcommittee. The results of the subcommittee's investigation were published as a congressional policy implication report that summarized the human rights violations under the Yusin government (United States House of Representatives, Committee on International Relations 1975).

Congressman Fraser was a vocal critic of Park Chung Hee's government in the 1970s and, with forty-one other concerned members of U.S. Congress, drafted a letter to President Jimmy Carter (dated August 23, 1978) complaining that South Korea's indirect presidential election system was "alarmingly similar to that of the Soviet Union" (UCLA Archive: Box 5, Folder 6). President Carter, for his part, even before he took office in 1977, "directly linked Park's record of human rights abuses to the issue of troop withdrawal" (Kim Y. J. 2011: 466). Known as the "human rights president," Jimmy Carter "introduced a new South Korea policy that diverged from the United States' traditional cold war stance . . . [putting] the issue of human rights abuses by President Park Chung Hee's *yushin* regime (1972–1979) at or near the top of the U.S. foreign policy agenda" (Kim Y. J. 2011: 457).

The agenda of the summit meeting between Presidents Carter and Park in 1979 centered on the American proposal (eventually rescinded) to withdraw a significant number of its troops from the Korean peninsula. Park Chung Hee promised to "make a significant move on human rights" if the United States reaffirmed its commitment to South Korea's national security. Partly as a result of these talks, 108 political prisoners were released following Carter's departure from Korea (Kim Y. J. 2011: 480).

Interestingly, President Carter's visit raised ambivalent feelings among the dissident community in Korea. Although some appreciated the U.S. effort to ameliorate the human rights problem in Korea, others worried that the summit meeting would further legitimate Park Chung Hee's government. Wary of this possibility, a group of family members of prisoners arrested under ED 9 gathered in front of the U.S. Embassy in Seoul on June 11, 1979, to question whether Carter was really "a human rights president" (KDF Events Dictionary: 646). A few weeks later, on June 27, students set fire to large portraits of Presidents Carter and Park that had been raised in central Seoul to mark the summit meeting (KDF Events Dictionary: 646). Two days after that, on June 29, family members of incarcerated journalists staged a rally in front of the Amnesty International office demanding to know why Carter was visiting Korea when so many human rights violations were committed by Park Chung Hee's government (KDF Events Dictionary: 646). Whether dissidents were encouraged by the U.S. interest in Korean human rights or critical that America was not doing enough, President Carter's visit fostered public debate about human rights and put additional pressure on the Yusin government.

HUMAN RIGHTS ORGANIZATIONS

The increasing saliency of human rights in protest events was an important development in the larger democracy movement. Protest discourse, as scholars have pointed out, constitutes a foundational element of mobilizing (Benford and Snow 2000; Benford and Hunt 1994; Snow and Benford 1988; Snow et al. 1986). In addition to movement frames, several studies have identified the important role that organizations play in providing material and human resources to social movements (McCarthy, McPhail, and Smith 1996; McCarthy and Zald 1977; Tarrow 1998; Tilly 1978). Human rights counseling centers were established in the postliberation period in South Korea, predominantly under the guise of government services. As noted earlier, however, these human rights centers were affiliates of larger government bureaucracies and did not possess the independence to address rights violations committed by the government itself.

Furthermore, those that were not de facto "token organizations" to begin with were sometimes coopted by the state to curb their effectiveness. For example, the International Human Rights League of Korea (Kukche Inkwŏn Ongho Hanguk Yŏnmaeng), founded on October 24–25, 1953, helped organize the annual Human Rights Week while providing counseling for 257 cases of rights violations between 1956 and 1961 (Lee 2009: 147). But by the 1970s, the League's ability to protect human rights, especially against violations committed by the government, was significantly compromised when it received formal endorsement by the Ministry of Justice on December, 17, 1976, during the height of state repression.[6]

In the Yusin period, a markedly different type of human rights organization emerged, founded by dissidents active in the democracy movement. Some were directly connected to international organizations such as the AKC; others were wings of religious groups, such as the NCCK's Human Rights Mission. Some human rights organizations addressed specific issues and supported particular social groups, such as the Peace Market Laborers' Human Rights Problem Council (P'yŏnghwa Sijang Nodongja Inkwŏn Munje Hyŏbŭihoe) and the National Committee for the Human Rights of Farmers (Chŏn'guk Nongmin Inkwŏn Wiwŏnhoe; KDF Events Dictionary: 556, 585). Others brought together diverse sectors of Korean society in formal coalitions, such as the Council for the Korean Human Rights Movement (Han'guk Inkwŏn Undong Hyŏbŭihoe), which was founded by Protestants, Catholics, educators, lawyers, media personnel, and laborers on December 29, 1977 (KDF Events Dictionary: 568). As state repression increased with the EDs, dissidents further developed the organizational foundations for human rights in South Korea.

Human rights organizations came to the fore of the democracy movement at significant points in time. As Figure 6.3 indicates, the number of protests organized by human rights groups varied over the decade. Human rights organizations played a minimal role before the EDs but became much more active after. During the lowest point of the anti-Yusin movement, in 1976, human rights organizations staged more protests than in any other year. And although the number of protests sponsored by human rights organizations tapered off after 1976, on average their levels were significantly higher in the ED era than before the repressive laws.

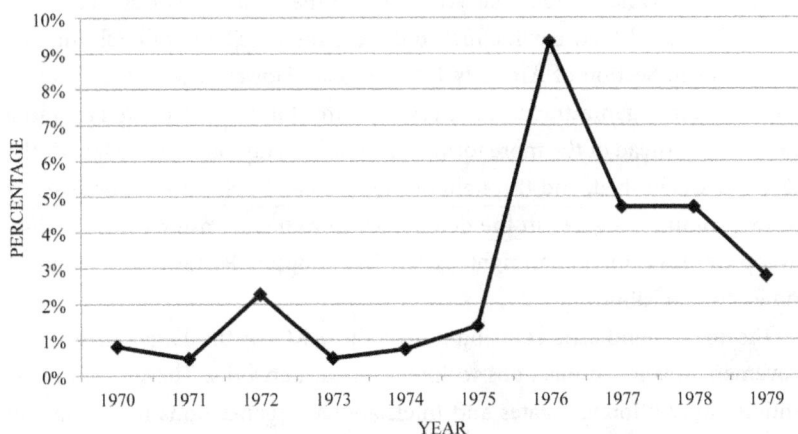

Figure 6.3. Participation of human rights organizations in protest events
DATA SOURCE: Stanford KDP Events Dataset (1970–1979).

Amnesty Korean Committee

Two of the most important human rights organizations active in the 1970s were the AKC and the NCCK Human Rights Mission. One of the first cases that Amnesty International adopted when it began its global human rights mission in 1961 was that of Korean journalist Song Chiyŏng, who was accused of disseminating communist doctrines and whose sentence, with Amnesty's help, was reduced from the death penalty to life imprisonment (*Kyunghyang Shinmun*, August 30, 1961).[7] Amnesty International's concern with the human rights situation in South Korea accelerated with the establishment of the AKC, which was formed in response to censorship and repression. On June 2, 1970, Park Chung Hee's government arrested poet Kim Chiha, publisher Pu Wanhyŏk, and editor-in-chief Kim Sŭnggyun, following the publication of Kim's satirical poem "Ojŏk" ("Five Bandits") in the previous issue of *Sasangge Monthly*. This eventually led to the popular intellectual journal being shut down permanently, prompting a strong reaction from the Korean literati and intelligentsia.

The thirty-seventh Annual Congress of PEN International, which opened on June 29, 1970, in Seoul, brought writers from sixty countries to South Korea. At this conference, Reverend Yun Hyŏn appealed to the foreign participants by personally delivering to their hotel rooms letters describing the Kim Chiha situation. One of the foreign participants informed Reverend Yun that he had also been approached by a professor of theology at Yonsei University and by a member of Amnesty International from Germany, Dr. Gerhard Breidenstein, regarding the same matter. That year, the two men, joined by Canadian missionary Reverend Fred Bayliss, met to discuss the possibility of establishing a South Korean Section of Amnesty International. However, due to the lack of monetary and organizational resources, the three founders requested to start a Committee instead of the more formal Section.[8] Finally, on March 28, 1972, the AKC was established, and throughout the 1970s and 1980s it was successively led by prominent figures in the democracy movement: Pastor Kim Chaejun, Bishop Chi Haksun, human rights lawyer Yi Pyŏngnin, Pastor Cho Hyangnok, and Pastor Na Kilmo.

The most significant contribution of the AKC to the larger democracy movement was its connections to international networks. The increasing attention paid by foreign states and international organizations to the human rights situation in South Korea led to tangible repercussions for Park Chung Hee's government, including the U.S. Congress and President Jimmy Carter

tying military aid to human rights. The ability of Korean dissidents to facilitate international pressure by adopting the human rights frame was recognized
by Park Chung Hee, whose government in March 1975 passed a law forbidding
Koreans from conveying to foreigners anything that might "harm the national
prestige" of the South Korean nation (United States House of Representatives,
Committee on International Relations 1975: 358). This "gag order" carried with
it a seven-year prison sentence for anyone who violated it.

The law was in part intended to discourage the AKC from hosting "missions"
by members of Amnesty International's general assembly and other concerned
foreigners, who came to South Korea to investigate the human rights situation.
One important visit, for example, was when Congressman Donald M. Fraser
and two Amnesty International members arrived in South Korea in the spring
of 1975 to meet with dissident leaders in the democracy movement (United
States House of Representatives, Committee on International Relations 1975:
357). Congressman Fraser returned to the United States with more information
and motivation to make human rights an integral part of the American policy
for South Korea.

Throughout the 1970s, more than one hundred South Korean prisoners of
conscience were "adopted" by Amnesty International, including high-profile
cases such as Kim Dae Jung and Kim Chiha (Amnesty International 1979).
Amnesty International and the AKC were also involved in some of the most
important court cases in the 1970s, including the PRP case and the many trials of students arrested during the Minch'ŏng incident. To investigate these related cases, Amnesty commissioned U.S. Attorney William Butler to visit South
Korea in July 1974. After completing his investigation, Butler concluded that the
prosecution lacked sufficient evidence for their claim that these were communist movements, and he argued that "even if such a threat did exist, the use of
torture by any government must be condemned as inhumane and barbarous
and not acceptable to any civilized nation" (Amnesty International 1975: 94).
Upon his return to the United States, Butler testified in front of Congressman
Fraser's subcommittee on the situation in South Korea (Kukche Aemnesŭt'i
Han'guk Chibu [Amnesty International South Korean Section] 2002: 32). On
the basis of his report, Amnesty cabled President Park demanding clemency for
prisoners associated with the PRP case and the Minch'ŏng incident. Although
their pleas fell on deaf ears, it was evident that the AKC, through its links with
Amnesty International, could garner powerful international support for victims of state repression.

An equally important visit was made by English lawyer Brian Wrobel and Danish surgeon Eric Karup Pederson in March and April 1975. During their visit, which was supported by the AKC and other progressive groups in the democracy movement, they were constantly harassed and discouraged by government officials, who refused to share information, rejected petitions to visit prisoners and facilities, and denied requests to meet members of the Ministry of Justice (Amnesty International 1977: 44–45). Wrobel and Pederson summarized what they had learned about the Korean human rights situation in their *Report of an Amnesty International Mission to the Republic of Korea: 27 March–9 April 1975* (Amnesty International 1977). The forty-five page report was subsequently used by the U.S. Senate Foreign Relations Subcommittee on Foreign Aid as a reference to ascertain how human rights would play a role in their policy suggestions (Amnesty International 1975: 95; United States House of Representatives, Committee on International Relations 1975: 49).

The AKC also ran its own programs in addition to hosting foreign delegations. One important project was the Prisoners of Conscience Fund, started in 1973 with seed money from Dr. Gerhard Breidenstein, which provided monetary resources to prisoners and to their family members (Han 2002: 143). Because of its activities, the Yusin government targeted the AKC, whose members often found themselves in prison alongside the very people they were trying to help. Although human rights violations continued throughout the 1970s, and although it was not especially effective in helping prisoners in the PRP and Minch'ŏng cases, the AKC played a pivotal role in publicizing the Korean situation to international groups during the most repressive years of the Yusin period.

NCCK Human Rights Mission

The most significant human rights organization in the 1970s was the NCCK Human Rights Mission. Following the arrest and trial of Pastor Pak Hyŏnggyu after his Easter Sunday protest in 1973, the NCCK formed an "executive committee" (*sirhaeng wiwŏnhoe*) consisting of advisors to Pastor Pak. It also hosted a conference titled "Faith and Human Rights" to discuss the escalation of state repression and the lack of an organized response by Christian churches (NCCK Archive Vol. 1: 295–300). As it became clearer that the Yusin Constitution was just the beginning of authoritarian consolidation, the NCCK's executive committee began preparations for establishing a formal human rights group. The Human Rights Mission was officially founded on April 11, 1974, just one week after ED 4 was declared and the Minch'ŏng incident began.

The NCCK Human Rights Mission was led by a governing body that included Christian clergy from six Protestant denominations as well as secular leaders from various professions, including law, media, and the academy (NCCK Archive Vol. 2: 470–471). Calling on churches "to assume the responsibility in the prevention and elimination of violation of human rights and to abide by Christian foundations in preserving dignity for humanity," the Human Rights Mission began to raise public awareness, provide legal advice and support for human rights victims, and hold Bible studies to rediscover Christian models for social engagement (NCCK Archive Vol. 2: 469). The Human Rights Mission's office was located at the famous Christian Building in the Jongno district of Seoul, which subsequently became the "Mecca of the Korean human rights movement" and a frequent site for state-Christian contention (Minjuhwa Undong Kinyŏm Saŏphoe 2009: 495).

In addition to engaging in research and counseling human rights victims, the Human Rights Mission provided a central network for diverse segments of the democracy movement. For example, it sponsored the Thursday Prayer Meeting, where dissidents received the latest news of political prisoners and planned further protest strategies (NCCK Archive Vol. 2: 822). A second related community that was supported by the Human Rights Mission was the Association of Family Members of Prisoners of Conscience. Similar to the Thursday Prayer Meeting, this association provided opportunities for family members of prisoners to share information and coordinate support for incarcerated dissidents, while also providing an audience to whom released prisoners could give their "testimonies" (Minjuhwa Undong Kinyŏm Saŏphoe 2009: 495). These organizations were important spaces from which to challenge the government, and it was at these meetings that Pastor George Ogle criticized the PRP case, which eventually led to his arrest and deportation (NCCK Archive Vol. 2: 516–529).

The Human Rights Mission was pivotal in some of the most important events in the Yusin period as well. The support that the Human Rights Mission gave to individuals involved in the PRP case, to students in the Minch'ŏng incident, to fired *Dong-A Ilbo* journalists, and to Y. H. Trading Company laborers (discussed in Chapter 7) solidified its place as a leading organization in the 1970s democracy movement. As an affiliate of NCCK, the Human Rights Mission enjoyed access to international organizations such as the Christian Conference of Asia (Baker 2007), and took strategic advantage of its global relationships by relying on foreign guests to smuggle censured information out of Korea in order to publicize the situation internationally. In these ways, the NCCK's Human Rights Mission helped to foster solidarity and popularize the human rights frame in the democracy movement.

REPRESSION AND THE EVOLUTION OF SOCIAL MOVEMENTS

The emergence of the human rights discourse and the mobilization of human rights organizations signaled an important transition in the democracy movement. The promulgation of the EDs limited the numbers of public protests against Park Chung Hee's government, but the movement evolved in tandem with the increasingly repressive state. In the ED era, dissidents altered their tactical strategies and raised issues that spoke directly to the harsh suppression of antigovernment protesters. These adaptive strategies were most notable in 1976, when the numbers of protests were at their lowest and, simultaneously, the proportions of nondisruptive tactics and human rights organizational involvement reached their highest peaks. Even though state repression was quite effective in subduing the total number of public protest events, dissidents found new ways to mobilize.

The evolution of the democracy movement in the ED era reflects the struggle by marginalized groups to "offset their powerlessness" (McAdam 1983: 735). Several studies have shown that increasing repression can trigger "tactical innovation" in social movements (McAdam 1983; Davenport 2005; Mottl 1980; Lichbach 1987; Moore 1998; Francisco 1995, 2005; Koopmans 1993; Johnston 2005). The assumption underlying this body of literature is that protesters are highly rational actors who "balance the costs and benefits of various tactics" (Lichbach 1987: 282). Hank Johnston (2005), for example, found that activists who mobilize against authoritarian regimes tend to use "speech acts" such as declarations, writings and literature, and other covert tactics rather than street rallies, demonstrations, and sit-ins. Similarly, Will H. Moore (1998) argues that dissidents are likely to change from violent to nonviolent tactics when the state responds quickly to disruptive protests.

Because disruptive protests invited greater repression (Chang and Vitale 2013), the shift to nondisruptive tactics helped to sustain Korea's democracy movement in the ED era. By pursuing new strategies and using less confrontational tactics, dissidents were better able to "elude repression while they continue to protest" (Francisco 2005: 72). Although speech acts, underground pamphlets, and other forms of nondisruptive protest can also be repressed by state authorities, they are less threatening than violent disruptive action. The ability of social movements to adapt has led some observers to suggest "that repression can be used to shape dissident behavior, but not to eliminate" it (Moore 1998: 870).

A less optimistic interpretation of movement adaptation might highlight the power of repressive states. As David S. Meyer and Suzanne Staggenborg note, "Of critical importance here is the recognition that movement development, tactics, and impact are profoundly affected by a shifting constellation of factors exogenous to the movement itself" (1996: 1633). Clearly, the repressive policies of the Yusin regime acted as the main exogenous factor influencing the transition to less disruptive protest tactics. It is possible that Park Chung Hee's government, having eliminated the student movement with ED 4, was relatively less concerned with the fewer number of protests in the ED era. That is, from the perspective of the Yusin regime, the EDs were quite successful at accomplishing that for which they were intended. This is not to downplay the significance of human rights organizations in the democracy movement, but rather to point out that, for Park Chung Hee, surely calling attention to human rights in small numbers of nondisruptive protests was a preferable situation relative to human rights mobilization *and* large disruptive student demonstrations.

Perhaps it is not necessary to pass judgment on whether shifts in tactical strategy reflect the acumen of Korean dissidents to adapt to heightened repression or the power of the Yusin regime to control dissent. Even if the EDs did reduce the number of disruptive protests in the 1970s, they triggered developments in Korea's social movement sector that would come to have long-lasting ramifications. Although the saliency of human rights was inevitably a time-dependent reaction to repression in the ED era, discursive and organizational remnants contributed to the democracy movement in the 1980s and are still relevant to contemporary civil society today (Shin and Chang 2011). As noted earlier, the ideal of human rights is invoked in a myriad of social movements in contemporary Korea. In tangible ways, social movements that use the rights frame today owe their discursive foundations to the legacy of the human rights movement in the 1970s.

Furthermore, the ability of the dissident community to continue to develop discursive and organizational resources at a time when public protests had declined speaks to the importance of reconsidering the relationship between repression and mobilization. If we move beyond simply counting the total number of protest events and instead look at how movement form changes following acts of repression, we are better able to discern the complex and often contradictory consequences of state action.[9] It is clear that the integration of human rights into the larger democracy movement occurred during the most repressive period in the Park Chung Hee era, which points to the qualitative progression of the movement, a possibility that cannot be captured by overall event counts. Repression was effective at stifling public protests, but the character of the movement evolved accordingly during the doldrums as dissidents raised the banner of human rights.

7 REPRESSION AND THE FORMATION OF ALLIANCES

We who are each involved in all levels of society . . . make this declaration in the name of all citizens.

Citizens' Conference for the Recovery of Democracy, 1974

At seven in the evening on April 8, 1970, twenty-five prominent individuals in the progressive community gathered in a conference room on the eighth floor of the YMCA building in downtown Seoul. The purpose of the gathering was to "pledge a response" (*kongmyŏng ŭl tajim*) to Park Chung Hee's successful attempt at pushing through the constitutional amendment that enabled him to run for a third presidential term in 1971. Troubled by this blatant disregard for the integrity of the democratic system, they read aloud the Declaration for the Protection of Democracy (Minju suho sŏnŏn) and formed a preparation committee to continue monitoring Park Chung Hee's political moves (KDF Events Dictionary: 81). The meeting's participants comprised an eclectic group who came from different sectors of Korean society, including educators, media personnel, lawyers, religious leaders, and literary figures. One year later, on April 19, 1971, this same group, in addition to others, formed the first coalitional organization in the 1970s dedicated to the "protection-of-democracy movement" (*minju suho undong*): the Citizens' Council for the Protection of Democracy (or Citizens' Council).

The Citizens' Council set an important precedent for the 1970s democracy movement by bringing together diverse individuals united in their opposition to the increasing authoritarianism of Park Chung Hee's government. Central leaders of the Citizens' Council included Pastor Kim Chaejun, the "father" of human rights law Yi Pyŏngnin, and Chŏn Kwanu, a director at *Dong-A Ilbo*. With the support of other prominent figures—such as novelist Lee Ho-Chul, Pastor Mun Ikhwan, Pastor Pak Hyŏnggyu, and poet Kim Chiha—the Citizen's Council fostered intergroup alliances between students and other dissident communities by providing a leadership structure for the larger democracy movement. Formal coalitions were still uncommon at the beginning of the Yusin period, when the majority of protest events were organized within social groups. With time, however, intergroup mobilization became a more frequent occurrence. These efforts to foster solidarity laid important foundations that paved the way for the rise of prominent national coalitional organizations in the 1980s.

In this chapter, I assess the impact of outgroup contention on ingroup solidarity in the 1970s democracy movement. I draw on archival sources and the Stanford KDP Events Dataset to show how the increasing severity of state repression galvanized the formation of alliances among dissident communities. The trend toward formal coalitions occurred in distinct stages. The visible repression of student street demonstrations alarmed the progressive community. Alarm gave way to shock as organizations such as the Association of Family Members of Prisoners of Conscience spread word of torture during interrogations, which in turn fueled a dramatic increase in the number of solidarity declarations during the most repressive years of the Yusin period. Eventually, declarations of solidarity motivated intergroup mobilization in which two or more groups organized a protest event together. This on-the-ground solidarity was then institutionalized in formal coalitions that reflected an increasingly cohesive antigovernment movement.

BUILDING SOLIDARITY

We saw in the previous chapter that the entry of multiple social groups into the democracy movement motivated the evolution of the tactical repertoire and the kinds of issues that activists pursued. In addition, movement diversification created the potential for alliances between different dissident communities. Similar to what Martin B. Shaffer found in the American environmentalist movement, the politicization of new social movement actors "provides an ideal setting for exploring the dynamics of coalition participation" (Shaffer 2000: 112). The importance of building coalitions has been noted by several scholars, who have shown that alliances between different groups working toward a common end can contribute to the vitality of a social movement by motivating protest events, increasing the pool of resources, and facilitating frame development (Rucht 2004; Shaffer 2000; Van Dyke 2003; Staggenborg 1986; Meyer and Corrigall-Brown 2005; McCammon and Campbell 2002; Bystydzienski and Schacht 2001). Indeed, some argue that the very success of mobilizing efforts is contingent upon the additional resources and leverage that coalitions bring to bear on a movement (Van Dyke 2003: 226; Meyer and Corrigall-Brown 2005: 337; Staggenborg 1986: 374; Shaffer 2000: 112; Rucht 2004: 197).

There are several mechanisms that facilitate coalition work between the different groups participating in a social movement. External forces can dictate the opportunities for coalition building depending on the larger political context. Political opportunities are, according to David S. Meyer and Catherine Corrigall-Brown, "critically important factors that affect the propensity of social movement organizations to cooperate in common cause" (2005: 327). Whereas earlier studies focused on expanding opportunities, recent work has identified repression as a significant external factor influencing movement development. On the basis of Jack A. Goldstone and Charles Tilly's (2001) reformulation of the political opportunity thesis, scholars have highlighted the potential of external threat to facilitate alliances (McCammon and Campbell 2002; Van Dyke 2003; Boudreau 2004; Almeida 2005; Alves 2001). Repression can motivate solidarity as movement actors adapt their tactical strategies to compensate for heightened threat.

The centralization of power in authoritarian governments, while contributing to a higher level of repressive capacity, offers diverse movement actors a unique motivation for cooperative work. As Sidney Tarrow points out, "In authoritarian settings . . . the centralization of power offers dissidents an odd sort of advantage—a unified field and a centralized target to attack" (1998: 82). Authoritarian states inadvertently motivate diverse challengers to work together because their policies affect all social sectors within their political jurisdiction, thus "unintentionally creat[ing] multiple oppositional groups by committing repressive acts against more than one sector" (Almeida 2005: 71). This cooperation can in turn develop into formal alliances against a "common enemy" (Van Dyke 2003: 228). In short, the very nature of dictatorship can engender solidarity among antigovernment forces, reflecting the dialectical relationship between repression and mobilization.

Participants in South Korea's democracy movement were well aware of the importance of creating alliances in their movement against Park Chung Hee's authoritarian government. Before the Yusin Constitution was enacted in 1972, the democracy movement was comprised primarily of students and a small group of social and political leaders. The entry of diverse socio-vocational groups into the movement, however, provided the opportunity for the various sectors of the progressive community in South Korean society to form intergroup alliances and develop coalitions. The advantages of developing a united front against the Yusin regime were readily apparent to dissidents, who recognized the strengths that could potentially be drawn from their cooperation, including greater legitimacy and a larger pool of material resources.

The relationship between students and journalists discussed in Chapter 5 is a case in point. In 1971, students staged many large demonstrations against the presidential election and the revision of the mandatory military training policy, but the efficacy of their movement depended in part on publicizing their grievances to Korean society at large. With the censoring of newspapers, however, students came to appreciate the critical role of journalists who were willing to defy the state and begin their own movement for a free press. Students extolled the bourgeoning mobilization of journalists and incorporated media freedom into their own protest events as well. The synergy created between students and Christian clergy was no different. Students valued the symbolic power that Christians carried in society, as well as their organizational resources and international networks. In appreciation of these advantages, students turned to Christian leaders to provide moral leadership and found sanctuary from state repression in their churches. For obvious reasons, then, dissidents attempted to facilitate solidarity within the democracy movement by participating in each other's protest events and forming organizations such as the Citizens' Council.

Alliances were formed within distinct social groups as well as between them. Intragroup alliances were both more practical and natural due to the frequency of contact between actors of similar backgrounds. As discussed in Chapter 3, it was especially important for students to create a national network to facilitate solidarity among the hundreds of student "circles" across the many universities nationwide. The formation of the National Alliance of Youth and Students for the Protection of Democracy (Students' Alliance) in 1971 and of the National Democratic Youth and Student Alliance in 1974 stand out as the most concerted attempts to unify the student movement, which explains the government's harsh repression of both mobilizing efforts.

But even within the ranks of student activists there were opportunities to create intragroup alliances based on unique interests. For example, 250 student journalists and editors of school newspapers came together on May 27, 1970. Led by Yonsei University's Kim Sŏnghwan and Sungkyunkwan University's Pak Ch'anwŏn, the students presented "progress reports" (kyŏnggwa pogo) that detailed the state of student newspapers and exhorted university administrators to allow for greater media freedom on university campuses (KDF Events Dictionary: 43). This was one of many instances of smaller divisional alliances within the student movement. Some alliances, such as the National Committee for the Human Rights of Farmers (founded May 1, 1978) and the Free Action Literary People Association (founded November 18, 1974), were formed on the basis of a combination of shared grievances and identities. While the former brought together farmers, the latter mobilized writers, poets, and other intellectuals (KDF Events Dictionary: 585). Other coalitional organizations were limited by geographical constraints—most notably the North American Coalition for Human Rights in Korea, headquartered in Washington D.C. (KDF Events Dictionary: 551). Organizations that fostered intragroup alliances helped to define the unique identities of particular social groups as well as clarify the issues and strategies pertinent to their positions in society.

Arguably more significant than the development of intragroup alliances was the growing solidarity among diverse sectors of the democracy movement. Intergroup alliances between distinct social groups contributed to a nascent united front against the Yusin regime that would come to represent a significant challenge to the legitimacy of Park Chung Hee's rule. It is important to understand the formation of alliances as a process. Solidarity is conceptualized in the literature on social movements in different ways, ranging from relatively "tight" formal coalitional organizations, such as the Citizens' Council, to event-specific alliances, such as when groups co-organize a demonstration (Rucht 2004: 203; Meyer and Corrigall-Brown 2005: 329). In either case, the preliminary step in alliance formation is the recognition and support of the mobilizing efforts of different social groups. Solidarity, according to Dieter Rucht, can develop in social movements "as long as these parts [different movement groups] deliberately seek to support each other" (2004: 202). This broad definition captures the early stages of alliance formation and is especially useful for identifying subtle forms of solidarity work in movements that emerge in highly repressive contexts.

Recognition of informal alliances in the 1970s is crucial because most formal coalitions did not emerge until after the promulgation of the EDs. Although a few coalitions, such as the Citizens' Council, were active in the early part of the decade, we would miss the initial foundation-building steps toward intergroup alliances if we focused only on formal organizations. The Stanford KDP Events Dataset allows us to analyze the preliminary stage of solidarity development between dissident communities because it includes a "link" variable that specifies the direct connections between protest events. On the basis of narrative accounts recorded in the KDF Events Dictionary, I coded for links if participants in an event *explicitly* identified and declared their support of a prior protest event. Most of these "solidarity statements" named the date and the specific actors or organizations (or both) involved in the prior event. "We support Seoul National University students who on June 16th staged an honorable demonstration against Park Chung Hee's dictatorship" is a representative example of a solidarity statement captured by the link variable.

Identifying links between protest events allows us to see how some protests inspired further mobilization. On August 23, 1971, for example, six hundred members of the SNU Faculty Association came together to criticize military presence on university campuses and to demand that the government stop interfering in academic affairs. As discussed, the state utilized preemptive strategies to stop students from engaging in antigovernment demonstrations by sending soldiers onto and around the campuses, cancelling classes or closing down colleges for a semester or an entire academic year, and suspending or firing professors who supported students. These actions enraged students and faculty alike, and the event on August 23rd sparked a smaller wave of protests around the issue of academic freedom. Two days later, on August 25, the Faculty Association at Chungnam University staged a similar protest and mentioned their support of the SNU faculty. Several other faculty associations on campuses across the nation modeled their protest events after SNU's, including the Pusan National University faculty on August 27, the Jeju National University faculty on September 4, and the National Regional Universities Faculty Association on September 13. The SNU faculty protest sparked intergroup solidarity as well. Inspired by the professors at South Korea's leading university, Pusan National University students made a declaration for academic freedom on August 25. In total, thirteen protest events specifically mentioned the August 23 SNU faculty event in statements of support and solidarity (KDF Events Dictionary: 137).

Of the 1,845 protest events recorded in the Stanford KDP Events Dataset, 327 involved statements of solidarity between different social groups. More interesting than the absolute number is the timing of the statements. Figure 7.1 reports the rate of intergroup solidarity statements as a percentage of the annual count of protest events in the 1970s. What is immediately apparent is that the rate of solidarity statements spiked in 1974, precisely when the state ratcheted up its repression of the student movement: half (50.18 percent) of the protest events in 1974 explicitly recognized the mobilizing efforts of another social group. Evidently, the driving force for intergroup solidarity was the consolidation of authoritarianism represented by increasing state repression. Although

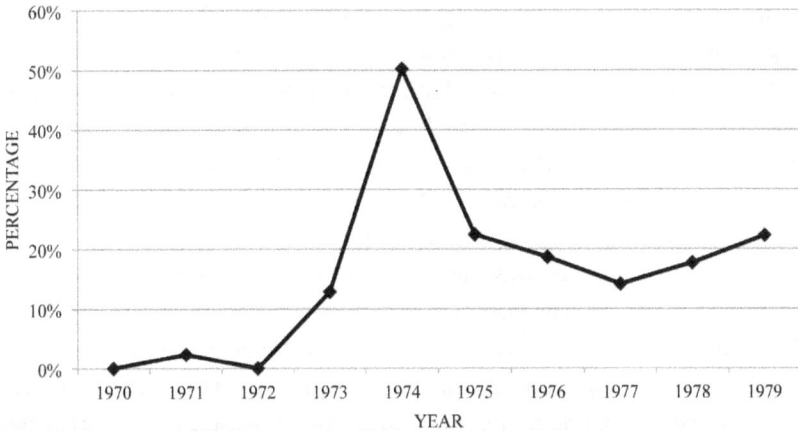

Figure 7.1. Percentage of intergroup solidarity statements in protest events
DATA SOURCE: Stanford KDP Events Dataset (1970–1979).

the state was successful in demobilizing students with the implementation of
ED 4, the number of solidarity statements rose rapidly during the Minch'ŏng
incident as new movement actors empathized with the repressed students. The
rate fell after 1974 but, overall, recognition and support between different dissident communities were more common during the ED era than prior to the
repressive laws.

FROM SOLIDARITY STATEMENTS TO FORMAL COALITIONS

The dramatic increase in solidarity statements in 1974 paved the way for the rise
of formal coalitions and intergroup mobilization. If the shock of the Minch'ŏng
incident motivated Christians and other groups to declare their support for students, this initial emotional reaction developed into a tactical strategy whereby
dissidents attempted to unify their movement under the umbrella of coalitional
organizations. An early model was the Citizens' Council, which was spearheaded by a group of progressive leaders in society who came together under
the general identity of *chaeya*, or the "dissident intelligentsia" (Park 2011: 373).
Although the majority of the *chaeya* were recognizable social leaders, they came
from different occupational, religious, and ideological backgrounds, and "there
was no one static *chaeya* to speak of during Park's rule" (Park 2011: 374). The motivation that brought *chaeya* leaders together was their resistance to "a common
enemy [that] provided them with a group identity despite their diverse ideological origins" (Park 2011: 375). Their high standing in society made them natural

leaders in the dissident community, and students and workers turned to them to provide leadership for the democracy movement. The *chaeya* led the earliest and the most important coalitional organizations in the 1970s. As discussed in Chapter 3, for example, in response to Park Chung Hee's bid for a third presidential term, *chaeya* leaders of the Citizens' Council supported the establishment of the Students' Alliance, the Christian Youth Council for the Protection of Democracy, and the Youth Council for the Protection of Democracy.

The Citizens' Council was the first major coalitional organization in the 1970s and became the template for more developed coalitions in the Yusin period, including the most important: the Citizens' Conference for the Recovery of Democracy (Minju Hoebok Kungmin Hoeŭi). As the democracy movement diversified in tandem with the government's increasing authoritarianism, these coalitions provided both leadership and resources for the various social groups participating in antigovernment protests. Organizational development was critical to movement solidarity, and the Citizens' Council that was active in 1971 evolved in 1974 into the Citizens' Conference for the Recovery of Democracy (or Citizens' Conference), which then became the central coalition in the ED era. The founding of the Citizens' Conference signaled a shift toward an increasingly "organized movement" (*chojikchŏk undong*) against Park Chung Hee's Yusin regime (KDF Organization Dictionary: 94).

Many of the *chaeya* leaders who founded the Citizens' Council also played instrumental roles in the Citizens' Conference, including Kim Chaejun, Yi Pyŏngnin, and Chŏn Kwanu. The change in the name of the organization, though subtle, was a significant one: the Citizens' Council was formed in the context of what was still a democratic system in order to "protect" (*suho*) democracy in the wake of the threat imposed by the possibility of Park Chung Hee's third presidential term, whereas the main objective of the Citizens' Conference was to "recover" (*hoebok*) democracy after the suspension of direct presidential elections and the transition to authoritarian government in 1972. As Lee Ho-Chul explains, "We changed the name from 'protecting' democracy to 'recovering' democracy because we already judged democracy to be lost" (interview with Lee Ho-Chul, December 16, 2004).

The *chaeya* leaders formed the Citizens' Conference at the height of state repression following the mass arrests of students during the Minch'ŏng incident, and when the state stepped up its effort to censor the media, culminating in the *Dong-A Ilbo* advertisement repression in December 1974. During the early part of the day on November 27, 1974, fifty *chaeya* leaders gathered on the second floor of the Christian Building in the Jongno district in Seoul. Present at this meeting were prominent senior advisors (*wŏllo*), including Quaker leader Ham Sok Hon, past president Yun Posŏn, and oppositional politician Kim Dae Jung[1] (NCCK Archive Vol. 1: 438, 440; KDF Events Dictionary: 306). Responding to the escalation of state repression, the participants articulated their resolve to fight for democracy in the form of a Citizens' Declaration (Kungmin sŏnŏn) signed by seventy-one *chaeya* leaders (including some signatures gathered before the meeting). The Citizens' Declaration provided justifications for antigovernment activities while explicitly declaring that theirs was a united movement that reflected the grievances and aspirations of the Korean people.

In addition to addressing a host of specific issues, such as the release of political prisoners and media censorship, the Citizens' Declaration made six major points:

1. Participants in the democracy movement are against communism.

2. The Yusin Constitution should be replaced with a democratic constitution.

3. The government is not the nation and an antigovernment stance does not mean we are anti-nation.

4. The state's economic policies have not secured basic living standards for the majority of workers and farmers.

5. Democracy will contribute to the possibility of unification with North Korea in the larger context of a polarizing world split between free democratic and communist nations.

6. The Citizens' Conference speaks for all citizens because its members come from all levels of society. (NCCK Archive Vol. 1: 438–440)

The Citizens' Declaration was, in short, a direct challenge to the state rhetoric legitimizing Park Chung Hee's rule. The *chaeya* not only clarified their stance on communism in response to the political framing of dissidents, but also expressed their awareness of Korea's precarious position in the larger context of the international Cold War: "We realize that our Korean democratic system has to take into consideration our historical realities but that means we need a democracy that fits our situation and we cannot use the north's [North Korea's] communism as an excuse to deny democracy" (NCCK Archive Vol. 1: 439).

Although participants in the Citizens' Declaration insisted that "we who are each involved in all levels of society [*kakkye kakch'ŭng*] share these beliefs and thoughts, and so we can make this declaration in the name of all citizens" (NCCK Archive Vol. 1: 439), it is fairly clear that the seventy-one signatories were not your usual "citizens." Indeed, as shown in Table 7.1, the Citizens' Declaration was signed by prominent leaders in South Korean society. Still, the Citizens' Conference was formally inaugurated on Christmas Day, 1974, at the YMCA building with the intent to provide a central organization through which the different elements of the democracy movement would be united. The Citizens' Conference was organized into "representative committees" (*taep'yo wiwŏn*) led by Yun Hyŏngjung and Yi Pyŏngnin and designated spokespersons (*taebyŏnin*), including Hong Sŏn'gu and Han Sŭnghŏn. In addition, the Citizens' Conference was counseled by an impressive advisory board (*komundan*) that included the likes of Kim Dae Jung, Yun Posŏn, Cardinal Kim Suhwan, Chŏng Kuyŏng, Hong Ikp'yo, Yu Chino, and Paek Nakchun (KDF Events Dictionary: 408). At the height of state repression, and in response to it, the Citizens' Conference emerged to provide senior leadership for the movement. Critically, the high social standing of its members further contributed to the legitimacy of the antigovernment movement, making it more difficult for the state to dismiss protestors as communist-influenced radical students.

Table 7.1. Signatories of the Citizens' Declaration

Occupation	Names of Individual Signatories
Senior political and social leaders (*wŏllo*)	Yun Posŏn, Paek Nakchun, Yi In, Kim Hongil, Yu Chino, Chŏng Irhyŏng, Chŏng Hwaam
Religious leaders	*Catholic:* Yun Hyŏngjung, Ham Seung, Sin Hyŏnbong, Kim T'aegam, An Ch'ungsŏk, Yang Hong, Yi Ch'angbok, Pak Sangnae
	Protestant: Kim Chaejun, Ham Sok Hon, Kang Sinmyŏng, Kang Wŏnyong, Kim Kwansŏk, Yun Pangung, Cho Hyangnok, Yi Sangnin, Pak Ch'anggyun, Kang Kichŏl, Kye Hunje, Sŏ Namdong, Mun Tonghwan, Ahn Byung-Mu
	Buddhist: Pŏpchŏng
Intellectuals/ literary figures	*Academics:* Yi Hwisŏng, Chŏng Sŏkhae, Chŏn Kyŏngyŏn, Yi Tonghwa, Pak Pongnang
	Writers: Yi Hŏn'gu, Kim Chŏnghan, Pak Yŏnhŭi, Kim Kyudong, Paik Nak-chung, Ko Un, Kim Yunsu, Kim Pyŏnggŏl, Hong Sajung
Journalists	Chŏn Kwanu, Yi Yŏnghŭi, Chang Yonghak, Kim Yonggu, Pu Wanhyŏk, Im Chaegyŏng
Lawyers	Yi Pyŏngnin, Hong Sŏn'gu, Hwang Inchŏl, Hang Sŭnghŏn, Im Kyŏnggyu
Politicians	Kim Young Sam, Yang Ildong, An P'ilsu, Ko Hŭngmun, Yun Chesul, Kim Chŏl, Chin Hŏnsik, Song Chinbaek, Hwang Hohyŏn
Others	Yi T'aeyŏng, Kong Tŏkkwi, Yi Ujŏng, Kim Chŏngnae, Kim Chaeho, An Chaehwan, Yu Sŏkhyŏn

DATA SOURCE: NCCK Archive, Volume 1: 440.

Facilitated by the status and networks of its leadership, the Citizens' Conference was able to establish nearly fifty branches across the nation in several cities and rural areas within three months of its founding (KDF Organization Dictionary: 92). Through its many regional branches, such as the Mokpo Citizens' Conference for the Recovery of Democracy[2] and the South Jeolla Province Citizens' Conference for the Recovery of Democracy,[3] the Citizens' Conference coordinated a nationwide movement against Park Chung Hee's Yusin regime (KDF Events Dictionary: 380–381). The Citizens' Conference also inspired organizations such as the Council of Prisoners for the Recovery of Democracy (Minju Hoebok Kusokcha Hyŏbŭihoe), which, under the leadership of Pastor Pak Hyŏnggyu, mobilized individuals arrested under EDs 1 and 4 upon their release from prison (KDF Organization Dictionary: 93).

The Citizens' Conference represented a significant threat to Park Chung Hee for two primary reasons. First, as discussed, the social status of the individuals who led this coalition made it difficult to frame it as a communist organization: leaders such as past president Yun Posŏn, Quaker Ham Sok Hon, and Cardinal Kim Suhwan brought considerable legitimacy to the Citizens' Conference and to the democracy movement at large. Second, the possibility of a nationwide coalition led by popular social leaders limited the state's ability to tailor repression tactics to isolated dissident communities, which explains in part the wide purview of ED 9, declared in May 1975. Because of their large numbers, students had been the only group to attempt a national coalition, but even they had limited their recruitment to other students. Notably, it was when students tried to develop a national network that the government's repression was most harsh. By working with students and other marginalized groups (such as laborers and farmers), the Citizens' Conference attempted to combine a large mass base with popular senior leadership. However, in the ED era, the connection between the Citizens' Conference and a mass base never materialized, mainly because the Yusin regime made a concerted effort to limit the diffusion of their movement.

Pursuing a preemptive strategy, the government identified and arrested individuals who were planning new branches of the Citizens' Conference. For example, on January 14, 1975, the police effectively stopped the founding of the Cheonan City branch when they took into custody Kim Sŭnggyŏng (a medical doctor) and Hwang Kyuyŏng (a minority-party politician), after they and several others met with the intent to form a local branch of the Citizens' Conference (KDF Events Dictionary: 381). The Yusin regime also targeted the leadership of the central Citizens' Conference in Seoul. On what many consider today to be trumped-up charges, a member of the Citizens' Conference's representative committee, lawyer Yi Pyŏngnin, was arrested for adultery on January 17, 1975, just a few weeks after the Citizens' Conference was founded (*Kyunghyang Shinmun*, January 21, 1975). Another lawyer, and designated spokesperson of the Citizens' Conference, Han Sŭnghŏn, was arrested on March 22, 1975, for violating the Anti-Communist Law. In addition to these arrests, university professors and other advisors to the Citizens' Conference were expelled from their academic posts (including Paek Nakchŏng and Kim Pyŏnggŏl) or given stern warnings by KCIA agents to stay out of politics (including Ahn Byung-Mu, Mun Tonghwan, Pak Pongnang, Sŏ Namdong, and Yi Ujŏng; KDF Organization Dictionary: 93).

The repression of the Citizens' Conference and its affiliated branches was intended to curb the growing solidarity in the democracy movement. The strategy backfired and instead fueled further coalitional activities. Coalitional organizations continued to spring up based on the original model set by the Citizens' Council in 1971. Memberships between old and new coalitions often overlapped because changing the names of the organizations was a common tactic to avert state repression. As described in the *KDF Dictionary of Organizations Related to the Democracy Movement*, new coalitions grew out of preceding organizations, which ensured some degree of continuity in the movement (KDF Organization Dictionary: 94). Figure 7.2 lists the most salient coalitions in the 1970s.

Growing solidarity and the emergence of coalitions had a tangible impact on street protests in the ED era. Although as early as 1971 students became interested in issues pertinent to other social groups (such as workers' rights after Chŏn T'aeil's self-immolation), their demonstrations almost exclusively involved students. Similarly, Christians were motivated to support other dissident communities, but clergy and lay leaders initially mobilized other progressive Christians through their church networks. The pattern of mobilizing one's own constituency began to change, however, as declarations of solidarity led to on-the-ground alliances. Figure 7.3 reports the annual percentage of joint protests organized by two or more distinct social groups.

Building on the spike in solidarity statements in 1974, the overall rate of intergroup mobilization accelerated after the promulgation of the EDs, with the exception of 1976.[4] In 1977, nearly one in every five protest events was co-organized by two or more groups. Attempts to create a unified front against Park Chung Hee's government were not new: the one million signatures petition campaign in 1973 and 1974 was essentially a strategy to show that the larger

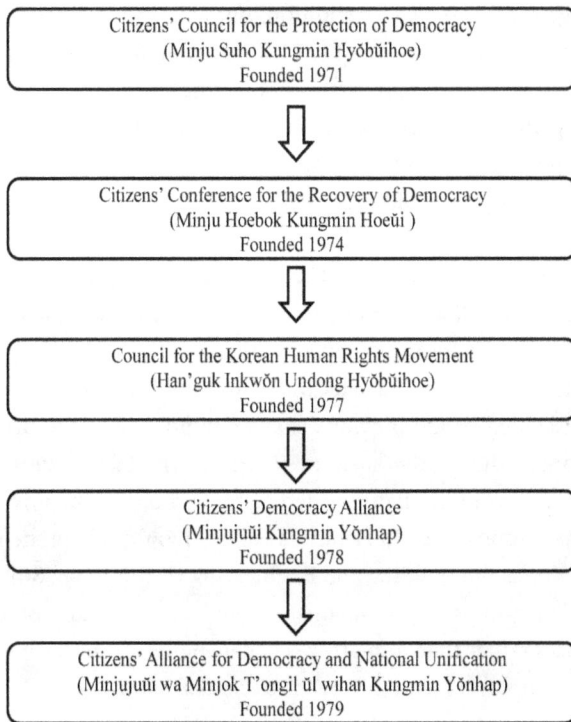

Figure 7.2. Salient coalitions during the Yusin period
SOURCE: KDF Organization Dictionary.

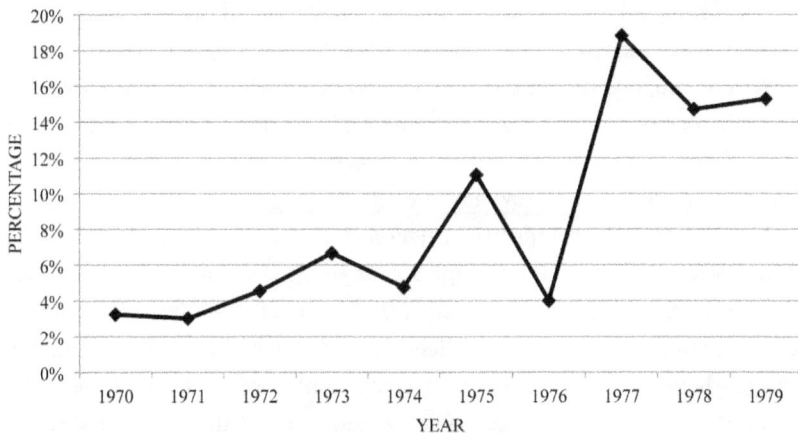

Figure 7.3. Percentage of intergroup protest events
DATA SOURCE: Stanford KDP Events Dataset (1970–1979).

public was against the Yusin Constitution. But with increasing repression embodied in the Minch'ŏng incident, the PRP case, and the mass firing of *Dong-A Ilbo* journalists, more dissident groups pooled their resources and staged protest events together. Repression continued to fuel solidarity in the ED era, and two labor disputes in particular provided the context for diverse sectors of the democracy movement to band together in common cause.

The Repression of Tongil Textile and Y. H. Company Women Workers

Notwithstanding the efforts by progressive Christians to raise the political consciousness of labor groups in the 1970s, workers for the most part limited their protest events to issues that related directly to their immediate work environments. As discussed in the previous chapter, almost all of the protest events staged by workers during the Yusin period dealt with labor issues. This is not to say that workers did not fight for democratic unions in the 1970s, and even before that, as demonstrated in Hwasook Nam's (2009) study of the 1960s labor union at the Korea Shipbuilding and Engineering Corporation. Still, relative to other protesting groups, they remained isolated, choosing to mobilize around local grievances rather than join others in challenging the authoritarian system that provided employers with the means to control labor.

There were, however, a few key labor disputes during the Yusin period that catapulted workers' issues to the forefront of the democracy movement. To be sure, these were sensational events that did not lead to the entry of workers en masse into the democracy movement "as a class" (Koo 2001). Instead, these disputes prompted other dissident groups to rally around the issue of labor repression. As discussed, throughout the 1970s the memory of Chŏn T'aeil was invoked in antigovernment protest events to make salient the connection between the democracy and labor movements. In addition to the "adoption" of Chŏn T'aeil's cause, two labor disputes involving women workers ignited the imagination of the democracy movement.[5]

Aided by the Urban Industrial Mission (UIM) and the Revered Cho Wha Soon, female employees at the Tongil Textile Company established a pro-labor union in 1972. Tongil Textile's management attempted to subvert their union activities, but the workers were resilient (Park 2005; Chun 2003; Koo 2001). The struggles between workers and management continued throughout the 1970s, including the time when female employees took their clothes off as a last resort to fend off the encroaching riot police, who did not hesitate to forcibly break up their meeting. This violation of propriety on July 25, 1976, shocked the workers and their immediate supporters, as well as the larger progressive community (Park 2005; Chun 2003).

The struggle at Tongil Textile also made headlines when on February 12, 1978, the candidate for union president preferred by the female employees was on the verge of winning a second term. Frustrated by their past success and fearing another year of dealing with a pro-labor union, the management of Tongil Textile hired street thugs to disrupt the election. Not only were the women violently accosted, but the hired strongmen threw human excrement on them to further render humiliation. After the altercation, 124 union members were fired on the spot, including the union leadership, for "causing damage to company property" (Ogle 1990: 86). Subsequently, workers associated with the Tongil Textile labor union were put on a blacklist and other companies refused to hire them or fired them upon learning of their past union participation (KDF Events Dictionary: 573).

Because of the violent nature of the repression surrounding its struggle, the Tongil Textile labor union became a rallying point for the larger democracy movement (Koo 2001). In the aftermath of the "human excrement incident," the fired workers joined members of the UIM, the NCCK's Human Rights Mission, the Ecumenical Youth Council, Dong-A T'uwi, and various Catholic organizations to begin a "fasting protest" at T'aptong Cathedral on March 12, 1978 (KDF Events Dictionary: 571). Participants in the protest criticized the company-endorsed election of Kim Yŏngt'ae as the Tongil Textile labor union president and the general mistreatment of workers.

In another solidarity event, on September 22, 1978, students, Christians, and former Tongil Textile workers came together to hold a prayer meeting to criticize the mass firing of the women workers. Roughly one hundred "plainclothes policemen" (*sabok kyŏngch'al*) were dispatched to disrupt the gathering, and after a violent exchange, thirty-one participants were taken into custody, with another twelve arrested later (KDF Events Dictionary: 573). News of the escalating violence spread far, even prompting clashes between the police and representatives of Amnesty International's Busan office and members of the Busan UIM who were trying to attend the court trials of the fired workers (October 19, 1978; KDF Events Dictionary: 573). And although all of the solidarity protests did not help the workers get their jobs or their union back, the Tongil Textile labor dispute led to the saliency of labor issues in the democracy movement and facilitated alliances between laborers, Christians, students, journalists, and human rights advocates.

The importance of the Tongil Textile incident for the development of the labor movement in the 1970s is rivaled only by the workers' struggle at the wig-manufacturing Y. H. Trading Company (Chun 2003). After depleting the company's capital reserves with irresponsible investments, the Y. H. Company's managers announced in March 1979 that the manufacturing firm would be closed down (Koo 2011: 89). Upon hearing the news, workers—again mostly women—began a series of protest events with the support of other labor groups, including the fired employees of Tongil Textile. The dispute came to a head when the women workers decided to politicize their struggle by holding a sit-in rally at the headquarters of the New Democratic Party (NDP; UCLA Archive: Box 09-1, Folder 09-1-06). On August 9, 1979, nearly 250 Y. H. Trading Company workers stormed into the NDP building and refused to leave until their demands were met. Their protest received the endorsement of the NDP when its leader, future president of South Korea Kim Young Sam, "declared his support for the striking workers" (Koo 2011: 90).

With the encouragement of company managers, the government sent one thousand policemen in full riot gear to break up the sit-in. During their raid on the complex on August 11, 1979, the police beat up the women workers and others who were there to support them, including NDP politicians and journalists. When the dust had settled, most of the women and twenty-five NDP politicians had been arrested, and one female worker, Kim Kyŏngsuk, was dead after falling from the fourth floor during the skirmish (UCLA Archive: Box 09-1, Folder 09-1-06; KDF Events Dictionary: 651).

Indignant because of the violence and the death of Kim Kyŏngsuk, several dissident groups joined the women workers in protest. Organizations such as the NCCK's Human Rights Mission, the Association of the Family Members of Prisoners of Conscience, Dong-A T'uwi journalists, and others staged protests and public forums decrying police brutality. Most important, the Y. H. Trading Company labor struggle directly linked institutional politicians to the labor movement and, in turn, to the larger democracy movement. Recognizing the potential threat of the alliance created between workers, *chaeya* leaders, Christian dissidents, journalists, and institutional politicians, Park Chung Hee ousted Kim Young Sam from the National Assembly.

The decision of the Y. H. Trading Company workers to hold their protest at the headquarters of the opposition party was a strategic one; they wanted to "escalate their economic struggle to a political struggle, and therefore . . . make a great impact on the entire society" (quoted in Koo 2001: 90). That labor problems were fundamentally related to the political situation was obvious to many in the democracy movement, because "it was the state that shaped the underdevelopment of free union activities in Korea" (Jeong 2007: 76). The government's control over the economy as a whole, and over union activities in particular, was evident in several policies, including the law that illegalized union strikes from 1972–1980, and the direct control of income inflation and wage setting (Kim and Bae 2004: 30; Jeong 2007: 69).

The suppression of labor motivated dissident communities to join the Tongil Textile and Y. H. Trading Company female employees in their fight for workers' rights. These alliances in turn "contributed to externalizing and politicizing labor struggles and to the fusion of labor struggles and pro-democracy political struggles" (Koo 2001: 91). The surprising success of the opposition NDP in the National Assembly elections in 1978 gave new confidence to politicians who were critical of the Yusin regime, and partly for this reason the Y. H. Trading Company workers sought their help (Kim B. K. 2011b: 142). The overall repressive conditions workers faced and the violent repression of female employees at Tongil Textile and Y. H. Trading Company catapulted labor issues to the forefront of the democracy movement in the ED era while fueling solidarity between diverse movement groups.

REPRESSION AND SOLIDARITY

The positive impact that repression had on alliance formation in Korea's democracy movement reflects the dialectical interplay between authoritarian regimes and social movements. In authoritarian polities, repression is a critical factor influencing the possibilities for collective action. Comparative studies of the consequences of repression for overall protest counts have yielded conflicting findings, suggesting the need to specify repression's impact on disaggregated components of a movement (Lichbach 1987; Hoover and Kowalewski 1992). Even when repression is successful at suppressing public acts of defiance, it can simultaneously facilitate the founding of social movement organizations (Loveman 1998), motivate new tactics (McAdam 1983; Lichbach 1987; Moore 1998; Titarenko et.al. 2001), and encourage frame development (Davenport and Eads 2001). Contributing to this growing body of literature on the unintended consequences of repression, this chapter has highlighted the influence of outgroup contention on ingroup solidarity in the case of South Korea's democracy movement.

If we limited our analysis to the number of protest events in the ED era (shown in Figure 2.2) we would only confirm the repressive efficacy of the Yusin regime and miss the dynamic ways that the democracy movement evolved in response to state repression. Although repression had a negative impact on the overall *quantity* of protest events, it facilitated the *quality* of movement solidarity. The process of alliance formation—from statements of support to formal coalitions and intergroup protest events—was fueled by the repression of students, journalists, and female workers. Along with universal issues, such as human rights and the torture of political prisoners, specific events such as the Minch'ong incident, the advertisement repression at *Dong-A Ilbo*, and the firing of Tongil Textile and Y. H. Company employees encouraged dissidents to "build cross-cutting coalitions" (Weiss 2006: 44).

The Korean case suggests important implications for the literature on protest cycles. Although Sidney Tarrow's (1998: 142) conceptual definition of protest cycles is not limited to a simple count of protests, high or low points in a cycle are often empirically operationalized by the frequency of protests occurring in a given period (Tarrow 1993; White 1993). Consequently, most scholars analyzing waves of contention have focused on movement development during high cycles by looking at the positive relationship between greater numbers of protest events and general diffusion processes (Tarrow 1993: 287; Tarrow 1998: 144–147; McAdam 1995: 235). In contrast, this chapter reveals that movements continue to evolve during the "doldrums," when the number of protest events is relatively small (Rupp and Taylor 1987; Armstrong 2002). This is another manifestation of the "repression paradox," namely that "repressive states depress collective action of a conventional and a confrontational sort, but leave themselves open to unobtrusive mobilization which can signal solidarity that becomes a resource when opportunities arise" (Tarrow 1998: 85).

Understanding how and why the democracy movement evolved during the highly repressive Yusin period also allows us to better appreciate the legacy of collective action in the 1970s for later social movements. The dialectical relationship between coercion and mobilization took on many forms. Key developments in the 1970s democracy movement included informal alliances between old and new movement actors, and the first formal coalitions in the authoritarian period, which became the foundations for critical relationships in the 1980s movement, including the student-worker alliance (Koo 2001; Lee 2007). Similar to how previous "failed" waves of dissent left an "organizational residue" that became resources for Poland's Solidarity Movement in the 1980s (Osa 2003), the alliances formed in 1970s Korea culminated in the national coalitions that led the movement in the summer of 1987 (Shin et al. 2011). Indeed, the strength and unity of Korea's democracy movement in the 1980s, reflected in broad-based coalitions such as the People's Movement Coalition for Democracy and Reunification (Minju T'ongil Minjung Undong Yŏnhap, abbreviated Mint'ongnyŏn) and the National Movement Headquarters for Securing a Democratic Constitution (Minju Hŏnpop Chaengch'wi Kungmin Undong Ponbu), were predicated on the "loose but powerful political alliance[s]" that were created in the 1970s (Choi 2011: 52).

CONCLUSION

The Legacy of the 1970s Democracy Movement

The past echoes in the epics of dissent; and from these epics new epochs emerge.

Nancy Abelmann, *Echoes of the Past, Epics of Dissent*

Civil society is an influential political force in contemporary South Korea (Shin and Chang 2011; Armstrong 2002; Kim 2000)—so influential that some have dubbed it the "fifth branch" of government in addition to the executive, legislative, and judicial branches, and following the media industry, the honorary "fourth branch." When asked about the historical origins of Korea's civil society, activists today are likely to fall back on a teleological narrative of "people's movements" that starts with the Tonghak Uprising of 1894, moves through the March 1, 1919, independence movement against Japanese colonialism, and includes in the postliberation period the April 1960 student revolution, the Gwangju Uprising in 1980, and the June protests in 1987. And although moral impetus and legitimacy are garnered from the historical continuity that this broad narrative engenders, it is important to appreciate both the qualitatively distinct contexts from which these movements arose and the specific mechanisms through which they are directly and indirectly connected.

The student revolution in April 1960 was the seminal moment of South Korea's democratization, yet it did not develop into a sustained movement for democracy. The reasons for this are straightforward. Notwithstanding the large protest cycle surrounding the reestablishment of diplomatic relations with Japan in 1964 and 1965, basic democratic structures were in place in the 1960s that deflected the need for a democracy movement. After two years of military rule following his 1961 coup, Park Chung Hee reinstated a civilian government, with presidential elections held in 1963 and 1967. Park's successful attempt to extend his rule in 1969 and the establishment of formal authoritarianism in 1972, however, transformed the foundations of the political process in South Korea, after which a *sustained* movement for democracy emerged.

The 1970s, as noted in the Introduction, are considered by many to be a "dark age" in South Korean political history, an era when authoritarianism and state repression reached new heights. A superficial analysis of macro indicators of movement vitality is consistent with this characterization of the Yusin period. As discussed in Chapter 2, the EDs had a profoundly negative impact on the number of public protests after 1975. Still, as I have argued throughout this book, dissidents were able to adapt to the repressive environment and further develop their movement in several ways. These developments would prove to have both immediate and far-reaching consequences for social movements in the 1980s and in contemporary civil society.

MOBILIZATION AND REPRESSION IN THE YUSIN PERIOD

The democracy movement that emerged in Korea in the 1970s went beyond criticizing government policies and instead challenged the very legitimacy of Park Chung Hee's rule. The nature of that challenge, however, evolved over the course of the Yusin period in response to the kinds of repression tactics the state used to quell antigovernment mobilization. The democracy movement was enriched by new social groups that joined students in protests. The central motivation for the diversification of movement actors was the expanding grievances associated with increasing state repression. As Quee-Young Kim puts it, "the greater the moral outrage toward violence by the state, the greater the participation by various sectors of society is likely to become" (1996: 1184).

The state responded to the nationwide mobilization of students against Park Chung Hee's successful run in the 1971 presidential election by systematically hunting down student leaders after declaring a garrison decree to preempt further demonstrations. The state fabricated conspiracy theories to frame student leaders and meted out long prison sentences after rounding up nearly two thousand student protesters. This heavy-handed repression led to the first fall of the student movement in 1971, and it wasn't until 1973 that students were able to remobilize. This time, however, they were protesting against the new authoritarian system that had been formalized with the passing of the Yusin Constitution in 1972. Wary of yet another large student protest cycle, Park Chung Hee resorted to special presidential Emergency Decrees that specifically targeted the student movement. The promulgation of EDs 4 and 7 justified the arrests of more than a thousand students in what became known as the Minch'ŏng incident. The students never fully recovered from this second fall and resorted to underground tactics and networks to sustain their movement after 1975.

The repression of the student movement had unintended consequences as many were alarmed at the harsh treatment of student protesters. In particular, prodded by students and their bereaved family members, a segment of the progressive wing of the Christian church mobilized to support the students, which in turn led to their own repression. Beginning with the arrest of Pastor Pak Hyŏnggyu in 1973, state repression motivated concerned Christian clergy and laity to join the democracy movement and directly engage in antigovernment protests. Christians, as it turned out, were better than other protesting groups at deflecting repression, because of the advantages they possessed, including moral status, organizational resources, and international networks. Partly because of these cultural and material resources, Christians and their organizations led the democracy movement in the ED era. Both clerical and lay leaders, such as Pastor Pak Hyŏnggyu, Pastor Mun Ikhwan, and Yi Ujŏng, along with theologians, such as Sŏ Namdong and Ahn Byung-Mu, worked through organizations such as the NCCK's Human Rights Mission to lead the antigovernment dissident community. With time, the justifications for their political participation were articulated in a Korean liberation theology.

Christian participation in antigovernment protests was part of a larger diversification process in the democracy movement. The student demonstrations in 1971 led indirectly to the politicization of journalists as they attempted to report on the domestic political situation. Fearful that media attention would fuel the diffusion of antigovernment sentiments, the state revised the Media Law to more effectively silence and discipline journalists who wrote sympathetic accounts of student protests. This galvanized the media freedom movement as journalists made a series of declarations for "freedom of the press." The state responded to this new challenge first by prohibiting businesses to advertise in the leading newspaper, *Dong-A Ilbo*, and then by pressuring the boards of newspapers to fire dissenting journalists. Once out of their jobs, journalists joined others in public protests and formed social movement organizations to publicize state censorship.

Similarly, lawyers were politicized through their experiences of defending students and individuals arrested under the various political control laws. The Yusin Constitution cemented Park Chung Hee's power over the judiciary by restructuring the process by which Supreme Court and lower court justices were appointed. The complete disregard for fair and transparent prosecution motivated lawyers and judges to challenge Park Chung Hee's dictatorial government, leading to the birth of the first generation of "human rights lawyers." As it did with Christians and journalists, state repression fueled the emergence of a small but visible group of lawyers who began to mobilize against the Yusin regime.

Because different protesting groups pursued particular mobilizing strategies and issues, the politicization of new actors transformed the overall character of the democracy movement in the ED era. This qualitative transformation was most evident between 1974 and 1975, when the demobilization of the student movement provided the opportunity and motivation for other social groups to lead public protests against Park's government. From 1975 to 1978, Christians organized more protest events than any other group, and this "changing of the guard" had direct consequences for the kinds of protest events that were staged. The movement after 1974 tended to be less disruptive because Christians, journalists, intellectuals, and politicians relied primarily on declarations, petitions, and prayer protest meetings instead of on the large, unruly demonstrations favored by students.

The expanding scope of the discursive challenge to Park's government was also a function of movement diversification as new dissident groups raised concerns relevant to their distinct positions in society. For example, as we saw in Chapters 5 and 6, journalists were primarily concerned with two issues: state repression and freedom of the press. While state repression was a concern for all groups, the issue of media freedom was particularly relevant to journalists. Another example is workers, whose concerns revolved almost exclusively around labor conditions. It is also not surprising that the state's intrusion into university affairs was a greater concern for students and intellectuals than for other groups, and that political governance was an issue raised mostly by oppositional politicians.

Another effect of diversification was the growing saliency of human rights. As a consequence of the severity of repression in the ED era, human rights became an important pillar of the discursive foundations of the democracy movement. Drawing on the global diffusion of human rights, and emboldened by the changing bilateral relationship between South Korea and the United States—after President Jimmy Carter made human rights an integral part of his foreign policy—Korean human rights organizations challenged the Yusin regime on the basis of "universally" accepted norms of governance.

Human rights provided a common motivation to create informal alliances and formal coalitions between diverse sectors of the democracy movement.

Repression played an integral part in fostering such alliances, as is evident in the spike in "solidarity statements" in 1974. These sentiments of support in turn paved the way for social groups to organize protest events together in the ED era. Also, coalitional organizations such as the Citizens' Conference for the Recovery of Democracy, the Council for the Korean Human Rights Movement, the Citizens' Democracy Alliance, and the Citizens' Alliance for Democracy and National Unification attempted to create a cohesive movement by providing centralized leadership. Admittedly, the ability of these coalitions to lead a large number of "citizens" was curbed by the repressive context; still, their efforts to establish branches across the country facilitated a unified front against the Yusin regime.

The empirical findings summarized here lend themselves to a reconsideration of current understandings of the relationship between repression and mobilization. The conflicting results in studies that look at repression's impact on the rate of protest events have been described as a "paradox" in the literature: some argue that repression reduces the number of protest events; others insist that it facilitates it (Olzak, Beasley, and Olivier 2003; White 1989; Khawaja 1993, 1994; Muller 1985; Weede 1987; Opp and Roehl 1990; Rasler 1996; Brockett 2005). To move beyond this impasse, scholars have suggested eschewing total event count as the single indicator of movement vitality (Hoover and Kowalewski 1992; McAdam 1996; Lichbach 1987; Davenport, Johnston, and Mueller 2005). In the Korean case, it is readily apparent that state repression had a negative impact on the number of protests. The annual count of protest events declined dramatically in 1972 when Park Chung Hee declared martial law before enacting the Yusin Constitution. And although the rate of protest events gradually increased, primarily driven by the reemergence of the student movement, the numbers fell again after the EDs and the Minch'ŏng incident.

Within that macro protest-repression dynamic, however, the democracy movement continued to evolve as repression facilitated the diversification of participating actors, which then led to developments in tactical repertoire, movement discourse, and solidarity formation. The Korean case encourages scholars to consider the possibility that movements can progress in a highly repressive context. Although innovation and expansion have been associated with high points in a protest cycle (Tarrow 1993, 1998), Korean dissidents were capable of advancing their movement further in important ways even as the number of protests dwindled. Indeed, as James C. Scott (1985) has shown, "weak" groups are quite creative in finding ways to resist oppression. Perhaps, then, repression does less to quell a movement than to motivate dissident groups to redirect their antigovernment activities along more inconspicuous paths (Tarrow 1998: 85).

The continuing development of the democracy movement during high periods of repression speaks to the "dialectical process of social change" (Koo 1993: 231). Several scholars have argued that we need better ways of analyzing the "reactionary element" in contentious politics (Mottl 1980; Meyer and Staggenborg 1996; Hoover and Kowalewski 1992; Davenport 2005). According to Tahi L. Mottl, "the analysis of reaction as an inevitable part of social conflict and change has not received sufficient analytical treatment in the social movements literature" (1980: 620). David S. Meyer and Suzanne Staggenborg also point out that "analysts have been slow to move beyond single-movement case studies to examine movement-countermovement interactions" (1996: 1630). Whether activists face countermovement mobilization by the state or by third parties, our ability to analyze the dynamic trajectory of a social movement is limited if we focus only on the movement itself. Contributing to this research program, this book has shown that the consolidation of Park Chung Hee's authoritarian regime was in part a reaction to the democracy movement that challenged his rule. Likewise, the countermobilization by the state, in the form of new repressive laws aimed specifically at protesters, became a catalyst for the movement's evolution. As Hagen Koo reminds us:

> Although the state has played a critical role in setting the dominant direction and framework of social transformation in Korea, concrete processes of social and political change have not been determined simply by the state's directives but have been intimately shaped by the specific ways in which individuals, groups, or social classes have reacted to state actions and to their experiences of social change . . . neither a state–centered nor a society–centered perspective is appropriate for comprehending the unique features of social change in contemporary Korea . . . we must go beyond the unnecessary dichotomy of these two approaches and direct attention to complex and dynamic relationships between the state and society and dialectic processes through which their relationships change. (1993: 231)

Recent assessments of Park Chung Hee have taken Hagen Koo's exhortation to heart by moving beyond a state-centered analysis of South Korea's modernization. In his introduction to a monumental study of the "Park Chung Hee era," Byung-Kook Kim highlights the multiple actors that made up the Korean state and society in the 1960s and 1970s, insisting on the need to "look at these actors as existing in a relationship of co-evolution, continually reshaping each other's political roles, identities, and strategies through their actions and counteractions" (2011a: 5). Although the 1970s democracy movement was in no way limited to elite intellectual leaders, Myung-Lim Park's comments about the *chaeya* can also be attributed to the movement as a whole: "What gave birth to it and accelerated its growth into a major force by the late 1970s was ironically Park himself. Every impetus for the *chaeya*'s growth came from Park's political choices: the signing of the normalization treaty with Japan in 1964,[1] the constitutional revision to introduce a third presidential term in 1969, the promulgation of the *yushin* constitution in 1972, and the declaration of nine EDs between 1973 and 1975" (2011: 398). Indeed, the diversification of movement actors, and their ability to adapt to an authoritarian state that became increasingly repressive in response to its critics, points to the "coevolutionary relationship" between state and society in the Yusin period (Oliver and Myers 2003: 15).

THE UNMAKING OF THE AUTHORITARIAN STATE

Despite their efforts, dissidents were not, in the end, the agents directly responsible for the fall of Park Chung Hee's regime. The catalyst instead came from within his government. On October 26, 1979, the director of the KCIA, Kim Chaegyu, shot and killed President Park and Ch'a Chich'ŏl, head of the Presidential Security Service, during an intimate dinner held at a KCIA safe house. The discrepant accounts of why Kim Chaegyu assassinated Park Chung Hee generally focus on Kim's personal rivalry with Ch'a Chich'ŏl and the immediate political situation surrounding that fateful dinner.[2] A long-term perspective, however, suggests that the assassination was the culmination of various interrelated structural strains that intensified throughout the Yusin period, including civil unrest fueled by the global economic recession in the late 1970s, growing divisions within Park's inner circle, and the ineffectiveness of government repression in quelling the democracy movement.

The success of Park's economic policies was reflected in double-digit GDP growth recorded in 1973 (12 percent), 1976 (10.6 percent), and 1977 (10 percent; Bank of Korea, quoted in Adesnik and Kim 2008). Economic growth was curtailed, however, in 1979 by a recession sparked by the second global oil crisis of the 1970s. In 1979, fear of a global fuel shortage was triggered by the political and religious revolution in Iran, which limited that country's oil production. Rising oil prices drove general inflation rates in South Korea to 18.3 percent, and the ensuing global recession slowed GDP growth to 6.8 percent in 1979 (Bank of Korea, quoted in Adesnik and Kim 2008). The economic downturn in 1979 motivated large protests by workers and social movement groups as "the bubble created by heavy and chemical industrialization (HCI) burst, intensifying the political opposition's challenge to Park's power" (Kim B. K. 2011b: 140).

Growing civil unrest was most evident in two related incidents in 1979. The Y. H. Company labor dispute discussed in the previous chapter had direct consequences for the political situation when Park Chung Hee ousted the leader of the opposition NDP, Kim Young Sam, from the National Assembly for supporting the women workers. The disciplining of Kim Young Sam drew both domestic and foreign criticism: all sixty-six members of the NDP resigned in protest and the United States recalled its ambassador to South Korea, William H. Gleysteen Jr. (Park 2011: 397). Originally from South Gyeongsang Province and the congressional representative of Busan, the region's largest and most important city, Kim Young Sam's expulsion from government sparked public outrage in his hometown and in the neighboring city of Masan. In October 1979, angered by Kim's predicament and expressing their frustration over the deteriorating economic situation, thousands of workers, students, and citizens in Busan and Masan began protests that quickly escalated into violent riots.

Although martial law was declared in Busan on October 18 and a garrison decree was issued in Masan on October 20, the core leadership of Park Chung Hee's government did not agree on how to respond to the growing unrest (Kim J. H. 2011: 196). The argument between Kim Chaegyu and Ch'a Chich'ŏl that immediately preceded Park's assassination was about how to handle the riots in Busan and Masan, with Kim advocating for "compromise and reform" (Eckert et al. 1990: 371) and Ch'a apparently willing to kill "100,000 to 200,000" citizens with tanks.[3] The contrasting positions of Kim Chaegyu and Ch'a Chich'ŏl represented the different poles of what Byung-Kook Kim interprets as the "fatal split" between "soft-liners" and "hard-liners" in Park's government over how to deal with the civil unrest in Busan and Masan specifically, and the democracy movement generally (2011a: 7).

For the Yusin regime, the problem of the persistence of antigovernment movements was only exacerbated by the growing strength of oppositional politicians. During the general elections in December 1978, the NDP, for the first time, won more votes than Park Chung Hee's ruling DRP. The 1978 National Assembly elections emboldened the NDP and its leader, Kim Young Sam, leading to fears that dissident groups would align themselves with institutional politicians in a united movement against Park's government. It was, in short, the combination of persisting social movements and growing institutional political threat that led Park Chung Hee to expel Kim Young Sam from the National Assembly in the aftermath of the Y. H. Company labor dispute.

If, as Myung-Lim Park argues, "the promulgation of ED no. 9 took the level of repression to new heights and gave the South Koreans only two options: acquiesce in the *yushin* regime or engage in a total struggle for the restoration of democracy" (2011: 394), the fresh wave of large and unruly demonstrations in Busan and Masan equally bifurcated the repression strategies from which the government had to choose. The "soft-liner" Kim Chaegyu had apparently lost faith in the types of harsh repression on which the Yusin regime had relied in the past, while Ch'a Chich'ŏl was willing to take repression to new heights. Although this difference in strategies was the essence of the argument that precipitated the shooting of Park Chung Hee, it was a disagreement based on years of diverging attitudes within the core leadership of the Yusin government.

At times the Yusin regime came down hard on antigovernment protesters, most notably with the repression of students after ED 4. But even then, just months after its promulgation in April 1974, Park Chung Hee "lifted ED no. 4, realizing that the measure had unexpectedly strengthened the *chaeya*'s resolve to resist" (Park 2011: 392). Park quickly returned in May 1975 to a hard-line repression strategy with ED 9, which he applied to all antigovernment groups and movements. Park's renewed commitment to heavy repression coincided with a series of critical events that significantly influenced his style of rule, including, most notably, the assassination of his wife, Yuk Yŏngsu, on August 15, 1974, and the communist victory in Vietnam in April 1975. Whereas the latter event reinforced the national security anxieties that had pervaded the years of Park's rule, the former paved the way for the rise of Ch'a Chich'ŏl, who replaced Pak Chonggyu as chief of the Presidential Security Service in the aftermath of First Lady Yuk's death.

Park's increasing reliance on the hard-liner Ch'a Chich'ŏl, especially after "Park's loss of confidence in the KCIA" due to Koreagate scandal in 1976 (Kim J. H. 2011: 195), compromised the quality and diversity of the advice that Park received from his inner circle. Carter Eckert notes that "by the late 1970s Park had become somewhat isolated, even from his own supporters" (in Eckert et al. 1990: 370). Park's dependence on Ch'a Chich'ŏl and his isolation from other key government figures limited his ability to deal with antigovernment movements. As Byung-Kook Kim puts it, "The way Park employed the strategy of repression became more clumsy as time progressed" (2011b: 166). In the late 1970s, Park's "clumsiness" was manifest in the growing power of the opposition NDP, the persistence of civil unrest, and the factional split in Park's inner circle. These forces came to a head on October 26, 1979, when Kim Chaegyu, with a single bullet to Park Chung Hee's chest, ended his eighteen-year reign.[4]

THE LEGACY OF THE 1970S DEMOCRACY MOVEMENT

Park Chung Hee's death brought new hope for democracy in Korea. That hope grew when Prime Minister Ch'oe Kyuha, after assuming the position of acting president on December 6, 1979, rescinded ED 9 and promised constitutional reforms and fair general and presidential elections (Eckert et al. 1990: 372). It was to be an ephemeral hope, however, as military forces reenacted the power play of Park Chung Hee's 1961 coup d'état. Major General Chun Doo Hwan, with the assistance of Major Generals Roh Tae Woo and Chŏng Hoyong, used his position as head of the investigation into Park Chung Hee's assassination and head of the Army Security Command to assume control over the military before violently suppressing student demonstrations in Seoul and Gwangju. By February 1981, after much bloodshed, Chun Doo Hwan had secured his place as South Korea's new despot.

Democracy advocates would have to wait another seven years before achieving the goals of direct presidential elections, civil liberties, and democratic governance. South Korea experienced a democratic opening, the "Seoul Spring," in the short period between Park Chung Hee's death and Chun Doo Hwan's seizure of power; but spring gave way to a harsh political winter that did not begin to thaw until 1984, when Chun relaxed laws on public gatherings and political campaigning (Shin et al. 2011: 36). The political environment between 1980 and 1984, set off by the Gwangju Uprising in May 1980, when Chun ordered the South Korean military into the city of Gwangju to put down demonstrations, was as repressive as anything South Koreans had experienced during the Yusin period. Hundreds were killed in that confrontation, forcing antigovernment protesters to go underground.[5]

The severe repression of the Gwangju Uprising was a wake-up call for the dissident community and led to important changes in the social movement sector in the 1980s. Namhee Lee (2007) argues that students and intellectuals were radicalized after the shock of Gwangju and turned to leftist theories, including

Marxism, Leninism, and Kim Il Sung's *chuch'e* ideology. In his study of South Korea's labor movement, Hagen Koo has shown that in the 1980s, workers developed the organizational capacity for militant mobilization, which set the stage for "the great labor offensive" in 1987 (2001: 153). Some argue that the radicalization of students and intellectuals and the increasing militancy of laborers negatively impacted the solidarity of the democracy movement. For example, students' increasing reliance on violent tactics and radical political ideologies made it difficult for Christians to join them in their fight against Chun Doo Hwan's regime. As a group, if not as individuals, Christians subsided from participating in protests in the 1980s (Shin et al 2011: 25).

Notwithstanding these significant developments, the anti-Yusin movement would have a lasting legacy for subsequent social movements. In both academic writing and popular understandings of South Korea's democracy movement, the focus has been on the Gwangju Uprising (Shin and Hwang 2003), the *minjung* (people's) movement (Lee 2007; Abelmann 1996; Wells 1995a), the participation of the middle class in the June 1987 protests (Chang and Shin 2011), and democratic consolidation after the reinstitution of direct presidential elections (Kim 2003; Diamond and Kim 2000). While recognizing the undeniable importance of the 1980s for Korea's democratization, we should also acknowledge the foundational "mobilizing structures" (McAdam 1996) that were created by dissidents in the 1970s. The democracy movement in the 1980s, and indeed civil society today, inherited significant material and cultural resources from the Yusin period, including leadership, tactical strategies, and movement ideology.

Leadership

One direct way that the 1970s democracy movement came to influence later social movements in South Korea was the provision of a generation of dissidents politicized while fighting the Yusin regime. This might possibly be the most significant legacy of the 1970s democracy movement, namely that a new generation of progressive leaders came of age in a period of heightened repression who then went on to direct the movement in the 1980s. These "modern *chaeya*" leaders (Park 2011) grew in popularity during the Yusin period, with some becoming even celebrity-like figures in the progressive community.

The poet Kim Chiha is an exemplary case. Although he was a known figure in the student movement in the 1960s, Kim Chiha was thrust into the spotlight in 1970 when the publication of his poem "Ojŏk" ("Five Bandits") in *Sasangge Monthly* prompted the state to close down the journal and arrest Kim Chiha and the journal's editor and publisher. Kim Chiha's popularity grew in the dissident community, especially among student activists, as he continued to publish satirical poems. His reputation as "a hero of Third World progressive intellectuals" (Sunoo 1976b: 18) was ultimately solidified after the public got ahold of his Declaration of Conscience,[6] which he wrote in jail following his re-arrest in 1974. His fame quickly grew beyond Korea—especially after winning the Afro-Asian Literary Lotus Award in 1975—and many renowned writers and intellectuals around the world, including "Jean-Paul Sartre, Simone de Beauvoir, Herbert Marcuse, Noam Chomsky, Edwin Reischauer, Jerome Cohen, Edo Shusaku, Oda Makodo, Tsurumi Shunsuke, as well as Willy Brandt of West Germany" (Sunoo 1976b: 18), petitioned Park Chung Hee for his release. Upon his release, Kim Chiha continued to pen popular dissident literature that ignited the imagination of the *minjung* movement in the 1980s.

State repression also popularized several other participants in the 1970s democracy movement. Kim Dae Jung was already a well-known politician in 1971, having almost defeated Park Chung Hee in that year's presidential election, but his reputation reached iconic proportions after the KCIA kidnapped him from his Tokyo hotel room in 1973. Protestant clergy and lay leaders—including Pastor Pak Hyŏnggyu, Pastor Mun Ikhwan, and Yi Ujŏng—were also catapulted to the forefront of the democracy movement after they were arrested for participating in sensational protest events, including the 1973 Easter Sunday protest and the March 1, 1976, Declaration for the Salvation of the Nation. Others became heroes in the dissident community because of their ability to resist repression. As the formal head of the Korean Catholic Church, Cardinal Kim Suhwan became a trusted leader of the democracy movement when he publicly criticized Park Chung Hee's dictatorship and opened the doors of Myeongdong Cathedral to student protesters on the run from the police and the KCIA.

These are just a few examples of the new leadership that emerged through the crucible of repression in the 1970s. The *chaeya* leaders represented diverse sectors of Korean society, including the academy, institutional politics, religious communities, the legal profession, and the media industry. Prominent individuals from these sectors facilitated the participation of their respective communities in the democracy movement. The emergence of the *chaeya*, who orchestrated some of the most important protest events in the 1970s, helped build solidarity for a movement that was diversifying. Later, the *chaeya* of the 1970s would lead the coalitions that pressured the transition to democracy in 1987. Indeed, when perusing the directory of leaders of the two most important social movement organizations in the 1980s—the People's Movement Coalition for Democracy and Reunification (PMCDR) and the National Movement Headquarters for Securing a Democratic Constitution (NMHSDC)—it is evident that almost all of the people who led the "coalitional surge" (Shin et al. 2011: 37) in the summer of 1987 had significant experiences of struggle and repression in the Yusin era (see Appendix C for a list of PMCDR and NMHSDC leaders and their experiences in the 1970s). Although Chun Doo Hwan dashed the hopes of these emerging leaders in 1980, "many of the same individuals would return to challenge the regime and force a transition to democracy" in 1987 (Adesnik and Kim 2008: 12).

Tactical Strategies

A second legacy of the anti-Yusin movement was the development of protest tactics and organizational strategies. Dissidents in the 1970s relied on what Sidney Tarrow calls "modular" tactics, such as demonstrations and declarations, which are "routines of confrontation" (1998: 37). Modular tactics were used in social movements prior to the 1970s and remained popular during the Yusin period. But with the diversification of movement actors came the possibility for tactical innovation. Christians, as discussed, popularized prayer protests as churches and religious meetings were transformed into spaces for political action. Although there were models for religion-based political mobilization before the 1970s—for instance, when Korean Christians and foreign missionaries resisted the Japanese colonial government's policy of Shinto Shrine worship in the 1930s (Kim 1997)—it was during the Yusin period that prayer meetings became part of the democracy movement's tactical repertoire. Various combinations of religious ritual and political protest are still common today.

If movement diversification made it possible for new relationships in the democracy movement, a critical precedent was set in the 1970s when various groups became interested in labor issues after the self-immolation protest of Chŏn T'aeil on November 13, 1970. In the Yusin period, secular and Christian students, along with organizations such as the Urban Industrial Mission and the Catholic JOC (Jeunesse Ouvrière Chrétienne, Young Christian Workers), began to experiment with the tactic of "going to the people," popularized by the Russian *khozhdenie v narod* movement.[7] In the Korean application, this meant that students and Christians "became workers" in order to pursue their "on-the-job-site" movement (*hyŏnjang undong*) or "factory volunteer activities" (*kongjang pongsa hwaltong*). A core group of dedicated students gained temporary employment in manufacturing factories during their summer vacations or as permanent employees after dropping out of school entirely, in order to mobilize workers from inside their respective companies.[8] Admittedly, there were not many of these students-turned-workers in the 1970s: Namhee Lee numbers them at less than one hundred (2007: 258). But this relatively novel mobilizing tactic[9] became a central strategy of the student movement in the 1980s that helped to define the critical relationship between students and workers in the *minjung* movement (Koo 2001; Lee 2007).

The push to foster movement solidarity continued to influence mobilizing strategies in the 1980s. Diversification made it possible and prudent to form alliances, as discussed in Chapter 7. It was not so much that the movement diversified but that diversity was coupled with the concerted effort to create alliances which helped the movement to survive in the ED era. Alliances between dissident communities were further institutionalized through formal coalitional organizations, such as the Citizens' Conference for the Recovery of Democracy and the Citizens' Alliance for Democracy and National Unification. The coalitional strategy pursued by *chaeya* leaders would have a lasting impact on the organizational capacity of civil society in the 1980s.

Scholars of Korea's democratization have pointed out that the formation of mass-based coalitions in the 1980s was one of the factors that pressured Chun Doo Hwan's government to reinstitute direct presidential elections in the summer of 1987 (Shin et al. 2011; Adesnik and Kim 2008). As discussed, the connections between organizations in the 1970s and those in the 1980s were often direct because many leaders of the 1970s movement continued in their leadership roles in the 1980s. Partly due to this direct connection, the strategies of the PMCDR—founded on March 29, 1985—overlapped with those used by coalitions in the 1970s such as the Citizens' Alliance for Democracy and National Unification, including the ideological position that the goals of democracy and unification between North and South Korea were intertwined.

The formation of coalitions was only one part of the expansion of the movement's organizational network in the 1970s. Although the emergence of new organizational types was often motivated by particular political situations that dissidents faced in the Yusin period, some have become standard form in the contemporary social movement sector. For example, the establishment of the Association of Family Members of Prisoners of Conscience paved the way for one of the most stalwart organizations in the 1980s democracy movement (and still active today): the Council of the Family Members' Movement for the Realization of Democracy (Minjuhwa Silch'ŏn Kajok Undong

Hyobŭihoe, abbreviated Min'gahyŏp).[10] Another leading organization in contemporary Korean civil society is Minbyŏn, the human rights lawyers' organization discussed in Chapter 5. Founded in 1988, Minbyŏn is the institutional culmination of the rise of human rights lawyering in the 1970s, which brought together lawyers active during the Yusin period with a new generation of lawyers in the 1980s democracy movement (Goedde 2011).

Movement Ideology

The development of the movement's discourse in the 1970s, in addition to providing tangible resources for subsequent activism, would fundamentally alter the cultural possibilities for political engagement. Many of the symbols and narratives that empowered the movement in the 1980s were first articulated in the 1970s. Dissidents developed their discursive critique of Park Chung Hee's government throughout the Yusin period as protests covered an increasingly wider range of social and political issues. Although social movements in the 1960s did raise paramount concerns, such as democracy, government corruption, and dependence on Japan, the explosion of new social issues in the 1970s reflected the tremendous changes brought on by Park Chung Hee's economic policies and political authoritarianism. Along with democracy, issues such as urban and rural poverty, workers' rights, freedom of education and religion, torture, and human rights became salient in both protests and the larger society. To be sure, new issues were raised in the 1980s as the political and social climate continued to shift, but as Myung-Lim Park argues, "With the exception of the issues of anti-Americanism, national unification, and socialism that dominated the *chaeya* movements of the 1980s, then, all major political, economic and social agendas of today's South Korea made their emergence during the early 1970s" (2011: 386–387).

With the benefit of hindsight, it is clear that the discourse of human rights is the most important issue to emerge from the 1970s. Human rights are invoked in a variety of contemporary social movements, including the gay and lesbian movement, the foreign migrant workers' movement, and the women's movement (Kim and Cho 2011; Piper 2004; Moon 2002; Jung 2013). Initially motivated by the repression that dissidents faced in the ED era, the issue of human rights is today a foundational discursive pillar of Korean civil society. By 2004 it was evident that human rights discourse had arrived in South Korea. In that year, South Korea hosted the 9th Annual Meeting of the Asia Pacific Forum of National Human Rights Institutions and the 7th International Conference for

National Human Rights Institutions. The latter event was attended by 150 global participants from seventy nations—the largest meeting to date—and was organized by the National Human Rights Commission of Korea with the support of the UN Office of the High Commissioner for Human Rights. The international meetings in 2004 solidified the National Human Rights Commission of Korea's position as a leading human rights institution just three short years after its founding and signaled to the world that South Korea was now a bastion for the protection of human rights (Cho 2002).

Other ideological concepts that first emerged in the 1970s became powerful master frames that shaped the 1980s democracy movement, even if they are less relevant today. Notwithstanding the differences that grew between students and other groups (primarily Christians) after the Gwangju Uprising in 1980, the democracy movement as a whole came together under the master *minjung* narrative (Lee 2007; Wells 1995a). The concept of the *minjung* was the cornerstone of the movement's ideology in the 1980s as activists struggled to realize a world in which the *minjung* were the subjects, and not objects, of history (CTC-CCA 1981).

In the 1970s, students were just beginning to incorporate the populist concept of the *minjung* into the larger movement discourse of nation (*minjok*) and democracy (*minju*). This "three *min* ideology" was articulated as early as April 3, 1974, on the eve of the Minch'ŏng incident, when student protesters at several different locations jointly declared the Declaration of People, Nation, and Democracy (Minjung-minjok-minju sŏnŏn). It is significant, however, that just a few years earlier, on September 9, 1971, the term *minjung* was absent from an important student declaration titled Raise High the Banner of the Nation, Democracy, and Reunification (Minjok-minju-t'ongil ŭi kitpal ŭl nop'i tŭlja; KDF Events Dictionary: 79). After the April 1974 "three *min*" declaration, *minjung* became an increasingly salient symbol in the democracy movement. Christians especially contributed to the development of the *minjung* concept as theologians debated the meaning of *minjung* and its application to Christian praxis in theological journals in the 1970s. The adoption of *minjung* as the defining feature of Korean liberation theology in the late 1970s subsequently helped spread the concept to diverse dissident communities (interview with Lee Ho-Chul, December 16, 2004).

The *minjung* frame found a wide variety of cultural expressions in the 1980s, igniting the imagination of an entire generation of progressive writers, artists, and musicians. Poets such as Pak Nohae published anthologies, such as his

Nodong ŭi saebyŏk (*Labor's Dawn*, 1984), that were circulated widely among students and labor groups. Writers such as Chŏng Hwajin, Kim Namil, Kim Insuk, and Sŏk Chŏngnam churned out novels with plots dramatizing the lives of the *minjung*. The premises, storylines, and characters that filled the pages of "*minjung* literature" (*minjung munhak*) were drawn from the real and imagined situation of the "oppressed" Korean people living under authoritarian rule. So much writing inspired by the *minjung* was produced in the 1980s that it became its own genre, and "minjung literature gained a unique place in the official literary sphere" (Choi 1995: 176).

Joining writers were artists, who conceived the idea of "*minjung* arts" (*minjung yesul*) as early as 1975.[11] However, it wasn't until the 1980s that the *minjung* art movement "blossomed" to become a ubiquitous part of public protests in the form of large banners and posters (Sung 2012: 192). In song also, the *minjung* were invoked. The songs that demonstrators sang at protest events were full of references to different *minjung* communities, including factory workers, farmers, political prisoners, and the urban poor. Songs such as "Nongmin'ga" (Farmer's Song) and "Kŭ nal i omyŏn" (When That Day Comes) inspired protesters with their themes of lament and hope. As the lyrics of the popular song "Sol a sol a p'urŭrŭn sol a" (O Pine! O Pine! O Green Pine!) demonstrate, it was this very combination of expressing heart-wrenching grievances and imagining a better world that was the essence of a "*minjung* song" (*minjung kayo*):

> In a fractured world where fierce winds blow,
> A mother's tears pierce my heart,
> For the freedom of a true world,
> Where the *minjung*'s spirit is master,
> I ply through the river waters,
> Though they are black with toil,
> O pine! O pine! O green pine!
> Don't waver in the east wind!
> Tied up behind prison bars,
> I live to meet you again.[12]

The *minjung* narrative would come to have wide cultural applications in literature, art, and song in the 1980s, but the three *min* ideology was a more focused political discourse that informed the movement's organizational strategies. The three *min* ideology, articulated in the student declaration of April 3, 1974, was merely an initial attempt to incorporate the populist *minjung* concept into the larger discourse on democracy and nation. As such, it was still underdeveloped. But after years of discussion and study, the three *min* ideology found clearer expression in several dissident communities. Students were the primary interlocutors of the three *min* debate and in March 1985 they formed the Committee for the Struggle for Three Min (Sammin T'ujaeng Wiwŏnhoe), under the auspices of the National Student Coalition (Chŏn'guk Haksaeng Ch'ongyŏnhap), in order to continue to mobilize on the basis of their commitment to the people, nation, and democracy.

The three *min* ideology also found expression in labor organizations when workers formed the National Workers' Committee for the Struggle to Secure a Three Min Constitution (Chŏn'guk Nodongja Sammin Hŏnpŏp Chaengch'wi T'ujaeng Wiwŏnhoe) in August 1985. Constitutional reforms based on the three *min* ideology became a matter for institutional politicians as well when Yu Sŏnghwan, a member of the newly organized progressive New Korea Democratic Party (Sinhan Minjudang), officially declared his commitment to the three *min* ideology at a plenary session of the National Assembly on November 14, 1986. Although assemblyman Yu was subsequently arrested for violating the National Security Law, his outspokenness was testament to the fact that the three *min* ideology had reached the very center of politics. As the importance of the three *min* ideology grew in the democracy movement, it became an effective frame, able to unite different dissident communities. If the solidarity of large-scale social movements is a function of a common ideology that can bring together disparate actors (Croteau and Hicks 2003), the three *min* ideology, based on the concept of the *minjung* first popularized in the 1970s, provided such a discursive common ground for the democracy movement in the 1980s.

·   ·   ·

It is not an exaggeration to say that Park Chung Hee's Yusin regime represented a highly, if not the most, authoritarian period in South Korean history. During this "dark period," however, dissidents fighting for democratization emerged and evolved. Both state and movement were locked in a mutually influencing relationship that defined the political landscape of 1970s Korea. Since democratic transition in 1987, there have been six presidents who were democratically elected in what most people would consider to be fair elections.[13] Among these presidents, there has been a balanced mix of conservative and progressive leadership. Furthermore, the transitions from conservative to progressive rule in 1997, and from progressive to conservative rule in 2007, were comparatively peaceful. These notable markers of South Korea's political stability are the fruits of seeds sown by advocates of Korean democracy as early as April 1960. A. David Adesnik and Sunhyuk Kim are of course right to point out that Korea "failed" to transition to democracy in 1979–1980 after Park Chung Hee's death (2008: 2). Although some might blame this failure on the 1970s dissidents, I have attempted in this book to show that the vitality and success of social movements are not always captured by the most obvious indicators. As Verta Taylor succinctly puts it, "movements do not die, but scale down and retrench to adapt to changes in the political climate" (1989: 772). In the face of tremendous repression, activists in the 1970s endured and adapted, ultimately contributing to the democracy that South Korea enjoys today.

REFERENCE MATTER

APPENDIX A
Data Sources

ARCHIVAL SOURCES

The Korea Democracy Foundation Sourcebooks

An important source of information about South Korea's democracy movement is the Korea Democracy Foundation (KDF; Minjuhwa Undong Kinyŏm Saŏphoe). The KDF was established in January 2002 by the South Korean government after the National Assembly passed the Korea Democracy Foundation Act the preceding year. The establishment of the KDF was motivated by the belief that the spirit of the democracy movement, and the historical lessons drawn from it, should be accessible to future progeny. The KDF's mission statement claims that "the Foundation's Archives will collect and preserve every form of historical data associated with Korea's democracy movement from the establishment of our government in 1948 to today. In addition, the Foundation wishes to be the source of information to the public for data and facts on the democracy movement" (http://www.kdemo.or.kr/en). As part of their effort to provide information to the public, the KDF, under the supervision of Oh Yusŏk and Yi Ch'angŏn, created two main sourcebooks on the democracy movement.

First, the *KDF Dictionary of Events Related to the Democracy Movement* (KDF Events Dictionary; *Minjuhwa undong kwallyŏn sakŏn sajŏn*) comprises nearly fifteen hundred pages of narrative accounts of events related to the democracy movement, covering the period from 1970 to 1992. This sourcebook provides detailed information on protest events, including date, types of participants, tactics used, and issues raised. In addition, the KDF Events Dictionary includes information on the state's response to protests, including the extent and severity of repression. Second, The *KDF Dictionary of Organizations Related to the Democracy Movement* (KDF Organization Dictionary; *Minjuhwa undong kwallyŏn tanch'e sajŏn*) is a detailed directory of social movement organizations that were active in the same period. It includes a host of information about social movement organizations, including date founded, main activities, organizational structure, and principal individuals involved.

To compile these sourcebooks the KDF drew from many sources, including newspapers, organizations' documents and publications, government records, personal memoirs, and secondary sources. To date, the KDF sourcebooks represent the most exhaustive effort to provide a comprehensive qualitative account of the democracy movement. Notwithstanding this monumental effort, it is important to note possible limitations in the KDF sourcebooks: events that were not recorded in any source (such as newspapers, memoirs, organizational histories, and so on) were not included simply because there was no information on them. Also, because the KDF sourcebooks used varied sources, the extent and reliability of the information is not consistent throughout the observation period. Rather than adjudicate the accuracy of the sources, the KDF in some cases provided discrepant accounts of a single event based on multiple references.

UCLA Archival Collection on Democracy and Unification in Korea

A second archive utilized in this book is the *University of California at Los Angeles Archival Collection on Democracy and Unification in Korea* (UCLA Archival Collection). This archive was compiled by the Korea Church Coalition for Peace, Justification, and Reunification (formally the North American Coalition for Human Rights in Korea), an important American organization that worked for Korean democracy in the 1970s and 1980s. The donation of this prodigious collection to UCLA was facilitated by Henry H. Em in the summer of 1995. The UCLA Archival Collection is currently housed in the UCLA Young Research Library's Department of Special Collections as part of UCLA's Richard C. Rudolph East Asian Library's Korea Collection. The archive contains ninety-five boxes of primary materials produced and collected by the North American Coalition for Human Rights in Korea from 1975 to the early 1990s. (Table of contents and archive finding aid are available at http://www.oac.cdlib.org/findaid/ark:/13030/kt9f59q833.)

The UCLA Archival Collection is a rich source for students of Korean democracy because it includes not only documents produced by the movement in Korea, but also materials related to the activities of organizations and groups outside of Korea who advocated for Korean democracy and human rights. The North American Coalition for Human Rights in Korea was formed in 1975 in the United States, and from its central location in Washington, D.C., it worked to support Korean democracy by lobbying the United States government, as well as by publicizing the repression of dissidents through the media. Included in this invaluable archive are various types of primary documents: printed materials produced by the North American Coalition, the National Council of Churches in Korea, and other social movement organizations; important statements by dissidents; and formal and informal documents produced by the U.S. Congress, U.S. State Department, and individual U.S. congressmen.

The National Council of Churches in Korea,
1970s Democracy Movement Collection

I also draw on the *1970s Democracy Movement* collection produced by the National Council of Churches in Korea (NCCK Archive; *1970-yŏndae minjuhwa undong*). This eight-volume collection was compiled by the NCCK Human Rights Mission and published in 1986. The NCCK Archive focuses on the contributions of Christian communities to the democracy movement in the 1970s while also including primary materials produced by secular groups. Christian participation is one of the significant subplots in the 1970s democracy movement, and Christian organizations such as the NCCK Human Rights Mission were critical in supporting dissident communities during the most repressive years of the Yusin period. The NCCK Archive includes publications by the NCCK Human Rights Mission, statements by prominent clergy and lay leaders, official histories of Christian social movement organizations, and descriptions of important protest events.

INTERVIEWS

In addition to the archival sources, I conducted in-depth interviews with twenty individuals who participated in the democracy movement in the 1970s in some significant way. Interviewees were identified on the basis of loose quota and snowball sampling methods in order to ensure some diversity in their backgrounds. Various groups are represented, including media personnel, lawyers, Christians, and intellectuals. The status of the interviewees also varies. Prominent individuals include Pastor Pak Hyŏnggyu, Professor Yi Ujŏng, lawyers Kang Sinok and Im Kwanggyu, photojournalist Yun Sŏkpong, and novelist Lee Ho-Chul. Others are from diverse communities, such as Christian seminary students, journalists working for Dong-A Media Corporation, a Korean professor at a Japanese university, and an American Catholic priest. Table A.1 provides descriptive information on the interviewees.

THE STANFORD KDP EVENTS DATASET (1970–1979)

The Stanford Korea Democracy Project (KDP) is a collaborative effort to understand the dynamic trajectory of South Korea's democracy movement from 1970 to 1992. Datasets consisting of attribute variables related to protest and repression events were created in order to summarize and analyze more efficiently the prodigious amounts of information in the KDF Events Dictionary described at the beginning of this appendix. With the financial support of the Walter H. Shorenstein Asia-Pacific Research Center, Stanford University, I created the first quantitative Stanford KDP Events Dataset, which includes records of nearly three thousand protest and repression events from 1970 to 1979. On the basis of a comprehensive codebook (see Appendix B) modeled after a coding manual for a different and independent dataset (Olzak and West 1995), I content-coded the KDF Events Dictionary to produce the Stanford KDP Events Dataset (1970–1979). The codebook was subsequently used by other members of the Stanford KDP to code protest and repression events from 1980 to 1992. The overall counts of events recorded in the Stanford KDP Events Dataset (1970–1979) are presented in Table A.2.

Table A.1. Description of interviewees

Name	Socio-Vocational Identity (Affiliations)	Date Of Interview
Christians		
Sinnott, James	American Catholic priest (Maryknoll Fathers and Brothers)	August 12, 2014
Kwŏn, Osŏng	Pastor (National Council of Churches in Korea)	December 24, 2005
Kim, Hong-Ki	Seminary professor (Methodist Theological University)	August 20, 2004
Yi, Kwangil	Pastor	August 30, 2000
Pak Kyŏngsŏ	Christian elder (Christian Academy)	August 25, 2000
Pak, Hyŏnggyu	Pastor (Chaeil Church, Christian Broadcasting System, Christian Academy, Seoul Metropolitan Community Organization)	August 23, 2000
Yi, Chŏlsun	Christian layperson	August 22, 2000
No, Ch'angsik	Christian student	August 22, 2000
Anonymous	Christian student	August 22, 2000
Yi, Ujŏng	Christian elder (Church Women United, Galilee Church)	August 17, 2000
Media		
Hong, Myŏngjin	Radio broadcaster (Dong-A Pangsongguk)	November 19, 2009
Han, Hyŏnsu	Radio broadcaster (Dong-A Pangsongguk)	November 19, 2009
Yun, Sŏkpong	Photographer (*Dong-A Ilbo*)	November 15, 2009
Chŏng, Tongik	Journalist (*Dong-A Ilbo*)	October 16, 2009
Sŏng, Yubo	Journalist (*Dong-A Ilbo*)	September 23, 2009
Legal Profession		
Im, Kwanggyu	Lawyer	March 12, 2010
Kang, Sinok	Lawyer	February 18, 2010
Kim, Hyŏngt'ae	Lawyer	December 8, 2009
Intellectuals		
Pae, Yŏnwŏn	Professor (University of Southern California)	June, 1 2006
Lee, Ho-Chul	Writer	December 16, 2004

Table A.2. Number of protest and repression events (1970–1979)

Event Type	Frequency	Percentage
Protest events	1,845	62.46
Repression events	1,043	35.31
Other	66	2.23
TOTAL	2,954	100

DATA SOURCE: Stanford KDP Events Dataset (1970–1979).

This dataset is unique for two reasons. Unlike most protest event datasets, it includes both protest and repression events, with a different set of variables associated with each event type. Thus the Stanford KDP Events Dataset (1970–1979) is a dyadic-structured database. A second unique feature of the dataset is that the substantive links between protest events, and between protest and repression events, are specified. That is, the dataset identifies which events were responses to prior events, consequently allowing for analysis of the interaction between protest and repression. Using the link variable, it is possible to map out the different clusters of connected events that make up the larger cycles of protest in the 1970s.

By creating and analyzing the Stanford KDP Events Dataset (1970–1979), I hope to satisfy critics of past studies of comparative social movements that utilized cross-sectional data or relied exclusively on newspaper accounts. Many scholars note the importance of longitudinal or cross-sectional time series data when analyzing movement evolution and change (Olzak 1989: 124; Oliver 1993: 283; Meyer and Staggenborg 1996: 1655; Hoover and Kowalewski 1992: 150, 156; Moore 2000: 116; Francisco 1995: 263, 280; Zwerman and Steinhoff 2005: 102). The Stanford KDP Events Dataset (1970–1979) was created with these concerns in mind and records start and end dates for all events. Also, the biases in newspaper accounts of protest events is well documented in the literature and this, as discussed in Chapter 5, is especially problematic for the case of South Korea in the 1970s (Barranco and Wisler 1999; Hocke 1998; McCarthy, McPhail, and Smith 1996; Smith et al. 2001; Oliver and Maney 2000; Woolley 2000). The Stanford KDP Events Dataset (1970–1979) addresses this concern by utilizing the KDF Events Dictionary, which includes pooled information from various sources. Univariate, bivariate, and temporal analyses of the Stanford KDP Events Dataset (1970–1979) are presented throughout the empirical chapters of the book.

APPENDIX B

Stanford Korea Democracy Project Events Dataset
Codebook

EDIT HISTORY

Name	Action	Date
Paul Y. Chang	Created	October 1, 2005
Paul Y. Chang	Revised through	June 1, 2006

EVENT ID AND DATE STAMP

Variable	Type	Code	Definition	Comments
ID	Continuous	1–99	Consecutive	Unique event ID
STYR	Continuous	1–99	Last two digits of year	Last two digits of year of incident
STDY	Continuous	1–3652	Number of days in the decade (1970–1979)	Number of day of event: 1 (Jan. 1, 1970) through 3652 (Dec. 31, 1979)
ENDYR	Continuous	1–99	Last two digits of year	Last two digits of year when incident ended
ENDDY	Continuous	1–3652	Number of day in the decade (1970–1979)	Number of day when event ended (see STDY)
TOTDAY	Continuous	1–9999	Number of days event lasted	ENDDY – STDY +1
AGENT	Categorical	0	Protest event	
		1	Repression event	

PROTEST EVENT CHARACTERISTICS

Variable	Type	Code	Definition	Comments
ISSUSPC1	Categorical	0	Not applicable	Specific issue raised in protest event
		1	Antigovernment sponsored elections	e.g. 1971 presidential and National Assembly elections
		2	Critique of PCH regime or antigovernment generally	e.g. critique of dictatorship (*tokchae*), governance, etc.
		3	Slum dwellings	e.g. removal or relocation issues
		4	Info collecting - fact finding	

Variable	Type	Code	Definition	Comments
		5	Anticensoring, freedom of press, or critique of media	
		6	Firing of teachers/professors	
		7	Antimilitary training in school	
		8	Labor conditions, rights, etc.	Also, related issues (e.g. unpaid wages, etc.)
		9	Japan policy	Critique of government's Japan policy
		10	Antirepression	Specifically mention past act of repression
		11	Educational freedom	e.g. closing down or surveillance of schools, revisions of school regulations, etc.
		12	Reinstatement of students	Reinstatement of expelled students
		13	Memorial event	Memorial event for fallen comrade
		14	Anticorruption	
		15	Civil rights and basic rights	e.g. right to life, living standard, etc.
		16	Return to democracy	
		17	Election corruption	e.g. election monitoring
		18	Reunification or NK issues	
		19	Yusin Constitution	Specifically mentioning revoking or revising Yusin Constitution
		20	Freedom of religion	Issues related to religion
		21	KCIA	Specifically mentioning KCIA
		22	Current situation	Civil unrest, state of emergency, etc.
		23	Political control laws	e.g. Anti-Communist Law, NSL, Emergency Decrees, Martial Law
		24	Critique of individuals	e.g. conservative Christians, individual politicians
		25	Regionalism	
		26	Foreign relations and issues	Critique of government foreign policy
		27	Anti-Vietnam War	
		28	Antitax laws	
		29	Control of merchant activity	e.g. local economic policies
		30	Antipoverty or increasing polarization of wealthy and poor	

Variable	Type	Code	Definition	Comments
		31	Movement organization	Issues internal to the movement
		32	Human rights	
		33	Housing issues	
		34	Prisoners of conscience	
		35	Sexual tourism	
		36	Solidarity with other activists	
		37	Refusing to conform to gov. mandate	e.g. military draft
		38	Save the nation, salvation	
		39	Justice and peace	
		40	National referendum	e.g. 1971 referendum for Yusin Constitution
		41	Torture	
		42	Government legitimacy discourse	e.g. criticizing "national security" or "economic development"
		43	Economic dependence on foreign nations	
		44	Privileged economic advantages to few	
		45	Farmers or rural issues	
		46	Rights of prisoners	Or general prison conditions
		47	"*minjung* liberation"	
		48	President Jimmy Carter visit	Criticizing U.S. President Carter's visit in 1979
		49	General economic failure	Failure of economic policies
		50	Separation of military from politics	
		99	Other	
ISSUSPC2–ISSUSPC8	See ISSUSPC1			
ISSUGEN1	Categorical	0	Not applicable	General issue that event is concerned about
		1	Political	
		2	Economic	
		3	Human rights	
		4	Internal to movement	
		5	Corruption	
		6	Media	
		7	Reunification or NK issues	
		8	Repression	

Variable	Type	Code	Definition	Comments
		9	Education	
		11	Local issue	
		12	Military	
		13	Civil rights/basic rights	
		14	Religion	
		15	Current situation	
		16	International relations	
		17	Regionalism	
		18	Urbanization	
		20	Nationalism	
		21	National security	
		22	Farming or rural issues	
		99	Other	
ISSUGEN2–ISSUGEN8	See ISSUGEN1			
EVTFORM1	Categorical	0	No particular event form	Tactic used in protest event
		1	Spontaneous disruption	Minimal amount of organization or planning
		2	Demonstration or rally	Public *temo*
		3	Meeting, internal discussion, determination (or meetings with target group)	Organized meeting not targeting the public (e.g. prayer meetings, organizational meetings, etc.)
		4	Picketing	
		5	Boycott	Specific action designed to prevent customers from obtaining services or products from some organization
		6	Vandalism	Defacing property
		7	Declaration	Rally where main protest tactic is the reading of a formal declaration
		8	Strike	Organized absence from work by employers of an organization
		9	Consciousness raising, debates, forums	Study groups or other consciousness raising activity (e.g. UIM labor laws class, Christian Academy night schools)
		10	Organization founding	Starting an SMO
		11	Sit-in, take over space (*nongsŏng*)	Sit-in protest
		12	Requests	Letters, signing petitions, or other forms of requests

Variable	Type	Code	Definition	Comments
		13	Self-inflicted harm, immolation, etc.	Protest by hurting oneself
		14	Silent rally	
		15	Memorial event	
		16	Symbolic protest/dramaturgy	Dramaturgical expression of protest (e.g. mock case, symbolic exorcism, play or reenactment, etc.)
		17	Propaganda	Spreading news, literature, placards, or other materials
		18	Parade or march	
		19	Fasting	
		20	Prayer or religious ceremony	e.g. protest prayer meeting targeting the public
		21	Protest via legal or formal channels	e.g. registering complaint legally or formally
		22	Violence	Attack on individuals or property, etc.
		23	Press conference	Meeting the press
		24	Monitoring elections	
		25	Resignation, quit work/job	
		26	Criticism or spoken protest	
		27	Investigation	
		28	Fundraising	
		29	Naked protest	Protest by taking clothes off
		30	Not trying hard at work	Slowing down the work process, dragging feet, etc.
		31	Take hostage	Kidnap or contain people against their wills
		99	Other	
EVTFORM2– EVTFORM4	See EVTFORM			In the case where protest event has more than one event form or tactic
GROUP1	Categorical	0	Not specified	Social group participating in the event
		1	Students or youths	
		2	Laborers	
		3	Christians	Protestant and Catholic
		4	Other religious	
		5	Intellectuals	Writers, professors, etc.
		6	Politicians	Also includes those who work with politicians, eg. Kim Dae Jung's secretary

Variable	Type	Code	Definition	Comments
		7	Farmers	
		8	Women	
		9	Economically poor	
		10	Journalists/media personnel	
		11	Christian students	
		12	General activists, civil groups	
		13	Professionals	e.g. lawyers, doctors, corporate, etc.
		14	Foreigners	Including Korean diaspora
		15	Citizens (general)	
		16	Judges, judicial workers	
		17	Educators, school officials	
		18	Merchants	Shopkeepers, entrepreneurs
		19	Family of political prisoners	
		20	Other religious students	
		21	Prisoners	
		22	Military personnel	
		23	Christian farmers	
		24	Christian prisoners	
		25	Student prisoners	
		99	Other	
GROUP2–GROUP7	See GROUP1			When there is more than one social group involved
GROUPNUM	Continuous	0–99	Total number of social groups involved	
NUMPART	Continuous	1–9999	Number of participants	Estimated number of participants in the event only for challenging group (e.g. excluding police or bystanders)
SIZE	Categorical	0	Not applicable	Estimated size of gathering
		1	Small (2–9)	
		2	Medium (10–49)	
		3	Large (50–499)	
		4	Very Large (500–999)	
		5	Massive (>1000)	
TARGET1	Categorical	0	No target specified	Main target of event
		1	Government (general)	Identify government (*chŏngbu*) without specifically mentioning PCH, ministries, etc.

Variable	Type	Code	Definition	Comments
		2	Park Chung Hee	Specifically aimed at Park Chung Hee
		3	Military	
		4	KCIA	
		5	Local general	Local external actors (e.g. university bureaucracy, local politicians, local police, urban poor, etc.)
		6	Employers	Or those who side with employers, such as company union
		7	Other challengers/movement activists, internally directed	Aimed at fellow challengers and activists
		8	Government specific	Specific branch of the government (e.g. particular politician or political party, or various Ministries, Department of Justice)
		9	Korean masses/general public	Aimed at the Korean people in general
		10	Judicial system	Members of the judicial system (e.g. judges, state prosecutors, etc.)
		11	Media	
		12	Church	
		13	Intellectuals	
		14	Foreigners	e.g. foreign embassies, U.S. Army soldiers
		15	Police, prosecutors, guards, prison system administrators	General law enforcement
		16	Legal system, judicial system	
		17	Independent parties or organizations	e.g. FKTU (independent labor organization, government sponsored but not necessarily controlled directly by government)
		99	Other	
TARGET2	See TARGET1			When multiple targets are identified in the event
ORGINV	Categorical	0	No organization involvement	Whether event was organized or sponsored by a formal organization
		1	Organization present	
ORGIND1	Categorical	0	No organization present	Type of social movement industry organization is from
		1	Student/youth groups and SMO	
		2	Church or denomination	

Variable	Type	Code	Definition	Comments
		3	Christian SMO	
		4	Labor union or groups	
		5	Women SMO	
		6	Political SMO	
		7	Formal political group/party	
		8	Farmers SMO	
		9	Civil rights SMO	
		10	Human rights SMO	
		11	Publishing company	
		12	Journalist SMO	
		13	Research or academic SMO	
		14	General religious SMO	
		15	Christian student SMO	
		16	Intellectual SMO	e.g. authors, writers, professors, etc.
		17	Land or housing SMO	e.g. related to urbanization
		18	International NGO	e.g. Amnesty International
		19	Family of prisoners or other support SMO	
		20	Student media organization	
		21	Student other religious organization	
		22	Newspaper or media group	
		23	Prisoners' association	
		24	Social or society committee	
		25	Professional SMO	e.g. lawyer groups
		26	Investigation committee	e.g. ad hoc groups
		27	Catholic or Protestant farmers SMO	
		28	Foreign government, embassy, state department, etc.	
		99	Other	
ORGTYPE1	Categorical	0	No organization present	Whether an organization participated in the event
		1	Semi-organization	e.g. student group, church, etc.
		2	Formal SMO or organization	
		3	Formal political party	
		4	Ad-hoc organization	e.g. founded only for specific issue such as voting, etc.
		99	Other	

Variable	Type	Code	Definition	Comments
ORGIND2–ORGIND5	See ORGIND1			
ORGTYPE2–ORGTYPE5	See ORGTYPE1			For additional organizations mentioned
ORGNUM	Continuous	0–99	Number of organizations present	
ORGNET	Categorical	0	Not applicable	Whether or not there are interorganizational linkages in the event
		1	Two or more organizations involved from same organizational industry	
		2	Two or more organizations involved from different organizational industries	
INT	Categorical	0	No international organization or group present	Whether or not there was support or participation by international organization or persons
		1	Support from international organization or persons	
PEOPLE	Continuous	0–999	Number of important persons mentioned in the event	
REPRESS	Categorical	0	No repression of event	Whether or not event was challenged by repressive forces
		1	Event repressed	

REPRESSION EVENT CHARACTERISTICS

Variable	Type	Code	Definition	Comments
IMMED	Categorical	0	Not applicable	Whether repression was immediate (happening at the same time as event), delayed, or independent
		1	Immediate repression	
		2	Deferred repression	
		3	Independent repression	e.g. not related to a specific event
GRPREP1	See GROUP1			The social group that was repressed
GRPREP 2–GRPREP 7	See GROUP1			In cases where multiple groups were repressed in a single event
REPTYPE1	Categorical	0	Not applicable	Type of repression
		1	Containment, barricade, garrison, disrupt, etc.	*taech'i*
		2	Enforce curfew	

Variable	Type	Code	Definition	Comments
		3	Violence	Physical violence against event participants (e.g. *ch'ungdol*, or *t'usŏk*, or bombings, etc.)
		4	Custody or arrest	Taken into custody, arrested, house arrest, etc.
		5	Surveillance, observation, spying	
		6	Censoring	
		7	Rummaging, stealing, investigating office, confiscating	
		8	Forced assimilation, brainwashing	e.g. forced into military or military training
		9	Suspended from school	
		10	Dissolving organization or party	e.g. closing down SMO
		11	Investigation or interrogation of individuals	
		12	Repressive laws	e.g. Emergency Decrees
		13	Denial of petition/request	e.g. not allowing use of school building for Chŏn T'aeil memorial event
		14	Closing down of school or stopping classes	
		15	Spoken critique or threat	including accusation or wanted signs, etc.
		16	Kidnapping	
		17	Propaganda	
		18	Death sentence	Persons given death sentence or ordered to be killed
		19	Killed	
		20	Not paying wages or limiting fundraising source	e.g. *Dong-A Ilbo* advertisement repression incident
		21	Deportation, denial of VISA	e.g. foreigners who have to leave country
		22	Creation of oppressive organization or government group	e.g. Hakto Hoguktan
		23	Legal channels or prosecution	e.g. suing
		24	Humiliation	
		25	Bribing	
		26	Harsher prison treatment	e.g. solitary confinement, moving prison cells, tying up prisoners, etc.
		27	Fired from job or forced resignation or not allowed to work	

Variable	Type	Code	Definition	Comments
		28	Harsher work conditions	e.g. relocation of job, given extra work, etc.
		29	Co-opted	e.g. when workers are forced to sign paper saying they will not participate in labor union
		30	Closing down of factory or company	e.g. when companies close down to quell labor protest
		99	Other	
REPTYPE2– REPTYPE5	See REPTYPE1			When multiple repression strategies were used
REPGRP1	Categorical	0	No repressive group present	Type of repressive group present at event
		1	Riot police	
		2	Normal police	
		3	Military	
		4	KCIA	
		5	Hired thugs	
		6	Legal or justice system	In case of court cases, the role of judges and prosecutors
		7	Government generally	In cases of political repression by other government parties, ministries, or persons
		8	Local authority	e.g. school bureaucrats
		9	Special police	e.g. *hyŏngsa* (detectives) trained in martial arts
		10	Protestant/Catholic students	
		11	Park Chung Hee	
		12	Specific individual	e.g. Kim Jong Pil, Minister of Education, etc.
		13	Employers	
		14	Foreigners	e.g. U.S. Embassy
		15	Security guards or prison guards	
		16	FKTU or other labor organizations	
		99	Other	
REPGRP2– REPGRP3	See REPGRP1			In cases where more than one repressive actor was involved
REPNUM	Continuous	1– 9999	Number from repressive group	Estimated number of repressive group members present at event (e.g. number of riot police)
REPSIZE	Categorical	0	No repressive group present	Estimates size of repressive group present at event
		1	Small (1–10)	

Variable	Type	Code	Definition	Comments
		2	Medium (11–50)	
		3	Medium-Large (51–100)	
		4	Large (>100)	
		5	Massive (>500)	
		99	Unable to estimate	
REPFORC	Categorical	0	No repressive group present	Level of repressive measure
		1	No force, or observe only	
		2	Little force used	e.g. barricade, most arrests, etc.
		3	Some force used	e.g. struggle with participants
		4	Force used	e.g. use of tear gas, fighting, etc.
		99	Other	
VIOLENCE	Categorical	0	No violence at all	Whether there was any violence in the event by challenger or challenged group
		1	Violence by challengers only	
		2	Violence by challenged groups	
		3	Violence by both	
		4	Limited violence	Only limited violence during event (e.g. slight scuffle between groups, stand-off lines, etc.)
PROP	Categorical	0	No damage to property	Assessment of physical damage to property or building
		1	Some level of damage	
INJURE	Categorical	0	No injuries mentioned	Injuries during event
		1	Injuries mentioned	
INJURNUM	Continuous	0–99	Number of injuries at event	Total number of injuries mentioned
KILL	Continuous	0–99	Number of people killed during event	
ARREST	Categorical	0	No arrest made	Or prosecuted
		1	Arrest made	
ARRSTNUM	Continuous	0–99	Number arrested at event	Or prosecuted
ARRSLAW1	Categorical	0	Not applicable	Law justifying arrest or prosecution
		1	National Security Law	
		2	Anti-Communist Law	
		3	Emergency Decrees	
		4	Antidemonstration law and anti-public gathering law	
		5	Antigovernment generally	
		6	Some other law	

Variable	Type	Code	Definition	Comments
		7	Garrison Decree or martial law	
		8	Overthrow of government	Accused of overthrowing government
		9	Media Law	
ARRSLAW2	See ARRSLAW1			
LEGALOUT1	Categorical	0	Not applicable	Legal outcome of case
		1	Conviction	
		2	Appeal	
		3	Reversal of conviction	
		4	Innocent/released	
		5	Death sentence	
LEGALOUT2	See LEGALOUT1			In case of multiple legal punishments
PRISON	Continuous	1–99	Number of years sentenced	Not necessarily number of years incarcerated
FIRE	Dummy	0	Not applicable or nobody fired from job	Whether anybody was fired or forced to resign from job/ occupation
FIRENUM	Continuous	0–99	Number of people fired or forced to resign from job	

LINKS AND REFERENCES

Variable	Type	Code	Definition	Comments
REACTION	Categorical	0	Not a reaction to previous event, novel event	
		1	Directly reacting to previous event	Participants at event specifically mention a past event
LINK1–LINK5	Continuous	1–999	ID of the previous event related to current event	ID number used to specify a different event in the dataset that proceeds and was mentioned specifically by current event
SEQ1–SEQ5	Continuous	1–999	Number of events in a linked series	Position in a sequence of linked events, starting from a seminal event.
KDFPAGE	Continuous	1–999	Page number in KDF sourcebook	Page corresponding to the description of event in the KDF sourcebook
NEWSTYP1	Categorical	0	No other reports	The print or other medium of other references in which event is documented (listed in KDF sourcebook)
		1	Book, research report, manuscript, etc.	
		2	*Dong-A Ilbo*	
		3	*Chosun Ilbo*	

Variable	Type	Code	Definition	Comments
		4	Website	
		5	Television	
		6	Other newspaper	e.g. Korean AP
		7	Journal or magazine	
		8	KDF research notes	
NEWSTYP2– NEWSTYP4	See NEWSTYP1			
NEWSNUM	Continuous	1– 999	Total number of references mentioned in KDF sourcebook	
COMMENTS	Script			Notes on events

APPENDIX C

Leadership Continuity in the Democracy Movement

I. PEOPLE'S MOVEMENT COALITION FOR DEMOCRACY AND REUNIFICATION (MINJU T'ONGIL MINJUNG UNDONG YŎNHAP), FOUNDED MARCH 29, 1985

NAME	VOCATION	POSITION IN PMCDR	1970s ACTIVITIES	DATE
Mun Ikhwan	Protestant pastor	Chairperson (*ŭijang*)	Drafted and arrested for March 1 Declaration for the Salvation of the Nation	3.29.1976
Kye Hunje	Social activist	Vice chairperson (*puŭijang*)	Participated in the National Restoration of Democracy Proclamation	11.27.1974
			Arrested for violating Emergency Decree 9	3.29.1976
Kim Sŭnghun	Catholic priest	Vice chairperson (*puŭijang*)	Indicted without detention for March 1 Declaration for the Salvation of the Nation	3.29.1976
Ham Sok Hon	Quaker leader and intellectual	Senior advisor (*komun*)	Indicted without detention for March 1 Declaration for the Salvation of the Nation	3.29.1976
			Indicted without detention for YWCA incident	12.27.1979
Kim Chaejun	Protestant pastor	Senior advisor (*komun*)	Chairperson of the Citizens' Council for the Protection of Democracy	4.19.1971
			First Chairperson of Amnesty Korean Committee	3.28.1972
Chi Haksun	Catholic bishop	Senior advisor (*komun*)	Arrested for violating Emergency Decrees	8.6.1974
Kang Hŭinam	Protestant pastor	Central committee chairperson (*chungang wiwŏnhoe ŭijang*)	Arrested for violating Emergency Decrees	11.5.1977
Ko Yŏnggŭn	Protestant pastor	Advisory committee member (*chido wiwŏn*)	Arrested for violating Emergency Decrees	3.12.1976
			Arrested for violating Emergency Decrees	11.27.1977
Yu Unp'il	Protestant pastor	Advisory committee member (*chido wiwŏn*)	Ordained minister at Wŏlgok Church (central location for Christian dissidents)	1979
Yi Sosŏn	Labor activist	Advisory committee member (*chido wiwŏn*)	Arrested for contempt of court	7.19.1977
Ham Seung	Catholic priest	Advisory committee member (*chido wiwŏn*)	Arrested for violating Emergency Decrees	12.25.1977

NAME	VOCATION	POSITION IN PMCDR	1970s ACTIVITIES	DATE
Mun Chŏnghyŏn	Catholic priest	Advisory committee member (*chido wiwŏn*)	Helped organize Catholic Priests' Association for Justice	9.26.1974
			Arrested for his speech "Our Thoughts on the State of the Nation"	7.26.1979
Yi Tonmyŏng	Lawyer	Advisory committee member (*chido wiwŏn*)	Defense attorney for Kim Chiha, accused of violating Anti-Communist Law	3.20.1975
			Defense attorney for participants in March 1 Declaration for the Salvation of the Nation	5.4.1976
			Defense attorney for Kim Chaegyu, head of KCIA, who assassinated Park Chung Hee	12.4.1979
Yu Kangha	Catholic priest	Advisory committee member (*chido wiwŏn*)	Collected "Donations for Freedom of Speech" for Andong *Dong-A Ilbo* branch	1.13.1975
			Sermon at the Korean Catholic Lay Association for Justice warning against printed materials that urged "everyone to submit to the authority of the state"	1975
Sin Hyŏnbong	Catholic priest	Advisory committee member (*chido wiwŏn*)	Helped organize Catholic Priests' Association for Justice	9.26.1974
			Participated in the National Restoration of Democracy Proclamation	11.27.1974
			Participated in March 1 Declaration for the Salvation of the Nation	3.1.1976
Song Kŏnho	Journalist	Advisory committee member (*chido wiwŏn*)	Representative at Inter-Korean Red Cross talks	8.29.1972
			Questioned by police about article concerning Seoul National University protests	10.231974
			Resigned as editor-in-chief after mass firing of reporters at *Dong-A Ilbo*	3.27.1975
Kim Pyŏnggŏl	Literary critic	Advisory committee member (*chido wiwŏn*)	Forced to resign as professor from Kyŏnggi Technical College for signing the National Restoration of Democracy Proclamation	12.1.1974
			Arrested for YWCA incident	12.27.1979
Yi Puyŏng	Journalist	People's chairperson (*minsaeng wiwŏnjang*)	Arrested for violating Emergency Decrees	6.17.1975
Kim Sŭnggyun	Journalist	Democracy–reunification chairperson (*minju t'ongil wiwŏnjang*)	Arrested for violating Anti-Communist Law	6.16.1970
Yi Ch'angbok	Social activist	Secretary general (*samu ch'ŏjang*)	Arrested for National Alliance of Young Democratic Students incident	5.27.1974
Ho Insu	Catholic priest	Supervisor (*kamsa*)	Ordained as Catholic priest and participated in various Catholic organizations	1976

NAME	VOCATION	POSITION IN PMCDR	1970s ACTIVITIES	DATE
Pak Chin'gwan	Buddhist monk	Supervisor (*kamsa*)	Ordained as Buddhist monk	1960
			Started literary career in the journals *Simunhak* and *Hyŏndae munhak*	1976
			Published poetry collection *Han charak namŭn maŭm*	1979
Chŏng Tongik	Journalist	Supervisor (*kamsa*)	Participated in the Declaration of Action for a Free Press	10.24.1974
			Founding member of Dong-A T'uwi	3.18.1975

II. NATIONAL COMMITTEE FOR A DEMOCRATIC CONSTITUTION (MINJU HONPOP CHAENGCH'WI KUNGMIN UNDONG PONBU), FOUNDED MAY 27, 1987

NAME	VOCATION	POSITION IN NCDC	1970s ACTIVITIES	DATE
Kim Suhwan	Catholic cardinal	Senior advisor (*komun*)	Appointed as South Korea's First cardinal	1969
			"Petition for the Restoration of Democracy" speech	12.13.1973
			Advocated for participants in the March 1 Declaration for the Salvation of the Nation (read at Myeongdong Cathedral)	3.15.1976
			Met with U.S. President Jimmy Carter to discuss Korea's human rights situation	7.1979
Kim Young Sam	Politician	Senior advisor (*komun*)	Participated in the National Restoration of Democracy Proclamation	11.27.1974
			Expelled from National Assembly for supporting Y. H. Company's women workers	1979
Kim Dae Jung	Politician	Senior advisor (*komun*)	Kidnapped by KCIA in Tokyo, Japan	8.8.1973
			Participated in the National Restoration of Democracy Proclamation	11.27.1974
			Arrested for March 1 Declaration for the Salvation of the Nation	3.29.1976
Ham Sok Hon	Quaker leader and intellectual	Senior advisor (*komun*)	Indicted without detention for March 1 Declaration for the Salvation of the Nation	3.29.1976
			Indicted without detention for YWCA incident	12.27.1979
Mun Ikhwan	Protestant pastor	Senior advisor (*komun*)	Arrested for March 1 Declaration for the Salvation of the Nation	3.29.1976
Pak Hyŏnggyu	Protestant pastor	Standing joint representative (*sangim kongdong taep'yo*)	Arrested for sedition and conspiracy after Easter Sunday protest	7.6.1973
			Arrested for collaborating with Minch'ŏng and violating Emergency Decree 4	8.10.1974
			Arrested for aiding Students-Religious Figures Demonstration	8.2.1975

NAME	VOCATION	POSITION IN NCDC	1970s ACTIVITIES	DATE
Kim Sŭnghun	Catholic priest	Standing joint representative (*sangim kongdong taep'yo*)	Indicted without detention for March 1 Declaration for the Salvation of the Nation	3.29.1976
Chisŏn	Buddhist monk	Standing joint representative (*sangim kongdong taep'yo*)	Completed training and received Buddhist name	1972
			Head monk at Pulgap Monastery at Yŏnggwang	1976
Kye Hunje	Social activist	Standing joint representative (*sangim kongdong taep'yo*)	Participated in the National Restoration of Democracy Proclamation	11.27.1974
			Arrested for violating Emergency Decree 9	3.29.1976
Yi Ujŏng	Protestant lay leader, professor	Standing joint representative (*sangim kongdong taep'yo*)	Participated in the National Restoration of Democracy Proclamation	11.27.1974
			Read the March 1 Declaration for the Salvation of the Nation	3.1.1976
			Arrested for participating in the March 1 Declaration for the Salvation of the Nation	3.29.1976
			Gave speech "For the Democratization of the Country" at Yun Posŏn's house	11.17.1979
Song Kŏnho	Journalist	Standing joint representative (*sangim kongdong taep'yo*)	Representative at Inter-Korean Red Cross talks	8.29.1972
			Questioned by police about article concerning Seoul National University protests	10.23.1974
			Resigned as editor-in-chief after mass firing of reporters at *Dong-A Ilbo*	3.27.1975
Pak Yonggil	Protestant lay leader	Standing joint representative (*sangim kongdong taep'yo*)	As Pastor Mun Ikhwan's wife, supported family members of those arrested in connection with the Minch'ŏng incident	1974-1975
			Supported participants in the March 1 Declaration for the Salvation of the Nation	1976
Ko Un	Poet	Standing joint representative (*sangim kongdong taep'yo*)	Participated in the National Restoration of Democracy Proclamation	11.27.1974
			Arrested for supporting Y. H. Company's women workers	9.10.1979
Yang Sunjik	Politician	Standing joint representative (*sangim kongdong taep'yo*)	Questioned but not detained in YWCA incident	12.27.1979
Kim Myŏngyun	Politician	Standing joint representative (*sangim kongdong taep'yo*)	Elected to 9th National Assembly (New Democratic Party)	1973
			Vice chairperson of the New Democratic Party	5.7.1973
Ch'oe Hyŏngu	Politician	Joint representative (*kongdong taep'yo*)	Elected to 9th National Assembly (New Democratic Party)	1973
			Elected to 10th National Assembly (New Democratic Party)	1978

NAME	VOCATION	POSITION IN NCDC	1970s ACTIVITIES	DATE
Pak Yŏngnok	Politician	Joint representative (*kongdong taep'yo*)	Elected to 9th National Assembly (New Democratic Party)	1973
			Elected to 10th National Assembly (New Democratic Party)	1978
Mun Tonghwan	Protestant pastor, professor	Joint representative (*kongdong taep'yo*)	Sermon "The Freedom to Proselytize" at the National Council of Churches	12.9.1974
			Forced to resign professorship at Korea Theological Seminary	6.11.1975
			Arrested for March 1 Declaration for the Salvation of the Nation	3.29.1976
			Arrested for supporting the Y. H. Company's women workers	9.10.1979
Yi Tonmyŏng	Lawyer	Joint representative (*kongdong taep'yo*)	Defense attorney for Kim Chiha, accused of violating Anti-Communist Law	3.20.1975
			Defense attorney for participants in March 1 Declaration for the Salvation of the Nation	5.4.1976
			Defense attorney for Kim Chaegyu, head of KCIA, who assassinated Park Chung Hee	12.4.1979
Chŏnghwa	Buddhist monk, poet	Joint representative (*kongdong taep'yo*)	Winner of the *Hankook Ilbo* Annual Spring Literary Contest with his poem "Ch'aesŏkchang p'unggyŏng"	1978
Lee Ho-Chul	Novelist	Joint representative (*kongdong taep'yo*)	Arrested for violating National Security Law (Literati Incident)	2.25.1974
Mun Pyŏngnan	Poet	Joint representative (*kongdong taep'yo*)	Poetry collection *Chuksun pat esŏ* banned for violating the Anti-Communist Law	1977
Cho Namgi	Protestant pastor	Joint representative (*kongdong taep'yo*)	Lectured on "Speech and Human Rights" at the National Council of Churches	12.10.1974
			Chairperson of the NCCK Human Rights Mission	4.8.1976
			Chairperson of the Council for the Korean Human Rights Movement	12.29.1977
Kim Kŭnt'ae	Protestant pastor	Joint representative (*kongdong taep'yo*)	Wanted for sedition and conspiracy	11.13.1971
			Wanted for violating Emergency Decree 9	1975

APPENDIX D

Timeline of Protest and Repression Events

DATE	PROTEST EVENTS	REPRESSION EVENTS	RELATED EVENTS
4.19.1960	April 19 student revolution against Synman Rhee		
5.16.1961		Park Chung Hee stages coup d'état	
6.19.1961		KCIA formed	
7.3.1961		Anti-Communist Law passed	
12.20.1961		*Minjok Ilbo* executive Cho Yongsu executed	
12.16.1963		Media Law passed	
March 1964	Student protests against normalization with Japan		
6.3.1964		Martial Law declared	
8.14.1964		First People's Revolutionary Party case begins	
8.26.1965		Garrison Decree declared	
1.21.1968			North Korean commandos attempt to assassinate Park Chung Hee
1.23.1968			North Korean Navy captures USS Pueblo
4.15.1969			North Korea shoots down U.S. reconnaissance plane
7.25.1969			Nixon Doctrine
9.14.1969			Amendment to the constitution allowing Park Chung Hee to run for a third term
12.11.1969			North Korea hijacks Korean Airline flight
4.8.1970	Declaration for the Protection of Democracy		
May 1970	Kim Chiha's poem "Ojŏk" published in *Sasangge Monthly*		
11.13.1970	Chŏn T'aeil self-immolates		

DATE	PROTEST EVENTS	REPRESSION EVENTS	RELATED EVENTS
1.27.1971		On-campus military training requirements revised	
4.15.1971	Coordinated nationwide student demonstrations		
4.15.1971	National Alliance of Youth and Students for the Protection of Democracy formed		
4.19.1971	Citizens' Council for the Protection of Democracy formed		
4.27.1971			Presidential election, Park Chung Hee wins third term
5.25.1971			National Assembly elections
6.25.1971		Election monitor Kim Ch'angsu dies from injuries related to torture	
7.9.1971			Henry Kissinger secretly visits China
8.10.1971	Protests in Gwangju, Gyeonggi Province, over removal of shantytowns		
8.18.1971		Mass student expulsions	
October 1971		Focused repression of student movement begins; 1,889 students arrested	
10.15.1971		Garrison Decree declared	
10.27.1971		SNU student Yi Sinbŏm interrogated and tortured	
12.6.1971		State of National Emergency declared	
12.27.1971		Act on Special Measures for National Security Censorship passed	
3.28.1972	Amnesty Korean Committee formed		
4.12.1972		Kim Chiha arrested for publishing "Groundless Rumors"	
5.1.1972		SNU students Cho Yŏngnac, Chang Kip'yo, and Sim Chaegwŏn convicted under NSL	
7.4.1972			NK-SK Joint Communiqué
8.3.1972			Emergency Decree for Economic Stability and Growth
10.17.1972		Martial Law declared; Special Declaration on the Reforms for National Resurrection	

DATE	PROTEST EVENTS	REPRESSION EVENTS	RELATED EVENTS
10.27.1972			Yusin Constitution announced
11.21.1972			National Referendum on the Yusin Constitution
12.24.1972	One-Million Signature petition drive against the Yusin Constitution		
4.22.1973	Pastor Pak Hyŏnggyu's Easter Sunday protest		
5.30.1973			Fifty Million to Christ campaign led by Billy Graham
7.6.1973		Pastor Pak Hyŏnggyu arrested	
10.2.1973	SNU Liberal Arts College student demonstration		
1.8.1974		Emergency Decrees 1 and 2	
3.27.1974	National Democratic Youth and Student Alliance formed		
4.3.1974	Declaration of People, Nation, and Democracy (three *min*) and coordinated nationwide student demonstrations	Emergency Decree 4 and start of the Minchŏng incident; 1,024 students taken into custody	
4.11.1974	NCCK's Human Rights Mission formed		
7.6.1974		Bishop Chi Haksun arrested for violating Emergency Decrees 1 and 4	
7.23.1974	Bishop Chi Haksun's Declaration of Conscience		
8.15.1974			First Lady Yuk Yŏngsu assassinated
10.24.1974	Declaration of Action for a Free Press by *Dong-A Ilbo* journalists		
11.22.1974			U.S. President Gerald Ford visits Korea
12.24.1974		*Dong-A Ilbo* advertisement repression	
12.30.1974	First advertisement to support *Dong-A Ilbo* journalists purchased		
3.8.1975		Mass firing of *Dong-A Ilbo* journalists	
3.22.1975		Lawyer Han Sŭnghŏn arrested for violating Anti-Communist Law	
3.30.1975			U.S. Congressman Donald Fraser visits Korea

DATE	PROTEST EVENTS	REPRESSION EVENTS	RELATED EVENTS
4.8.1975		Emergency Decree 7	
4.10.1975		Eight individuals related to the People's Revolutionary Party case are executed	
4.11.1975	SNU student Kim Sangjin commits suicide		
4.30.1975			Fall of Saigon
5.13.1975		Emergency Decree 9	
3.1.1976	Declaration for the Salvation of the Nation		
7.25.1976	Tongil Textile's women workers' struggle		
12.29.1977	Council for the Korean Human Rights Movement formed		
1.6.1978	Former president Yun Posŏn addresses 500 people regarding government's human rights violations		
12.12.1978			New Democratic Party wins majority in National Assembly elections
6.27.1979	Students set fire to portraits of U.S. President Jimmy Carter and Park Chung Hee in central Seoul		
6.29.1979			U.S. President Jimmy Carter visits Korea
8.9.1979	Y. H. Company's women workers' struggle		
10.18.1979	Busan protests begin	Martial law declared for Busan	
10.20.1979	Masan protests begin	Garrison Decree declared for Masan	
10.26.1979			Park Chung Hee assassinated by Kim Chaegyu
5.18.1980	Start of the Gwangju Uprising		
2.25.1981		Chun Doo Hwan assumes presidency	

NOTES

1. At the Cairo Conference (November 22–26, 1943) the United States, Great Britain, and China agreed that Korea, after thirty-six years of Japanese colonial rule, should be an independent nation "in due course," but date and timing were not specified. Similar statements by the superpowers were made in Teheran (November 28–December 1, 1943), Yalta (February 4–11, 1945), and Potsdam (July 17–August 2, 1945).

2. Common narratives of social movements in post-liberation Korea emphasize state repression and authoritarianism in the 1970s, and sometimes skip over this decade altogether. For example, Kenneth Wells argues that "from the Yŏsun rebellions in 1948 to the 1960 student uprising and 1980 Kwangju rebellion, South Korea's history has been marked by bloody clashes between military regimes and a disaffected populace" (1995b: 3).

3. The 1980 Gwangju Uprising consisted of protests that arose in the city of Gwangju, located in South Jeolla Province. Initiated by students at Chonnam National University against General Chun Doo Hwan, who assumed power after Park Chung Hee's death in 1979, the struggle quickly escalated to include Gwangju citizens who took up arms against the encroaching military. To this day it is uncertain how many citizens were killed by the military during the struggle.

4. Unless otherwise noted (as in North Korea), Korea refers to South Korea throughout the book.

5. Some studies look at social movements in the 1970s but do not provide a comprehensive analysis of the democracy movement in that decade. Instead, they focus on specific groups, including Christian activists (Sunoo 1976; Kang 1997); on the relationship between Christians and the labor movement (Ogle 1990); and on the contributions of foreign missionaries (Stentzel 2006), women workers (Park 2005), and Chŏn T'aeil, whose suicide protest is discussed in Chapter 3 (Cho 2003).

6. Assessments of when the democracy movement "actually" began depend on the definition of *democracy* employed. In the activist community in South Korea today it is common to hear of the long history of the *minjung* movement. The Tonghak Uprising in 1894—the largest peasant uprising in premodern Korea—is often cited as the beginning of this history, which moves through the March 1, 1919, independence movement against

Japanese colonialism, the 1960 student revolution, the 1970s anti-Yusin movement, the Gwangju Uprising in 1980, and the massive protests in June 1987. While this teleological understanding of Korean social movements contributes to a feeling of continuity, legitimacy, and moral justification, it also overlooks important distinctions between the different movements. It is not so much my intention to challenge this narrative, or to identify a starting time for the democracy movement, as to point out the distinct political context that gave rise to a sustained democracy movement in the 1970s.

7. Juxtaposing colleges and prisons, the latter representing the potential cost of political engagement, Ham Sok Hon writes, "That is why I call college a prison and prison a college. In college, rather than learning, people lose their good nature. In prison, people have the outside world completely taken away from them. Ironically, people only seek their God-given humble heart no longer influenced by the physical, because there is nothing else left" (Ham 1959: 192). Ham Sok Hon's message was not an unusual one for the *Sasangge Monthly*: at around the same time that Ham's article was published, Chang Chunha—the journal's founding editor—demanded in the preface of the one hundredth issue that students "'stand up against [the] injustice and immorality' of the Rhee regime" (quoted in Robinson 2012: 14).

8. The reference to the "five bandits" in Kim Chiha's poem was a play on the "five traitors" who were the officials of the Chosŏn Dynasty who signed the Ŭlsa Treaty of 1905, which made Korea a protectorate of the Japanese Imperial Empire and paved the way for formal colonization in 1910. The five bandits represent the network of corporate, government, and military elites who during Park Chung Hee's rule were responsible for the oppression of the Korean people generally and of Korean workers specifically. In Kim Chiha's words, the five bandits were the "ConglomerApe, AssemblyMutt, TopCivilSerpent, General-in-Chimp and HighMinisCur" (Kim 1970, translated by Brother Anthony of Taizé, available at hompi.sogang.ac.kr/anthony/FiveBandits.doc, retrieved April 13, 2013).

9. Myung-Lim Park argues that the intellectuals writing in *Sasangge Monthly* in the 1950s, who became the first generation of "dissident intelligentsia" (2011: 373), initially supported Park Chung Hee's coup in May 1961 because of their "staunchly anticommunist" political views.

10. After granting an interview in 2000, Yi Ujŏng passed away on May 30, 2002. Other prominent leaders, including Kim Kwansŏk, General Secretary of the National Council of Churches in Korea in the 1970s, have also passed away.

CHAPTER 1

1. Although it is obviously not a rigorous methodology for ascertaining the public's opinion of Park Chung Hee, I often ask drivers what they think about President Park when I am in a taxi in South Korea. The immediate reply of the great majority of drivers is that he "saved" the country from poverty and should be recognized as a great leader who modernized South Korea and brought wealth to the nation. When I quickly follow

up with the question about Park's human rights record, the same drivers usually unhesitatingly exclaim that he was a "terrible dictator." And herein lies the oxymoronic legacy of Park Chung Hee. The fascinating aspect of these responses, from a psychological standpoint, is that both evaluations of Park Chung Hee are held simultaneously without producing the cognitive dissonance one would expect from such diametrically opposing opinions of the same man.

2. As one participant puts it, following the April 1960 student revolution and in the absence of government, students enjoyed a period of "paradise" when they took on the duties of keeping public order through crime and traffic control (interview with Pae Yŏnwŏn, June 1, 2006). The "student paradise" quickly ended, however, with the establishment of a parliamentary democracy with Chang Myŏn as prime minister and Yun Posŏn as president: real power was vested in the former position and the latter acted as a ceremonial figurehead. This parliamentary system lasted for only one year, until Park Chung Hee's coup d'état in May 1961.

3. Critics of Park Chung Hee speculate that, if not for U.S. pressure, Park would have continued to rule through the military government. If this is so, the "democratic" government in the 1960s was a forced compromise, because Park Chung Hee was constrained by South Korea's economic and military dependence on the United States.

4. From an August 22, 2000, interview with a Christian student activist of the 1970s who wished to remain anonymous.

5. According to Bruce Cumings, as late as June 1950, "the United States military consistently maintained the position that the Korean peninsula had no strategic value to the United States in time of general world conflict," while the U.S. State Department entertained "competing visions" of its commitment to South Korea's security (1981: 120, 116).

6. One example was a public declaration by university professors in their statement "Declaration of Professors Against the Korea-Japan Normalization of Diplomatic Relations" (Han-Il kukkyo chŏngsanghwa pandae kyosu sŏngmyŏngsŏ) made on July 12, 1965.

7. This incident came to be known as the 6.3 student movement, after the especially harsh crackdown on June 3, 1964. It was followed on August 26, 1965, by a garrison decree, which reestablished social stability in the country.

8. Other sources indicate an even smaller range of victory for Park Chung Hee. Relying on newspaper data, Hak-Kyu Sohn (1989: 31) reports that Park won only 51.2 percent of the popular vote.

9. World Bank data. Retrieved June 2012 from http://data.worldbank.org.

CHAPTER 2

1. Although the technical distinction between garrison decrees (*wisuryŏng*) and martial law (*kyeŏmryŏng*)—the former indicating the deployment of the military under the control of civilian government and the latter meaning the suspension of all civilian authority—is lost in the context of Park Chung Hee's absolute control over both the

military and the civilian government, these were nominally distinct strategies employed by Park.

2. The KCIA was led by several other military officers for shorter periods, including Kim Yongsun (January 1963 to February 1963, three-star lieutenant general), Kim Chaech'un (February 1963 to July 1963, two-star major general), and Kim Kyewŏn (October 1969 to December 1970, four-star general) (http://www.army.mil.kr/english/sub06/sub06_03_01.jsp, accessed April 3, 2012).

3. After losing to Park Chung Hee by a small margin in the 1971 presidential election, Kim Dae Jung was kidnapped by KCIA agents on August 8, 1973. He was released five days later, presumably after U.S. Ambassador to South Korea Philip Habib pressured the Korean government to do so.

4. It was discovered in U.S. congressional investigations that the KCIA, through Korean businessman Pak Tongsun, bribed U.S. congressmen in 1976 and 115 members of the U.S. Congress and the American CIA were consequently implicated in the incident (UCLA Archival Collection: Box 6, Folder 1, and Box 20, Folder 4; "Ending the Korean Probe," *Washington Post*, October 10, 1978).

5. Other political control laws included the Law of Purification of Political Activities, the Social Safety Law, the Law on Public Gatherings and Demonstrations, the Special Law on the Punishment of Crimes Under Emergency Situations, and the Special Law on the Protection of the State.

6. After the assassination of Park Chung Hee in 1979, the ACL was merged with the NSL on December 31, 1980, and the newly emboldened NSL was used in the 1980s to arrest and incarcerate individuals who the government felt were a threat to South Korea's national security, including those participating in the democracy movement.

7. Because of his association with *Sasangge Monthly*, Chang Chunha was one of the leading intellectuals at the time and an outspoken critic of Park Chung Hee's government. He was part of a small group of senior leaders in the progressive dissident community that also included, among others, Ham Sok Hon, Paek Nakchun, Yi Pyŏngnin, Kim Chaejun, and Ch'ŏn Kwanu. On August 17, 1975, Chang Chunha was found dead at the bottom of Yaksa-bong (peak), where he supposedly fell while hiking. On March 26, 2013, however, forensic experts declared that, on the basis of a reexamination of his cranium, Chang Chunha was most likely killed from a blow to the head. The new report has fueled the opinion that Chang was murdered by Park Chung Hee's government (*Hankyoreh Newspaper*, March 27, 2013, and August 16, 2012).

8. Lee Ho-Chul was a senior member of the Citizens' Council for the Protection of Democracy (introduced in Chapter 3 and discussed in detail in Chapter 7) and helped lead the campaign for a fair presidential election in 1971. In 1973 he joined Chang Chunha and others in criticizing the establishment of the dictatorial system under the Yusin Constitution. He was arrested for violating ED 1 on January 14, 1974.

9. The third ED, issued on January 14, 1974, aimed to stabilize the economy by eas-

ing the tax burdens of low-income earners. The fifth ED, issued on August 23, 1974, annulled the first and the fourth decrees. The sixth ED, issued on December 31, 1974, annulled the third ED, and the eighth ED, issued on May 13, 1975, annulled the seventh ED.

10. See Stentzel (2006) for an English translation of ED 9.

11. Incidentally, the Constitutional Court of the Republic of Korea delivered a ruling in March 2013 stating that the promulgation of EDs 1, 2, and 9 in the 1970s violated basic rights protected in the constitution, and that all individuals convicted under these EDs will have the right to a retrial. The ruling passed with all eight Constitutional Court justices voting unanimously ("Court Says South Korean Dictator, Father of Current President, Violated Constitution," *New York Times*, March 22, 2013, A6).

12. The state sometimes mobilized its own supporting organizations, such as when Park Chung Hee reestablished the National Defense Student Corps (Hakto Hoguktan) on May 21, 1975, just nine days after the promulgation of ED 9. Originally formed by Syngman Rhee in 1949 to mobilize students and youth for political purposes, the reactivated National Defense Student Corps was supposed to show the larger public that students did in fact support the Yusin government and that demonstrating students were aberrations.

13. Three laws that were passed on April 17, 1963—the Labor Union Law (Nodong chohappŏp), the Labor Dispute Adjustment Law (Nodongjaeng ŭi chojŏngpŏp), and the Labor Relations Commission Law (Nodong wiwŏnhoepŏp)—were effectively used by Park's first administration to regulate and control attempts at labor organizing (Lee 2006).

14. Korean companies holding foreign investments were given special status by Park Chung Hee's government because of their vital role in the national economy (*kungmin kyŏngje*), and labor relations at these companies were not subject to the normal procedures governing employer-employee relations.

15. The Act on the Establishment of Free Export Zones (Such'ul chayu chiyŏk sŏlch'ipŏp), which took effect on January 1, 1970, along with the Act on Special Measures for National Security, was intended to attract foreign investment by limiting the leverage of workers in labor disputes.

16. The FKTU was reconstituted on August 31, 1961—within months of Park Chung Hee's coup in May—when "workers' representatives proclaimed their complete endorsement of the military coup and their unreserved commitment to the 'revolutionary task'" (Choi 1989: 31).

CHAPTER 3

1. It should be noted that not all former participants in the 4.19 student revolution consider it to have been a successful revolution. As one participant observes, "Even though the student movement was able to force a political transition, students did not end up in the center of the new power. Therefore, I do not see the student movement as a completely successful revolution. . . . The students started the 4.19 revolution, but in the end it was the politicians who took power" (anonymous interview, August 22, 2000).

2. Labor movements and the development of pro-worker labor unions varied across industries, with some better organized than others. As Hwasook Nam (2009) has shown, laborers in the shipbuilding industry were relatively better organized than most workers in the 1960s. Overall, however, the state was highly effective in repressing labor unrest during the Yusin period, and the power of laborers in the 1970s was quite weak compared to labor movements in the 1980s and 1990s. According to Hagen Koo, it wasn't until the 1980s that we began to see the formation of a working class, when "a significant change occurred in Korean workers' collective identity and consciousness" (2001: 13).

3. According to Nohlen, Grotz, and Hartmann (2001), Kim Dae Jung won an impressive 59.4 percent of the votes from the city of Seoul compared to Park Chung Hee's 40 percent. This strong showing from South Korea's most important city, along with the majority of votes from his hometown in Jeolla Province, constituted the two sources of support for Kim Dae Jung.

4. Minister of Culture and Education Min Kwansik confronted students at the Nationwide Meeting of University Students (Chŏn'guk Taehak Ch'ong Haksaeng Hoeŭi) on June 21, 1971, to inform them of the reduction in mandatory military training hours and the reopening of schools starting with SNU on June 23, 1971 (KDF Events Dictionary: 117).

5. The schools that were permanently shut down were SNU, Korea University, Yonsei University, Sogang University, Sungkyunkwan University, Kyung Hee University, Hankuk University of Foreign Studies, and Chonnam National University (KDF Events Dictionary: 157).

6. As in many other cases of exaggerated prison sentences, the four students did not serve their entire jail terms and were released after two years of incarceration.

7. Throughout the 1960s and 1970s and into the 1980s, students organized themselves into small cells or study groups that acted as the foundational organizational units on which the larger student movement was built. Younger students (*hubae*) were often recruited into these circles by their seniors (*sŏnbae*) for multiple purposes, including studying banned political books and organizing protest events (see Lee 2007).

8. Further biographical information on the four SNU students can be found in *Kyunghyang Shinmun* 2003.

9. In the heightened repressive context of the "national security state," students took their movement underground. The main tactic they relied on to maintain their networks and some momentum after the garrison decree and the mass arrests was underground circulation of student pamphlets. At Korea University, for example, publications such as *Minuji* (*Friend of the Minjung*) and *Yasaenghwa* (*Wildflower*) were disseminated among the student activist community. Some publications, such as *Hamsŏng* (*Battle Cry*), produced by students at Chonnam National University, were circulated widely among student groups in cities such as Seoul, Daegu, and Busan. *Hamsŏng* and other publications of this sort helped maintain the national network of student dissidents that was established through the now defunct Students' Alliance (Yi 2011: 323–324).

10. Quoted at http://en.wikipedia.org/wiki/People's_Revolutionary_Party_Incident.

11. The Chief Prosecutor of the Republic of Korea is equivalent to the Attorney General of the United States of America.

12. Key government officials played important roles in both the 1964 and 1974 PRP cases: Sin Chiksu, who was the nation's chief prosecutor in 1964, was director of the KCIA in 1974; Yi Yŏngt'aek, who was a central KCIA agent investigating the PRP in 1964, was the sixth bureau director of the KCIA in 1974. The National Council of Churches in Korea has speculated that "the 1974 case may be an act of revenge by the two [Sin Chiksu and Yi Yŏngt'aek] as they were humiliated by the Ministry of Welfare and Security prosecutors due to their sloppy litigation preparations in 1964 and the refusal [of government prosecutors] to sign the indictment [and] coercion only caused the prosecutors to resign and challenge them" (NCCK Archive Vol. 1: 452).

13. Incidentally, on September 12, 2002, a government Truth-Fact Finding Commission announced that the PRP case was a fabrication of Park Chung Hee's government. On January 23, 2007, the Seoul Central District Court formally exonerated the eight executed individuals of violating the Emergency Decrees, the National Security Law, the Anti-Communist Law, and the Prohibition on Conspiracy and Preparation to Commit Rebellion. A federal court went further when on August 21, 2007, it "ordered the South Korean government to pay almost US$26 million in compensation to [the] families" of the eight victims in the PRP case (AFP Seoul, "Seoul Court Orders Compensation for Executed Activists," retrieved August 22, 2012, from http://www.taipeitimes.com/News/front/archives/2007/08/22/2003375264).

CHAPTER 4

1. The monarchs of the Chosŏn Dynasty (1392–1910) severely persecuted Korean Catholics in the 1800s, leading to the deaths of eight to ten thousand believers (Choi 2006). Consequently, 103 martyrs were canonized by Pope John Paul II in 1984.

2. The first "modern" hospital in Korea was started by missionary doctor Horace Allen when, after saving the life of Queen Min's nephew, he was granted land and resources by King Kojong to start the House of Extended Grace (Gwanghyewon), which evolved into Severance Hospital. Other missionaries—Horace G. Underwood, Mary F. Scranton, and Henry Appenzeller—started schools that grew into some of the most prestigious universities in Korea today, including Yonsei University and Ewha Womans University.

3. Although Pastor Pak Hyŏnggyu's Easter Sunday protest facilitated the politicization of the progressive Christian community, it is important to note that prominent Christian individuals did play a significant part in political campaigns before 1973. Most conspicuous was Pastor Kim Chaejun, a founding member of the Citizens' Council for the Protection of Democracy, who became a vocal critic of Park Chung Hee after the 1969 constitutional amendment that allowed Park to run for a third presidential term. Furthermore, Pastor Pak's Easter Sunday protest was not the first Christian protest

against the Yusin Constitution. In 1972, "the Reverend Ŭn Myŏnggi, a liberal pastor in Jeonju, North Jeolla Province, criticized the Yusin system in an all-night prayer meeting at his church and became the first clergyman arrested by the government during the Yusin period (1972–1979)" (Park 2003: 193).

4. Pastor Pak Hyŏnggyu's status as a senior leader in the democracy movement culminated with his appointment as the first president of the Korea Democracy Foundation in 2002.

5. Preeminent theologian Paul Tillich left Union Theological Seminary for Harvard Divinity School just before Pastor Pak arrived. Although Pastor Pak wanted to transfer to Harvard to study with Tillich, he eventually decided to remain at Union Theological Seminary (interview with Pak Hyŏnggyu, August 23, 2000).

6. Because of the International Date Line and the country's various time zones, America is roughly a half day behind Korea.

7. It should be noted that there is an ongoing friendly debate about who the first "*minjung* theologian" is. Some say it is Ahn Byung-Mu because his speech celebrating the release of political prisoners on March 1, 1975, was the first public use of the term *minjung* by a Christian theologian (Hyŏn 1985). Others say that although Sŏ Namdong may not have used the term in the title of the lecture he gave at Yonsei University's faculty retreat in December 1974, the content was Minjung Theology in every way but name (Song 1984). What is more pertinent, however, is that Minjung Theology is a fundamentally communitarian endeavor and was not created by any one individual, but rather arose from the experiences of an oppressed community.

CHAPTER 5

1. Field notes, October 23, 2009.

2. After the unprecedented show of Korean nationalism on March 1, 1919, in what became known as the 3.1 Independence Movement (3.1 *tongnip undong*), the Japanese colonial government, under a new governor-general, Saitō Makoto (1919–1927 and 1929–1931), instituted a drastically different policy for governing Korea. The Cultural Policy (in Japanese, *bunka seiji*) ushered in a period of "cultural and political renaissance" that lasted until the Manchurian Incident in 1931, when Japan began to mobilize for total war with China (Eckert et al. 1990: 286).

3. John R. Hodge and the XXIV Corps arrived in Korea to occupy the southern half of the peninsula on September 8, 1945, following an agreement between the United States and the Soviet Union to a two-party trusteeship of the Korean peninsula (Cumings 1981: 137).

4. These and other solidarity ads are available at http://blog.naver.com/happy24nara /100188774995; accessed February 22, 2014.

5. Although there may have been "hatred" between journalists who sided with the company and those who were fired for participating in the free press movement, with

the benefit of time and hindsight Hong Myŏngjin acknowledges that the journalists who stayed in the company may have had valid reasons for not joining the free press movement: "I think they had their own reasons, like being a breadwinner. They had to earn money. Now, I realize that I did not need to return to the company as I could manage to live without earning money because my parents supported me. So I think I understand that they had their own reasons and now I understand them" (interview with Hong Myŏngjin, November 19, 2009).

6. The state, not unlike in its approach to students, fabricated a conspiracy story involving a clandestine communist organization called the Blue Friend Group (Chŏng Uhoe) that was purportedly to be a gathering of communists whose goal was to "overthrow the Yusin dictatorship" (Dong-A T'uwi 2005: 226). The government then accused Sŏng Yubo of being a member of the Blue Friend Group and arrested him.

7. In the 1970s, the bachelor's degree in law, unlike in the American system, qualified Koreans to take the national bar examination. In addition, one had the choice to become a judge or a lawyer upon passing the relevant examination. Recently, law education in South Korea converted to a graduate law school system based on the American model.

8. Sin Yŏngbok was sentenced to death by the military court before the Supreme Court reduced his sentence to life imprisonment.

9. The Great West Gate Prison was infamous as the central facility where the Japanese colonial government incarcerated and tortured Koreans who participated in independence movements during the colonial period.

10. Diversity is calculated using the Simpson Diversity Index (see Olzak and Ryo 2007), a proportional statistic with values ranging between 0 (no diversity, only one group participating that year) and 1 (only a theoretical possibility of complete diversity). It is calculated with the following equation:

$$S = 1-[(A/year\_total)^2 + (B/year\_total)^2 + (C/year\_total)^2 + \ldots]$$

where A is the number of events organized by group A in a year's time, and B is the number of events organized by group B, and so on. The denominator "year total" is the total sum of the number of events by all groups and thus can exceed the number of actual events (such as when two or more groups participate in a single event together).

11. In 1988, lawyers associated with two organizations, Lawyers for the Realization of Justice (Chŏngŭi Sirhyŏn Pŏpchoinhoe) and Young Lawyers Association (Chŏngnyŏn Pyŏnhosahoe), came together to form the Lawyers for a Democratic Society (Goedde 2011).

12. For example, during the so-called Yongsan Tragedy in 2009, when five individuals and one policeman were killed during a skirmish between authorities and tenants who refused to be evicted, Minbyŏn and Duksu lawyers such as Kwŏn Yŏngguk, Kim Hyŏngt'ae, and Sin Tongmi represented the grieved tenants and criticized the government's denial of their basic rights.

CHAPTER 6

1. Nondisruptive tactics include declarations, resolution meetings, boycotts, consciousness raising, debates, organizational foundings, requests, propaganda, fasting, prayer or religious ceremonies, legal or formal channels, press conferences, monitoring of elections, resignations, critique or spoken protests, investigations, fundraising, not trying hard at work, and cultural events. Disruptive tactics are rallies and demonstrations, spontaneous disruptions, picketing, rioting and vandalism, strikes, sit-ins, self harm and suicide, symbolic and dramaturgical protests, parades and marches, violence, naked protest, and taking hostages.

2. Although many scholars highlight the role played by Christians and students in the 1970s labor movement, the data presented here confirm other studies of South Korean workers that have identified the 1980s as the period when labor movements and the democracy movement came together in significant ways (Koo 2001; Lee 2007).

3. Although Lee Jeongeun (2009) reports that Human Rights Week was first established in 1953, archival data from *Dong-A Ilbo* include a story published on December 5, 1951, describing the first "Human Rights Support Week" (*inkwŏn ongho chugan*), which was hosted by the United Nations Korean Association (Kukche Yŏnhap Han'guk Hyŏphoe), the Korean Bar Association, the Ministry of Justice, and the Bureau of Public Information.

4. Predictably, both George Ogle and James Sinnott did not stop advocating for the PRP defendants after leaving Korea and were able to talk more freely about the case in the United States (Ogle 2006; interview with James Sinnott, August 12, 2014).

5. The Foreign Assistance Act of 1973 built on the Foreign Assistance Act of 1961, which was "a statement of policy regarding development assistance authorizations" (Bill Summary & Status, 93rd Congress, available at http://thomas.loc.gov/cgi-bin/bdquery/z ?d093:SN01443:@@@L&summ2=m&, retrieved March 11, 2013).

6. IHRL of Korea website, retrieved August 2011.

7. Song Chiyŏng was one of three executives at the newspaper *Minjok Ilbo* who were arrested for advocating communist ideology "similar to that of North Korea" (see Chapter 5). Song did not serve his full sentence and instead was released in 1969.

8. The Amnesty International Section in South Korea was later approved in 1993.

9. Namhee Lee (2007) argues, for example, that South Korea's student movement continued to develop its underground networks in the highly repressive period immediately following the Gwangju Uprising in 1980. Though students were not able to hold public demonstrations between 1980 and 1984, after which the Chun Doo Hwan regime relaxed its policies, they continued to hone their ideological positions and organizational structures, which became the foundations for mobilization in the late 1980s.

CHAPTER 7

1. The Citizens' Council for the Protection of Democracy did not include politicians as members because of its goal to ensure fair presidential elections in 1971. With the "loss

of democracy," however, the Citizens' Conference for the Recovery of Democracy welcomed the addition of marginalized opposition politicians such as Yun Posŏn, Kim Dae Jung, and Kim Young Sam (interview with Lee Ho-Chul, December 16, 2004).

2. The Mokpo Citizens' Conference for the Recovery of Democracy was founded by lawyer Kim Kiyŏl, Catholic priest Chang Chigwŏn, and past editor of *Jeonnam Ilbo* Myŏng Chaeyong.

3. The South Jeolla Province Citizens' Conference for the Recovery of Democracy was founded by Catholic priest Yi Sangt'aek, YMCA representative Pak Chaebong, YWCA representative Cho Ara, lawyer Hong Namsun, and past member of the National Assembly Pak Min'gi.

4. There are possible methodological and substantive reasons for the low rate of intergroup mobilization in 1976. Because the rate of intergroup protest events is a function of the total number of events, the rate might be low because the total number of protest events that year was small. Substantively, the repressive climate immediately following ED 9 could have diminished both the rate of intergroup protest events and the total number of events in 1976.

5. As Seungsook Moon (2005) argues, the impact of the state's "militarized modernization" program was different for female and male workers conscripted into South Korea's economy. While the state encouraged most citizens to contribute to economic development in some way, women were overrepresented in key industries, including textile manufacturing, that were the drivers of Korea's economy in the 1960s.

CONCLUSION

1. The treaty to normalize relations with Japan was signed in 1965, the culmination of negotiations that started in 1964.

2. Most explanations of the assassination revolve around Kim Chaegyu's rivalry with Ch'a Chich'ŏl and the increasing influence the latter had on President Park. Some speculate that Kim acted impulsively at the dinner following an argument about how to handle the civil unrest in the southeastern cities of Busan and Masan; others believe that it was a carefully orchestrated coup. Some cite Kim Chaegyu's frequent meetings with the United States' CIA chief in Korea, Robert G. Brewster, and a meeting with U.S. Ambassador William H. Gleysteen Jr. on the same day as the assassination as evidence that the United States was somehow involved or supported Kim's actions. The United States, for its part, has consistently denied any involvement in Park Chung Hee's death. For a summary of the assassination, see Kleiner (2001).

3. As recreated from testimonies by Kim Chaegyu and Chief Presidential Secretary Kim Kyewŏn—who along with female singer Sim Subong and model Sin Chaesun attended the dinner at which Park was assassinated—Ch'a Chich'ŏl, in response to the question of what to do about the demonstrators in Busan and Masan, is reported to have said, "It wasn't a big deal to kill a few million in Cambodia. It's only 100,000 or 200,000,

let's mow them down with tanks" (*Sisa onŭl sisa ON*, March 22, 2011: http://www.sisaon .co.kr/news/articleView.html?idxno=7700, retrieved August 21, 2012).

4. After shooting Ch'a Chich'ŏl in the arm and Park Chung Hee in the chest, Kim Chaegyu's gun jammed. He went out of the room to get a second gun, with which he proceeded to shoot and kill Ch'a. He then shot Park Chung Hee in the head. Reports indicate that Park Chung Hee was dead before the second shot (*Kyunghyang Shinmun*, December 4, 1979).

5. It is still uncertain how many people died during the Gwangju Uprising, with some arguing as few as several hundred and others arguing that the death toll reached over two thousand (see Shin and Hwang 2003).

6. Kim Chiha's Declaration of Conscience was smuggled out of his jail cell and circulated among the dissident community. In addition, "through the efforts of Congressmen Donald M. Fraser of Minnesota and Frederick W. Richmond of New York" (Sunoo 1976b: 18), the declaration was included in the materials that the U.S. House of Representatives Subcommittee on International Organizations considered during their hearings on the human rights situation in South Korea in 1975 (United States House of Representatives, Committee on International Relations 1975).

7. The *khozhdenie v-narod* movement, which was "all that was finest" in the early socialist revolution in late nineteenth-century Russia, was "based on a firm belief in the Russian peasants and . . . the need for a vast social revolution—carried out by the people themselves" (Pedler 1927: 130).

8. Other applications took the form of "rural volunteer activities" (*nongch'on pongsa hwaltong*) and "mining volunteer activities" (*kwangsan pongsa hwaltong*) in which students aided farmers and miners with the season's harvest and the extraction of minerals, respectively, as well as engaging in political discussion. Together these three activities came to be known as the "3-*hwal*" movement: *konghwal, nonghwal*, and *kwanghwal*.

9. The tactic of "going to the people" was introduced to Korea as early as the colonial period, when "Tonga ilbo in the 1930s [sent] educated youth to the countryside to spread literacy" (Robinson 2012: 12).

10. For Min'gahyŏp's history and current activities, see http://minkahyup.org/in-dex_bak.htm, retrieved August 27, 2012.

11. According to Wan-kyung Sung (2012: 192), art critic Won Dong-sŏk first used the term *minjung* arts in 1975.

12. The lyrics to "Sol a sol a p'urŭrŭn sol a" were initially penned as a poem by the poet Pak Yŏnggŭn in the early 1980s before a Yonsei University student, An Ch'ihwan, put it to music in 1986. This song quickly became a favorite in the 1980s *minjung* movement (lyrics reprinted here with the permission of An Ch'ihwan).

13. It should be noted that, at the time of this writing, there was a scandal about the 2012 presidential election, with the National Intelligence Service (the contemporary version of the KCIA) accused of trying to manipulate public opinion through digital technology in favor of President Park Geun-hye, daughter of Park Chung Hee.

REFERENCES

ARCHIVES AND OFFICIAL SOURCES

Amnesty International. 1975. *Amnesty International Annual Report 1974/5.* London: Amnesty International Publications.

——. 1977. *Report of an Amnesty International Mission to the Republic of Korea: 27 March–9 April 1975.* 2nd ed. London: Amnesty International Publications.

——. 1979. *Amnesty International Report 1979.* London: Amnesty International Publications.

Chinsil/Hwahae rŭl wihan Kwagŏsa Chŏngni Wiwŏnhoe [Truth and Reconciliation Committee, Republic of Korea]. 2010. "9-kwŏn 7: Inmin Hyŏngmyŏngdang sakŏn [Volume 9 Number 7: People's Revolutionary Party Incident]." Seoul: Truth and Reconciliation Committee, Republic of Korea. Available at http://www.jinsil.go.kr/app-dealing/databoard/app_read.asp?num=390&pageno=1&stype=content&sval=%C0%CE%B9%CE%C7%F5%B8%ED&data_years=&data_month=

Kukche Aemnesŭt'i Han'guk Chibu [Amnesty International South Korean Section]. 2002. *Han'guk Aemnesŭt'i 30-yŏn! Inkwŏn undong 30-yŏn! Kukche Aemnesŭt'i Han'guk Chibu 30-yŏn yaksa* [30 years of Korea's Amnesty International! 30 years of human rights activities! 30-year historical outline of Amnesty International's South Korea Section]. Seoul: Amnesty International South Korean Section.

Minjuhwa Undong Kinyŏm Saŏphoe [Korea Democracy Foundation]. n.d. *Minjuhwa undong kwallyŏn sakŏn sajŏn* [KDF Dictionary of Events Related to the Democracy Movement]. Seoul: Korea Democracy Foundation Research Center.

Minjuhwa Undong Kinyŏm Saŏphoe [Korea Democracy Foundation]. n.d. *Minjuhwa undong kwallyŏn tanch'e sajŏn* [KDF Dictionary of Organizations Related to the Democracy Movement]. Seoul: Korea Democracy Foundation Research Center.

Han'guk Kidokkyo Kyohoe Hyŏbŭihoe [National Council of Churches in Korea Human Rights Mission]. 1987. *1970-yŏndae minjuhwa undong* [1970s Democracy Movement]. 8 vols. Seoul: National Council of Churches in Korea.

Kukka Inkwŏn Wiwŏnhoe [National Human Rights Commission of Korea]. 2002. *Kukka poanpŏp chŏgyongsang esŏ nat'anan inkwon silt'ae* [Human rights practices in the application of the National Security Law]. Seoul: National Human Rights Commission of Korea.

Olzak, Susan, and Elizabeth West. 1995. *Ethnic Collective Action in Contemporary Urban U.S.—Data on Conflicts and Protests*. Stanford, CA: Stanford University. Available at http://data.stanford.edu/urban_ECA

Park, Chung Hee. 1962 (1970). *Our Nation's Path: Ideology of Social Reconstruction*. Seoul: Hollym Corporation.

———. 1970. *Major Speeches by Korea's Park Chung Hee*. Seoul: Hollym Corporation.

———. 1973. *Major Speeches by President Park Chung Hee, Republic of Korea*. Seoul: Samhwa.

United States House of Representatives, Committee on International Relations. 1975. *Human Rights in South Korea and the Philippines: Implications for U.S. Policy*. Washington, DC: U.S. Government Printing Office.

University of California at Los Angeles (UCLA) Archival Collection on Democracy and Unification in Korea. Housed at the UCLA Charles E. Young Research Library's Department of Special Collections: http://www.library.ucla.edu/libraries/eastasian/korean-studies-collections

SECONDARY SOURCES

Abelmann, Nancy. 1996. *Echoes of the Past, Epics of Dissent: A South Korean Social Movement*. Berkeley: University of California Press.

Abramowitz, Stephen I., and Alberta J. Nassi. 1981. "Keeping the Faith: Psychological Correlates of Activism Persistence into Middle Adulthood." *Journal of Youth and Adolescence* 10(6): 507–523.

Adesnik, A. David, and Sunhyuk Kim. 2008. "If At First You Don't Succeed: The Puzzle of South Korea's Democratic Transition." CDDRL Working Papers, no. 8. Stanford, CA: Center on Democracy, Development, and the Rule of Law, Stanford University.

Ahn, Byung-Mu. 1975. "Minjok, minjung, kyohoe [Nation, Minjung, Church]." *Kidokkyo sasang [Christian Thought]* 203(April): 78–84.

Almeida, Paul D. 2003. "Opportunity Organizations and Threat-Induced Contention: Protest Waves in Authoritarian Settings." *American Journal of Sociology* 109(2): 345–400.

———. 2005. "Multi-Sectoral Coalitions and Popular Movement Participation." *Research in Social Movements, Conflicts and Change* 26: 65–99.

———. 2008. *Waves of Protest: Popular Struggle in El Salvador, 1925–2005*. Minneapolis: University of Minnesota Press.

Alves, Maria Helena Moreira. 2001. "Interclass Alliances in the Opposition to the Military in Brazil: Consequences for the Transition Period." In *Power and Popular Protest: Latin American Social Movements*, edited by Susan Eckstein, 278–298. Berkeley: University of California Press.

Andrews, Kenneth T., and Michael Biggs. 2006. "The Dynamics of Protest Diffusion: Movement Organizations, Social Networks, and News Media in the 1960 Sit-Ins." *American Sociological Review* 71(5): 752–777.

Armstrong, Charles K., ed. 2002. *Korean Society: Civil Society, Democracy and the State.* London: Routledge.

———. 2003. *The North Korean Revolution, 1945–1950.* Ithaca, NY: Cornell University Press.

Baker, Donald. 2007. "The International Christian Network for Korea's Democratization." In *Democratic Movements and Korean Society: Historical Documents and Korean Studies,* edited by Sang-young Rhyu, 133–161. Seoul: Yonsei University Press.

Barranco, José, and Dominique Wisler. 1999. "Validity and Systematicity of Newspaper Data in Event Analysis." *European Sociological Review* 15(3): 301–322.

Barvosa-Carter, Edwina. 2001. "Multiple Identity and Coalition Building: How Identity Differences Within Us Enable Radical Alliances Among Us." In *Forging Radical Alliances Across Difference: Coalition Politics for the New Millennium,* edited by Jill M. Bystydzienski and Steven P. Schacht, 21–34. London: Rowman and Littlefield.

de Bary, William Theodore, and Tu Weiming. 1998. *Confucianism and Human Rights.* New York: Columbia University Press.

Benford, Robert D., and Scott A. Hunt. 1994. "Social Movement Counterframing and Reframing: Repairing and Sustaining Collective Identity Claims." Paper presented at the Midwest Sociological Society Conference, St. Louis, MO.

Benford, Robert D., and David A. Snow. 2000. "Framing Processes and Social Movements: An Overview and Assessment." *Annual Review of Sociology* 26: 611–639.

Biggs, Michael, and Kenneth T. Andrews. 2010. "From Protest to Organization: The Impact of the 1960 Sit-Ins on Movement Organizations in the American South." In *The Diffusion of Social Movements: Actors, Mechanisms, and Political Effects,* edited by Rebecca Kolins Givans, Kenneth M. Roberts, and Sarah A. Soule, 187–203. Cambridge, UK: Cambridge University Press.

———. 2004. *Resisting Dictatorship: Repression and Protest in Southeast Asia.* Cambridge, UK: Cambridge University Press.

Brazinsky, Gregg. 2007. *Nation Building in South Korea: Koreans, Americans, and the Making of a Democracy.* Chapel Hill: University of North Carolina Press.

Brockett, Charles D. 1995. "A Protest-Cycle Resolution of the Repression/Popular-Protest Paradox." In *Repertoires and Cycles of Collective Action,* edited by Mark Traugott, 117–144. Durham, NC: Duke University Press.

———. 2005. *Political Movements and Violence in Central America.* Cambridge, UK: Cambridge University Press.

Bystydzienski, Jill M., and Steven P. Schacht, eds. 2001. *Forging Radical Alliances Across Difference: Coalition Politics for the New Millennium.* London: Rowman and Littlefield.

Carnegie, Dale. 1932. *Lincoln the Unknown.* Forest Hills, NY: Forest Hills Publishing.

Chang, Paul Y. 2006. "Carrying the Torch in the Darkest Hours: The Sociopolitical Origins of Minjung Protestant Movements." In *Christianity in Korea,* edited by Robert E. Buswell and Timothy S. Lee, 195–220. Honolulu: University of Hawai'i Press.

————. 2008. "Unintended Consequences of Repression: Alliance Formation in South Korea's Democracy Movement (1970–1979)." *Social Forces* 87(2): 651–677.

Chang, Paul Y., and Alex S. Vitale. 2013. "Repressive Coverage in an Authoritarian Context: Threat, Weakness, and Legitimacy in South Korea's Democracy Movement." *Mobilization* 18(1): 489–511.

Chang, Paul Y., and Byung-Soo Kim. 2007. "Differential Impact of Repression on Social Movements: Christian Organizations and Liberation Theology in South Korea (1972–1979)." *Sociological Inquiry* 77(3): 326–355.

Chang, Paul Y., and Gi-Wook Shin. 2011. "Democratization and the Evolution of Social Movements in Korea: Institutionalization and Diffusion." In *South Korean Social Movements: From Democracy to Civil Society*, edited by Gi-Wook Shin and Paul Y. Chang, 3–18. London: Routledge.

Cho, Chunhyŏn. 2006. "Minch'ŏng Hangnyŏn sakŏn [The Minch'ŏng Hangnyŏn incident]." Retrieved February 19, 2013, from http://contents.archives.go.kr/next/content/listSubjectDescription.do?id=000996&pageFlag=

Cho, Wha Soon, Sun Ai Lee, and Sang Nim Ahn. 1988. *Let the Weak Be Strong: A Woman's Struggle for Justice*. Bloomington, IN: Meyer-Stone Books.

Cho, Yong-Whan. 2002. "The National Human Rights Commission: Law, Reality, and Its Future Tasks." *Korea Journal* 42: 228–262.

Cho, Young-rae. 2003. *A Single Spark: The Biography of Chun Tae-Il*. Seoul: Dolbegae.

Choi, Hyun-moo. 1995. "Contemporary Korean Literature: From Victimization to Minjung Nationalism." In *South Korea's Minjung Movement: The Culture and Politics of Dissidence*, edited by Kenneth M. Wells, 167–178. Honolulu: University of Hawai'i Press.

Choi, Jai Keun. 2006. *The Origin of the Roman Catholic Church in Korea: An Examination of Popular and Governmental Responses to Catholic Missions in the Late Chosŏn Dynasty*. Cheltenham, PA: Hermit Kingdom Press.

Choi, Jang Jip. 1988. *Han'guk ŭi nodong undong kwa kukka* [Korean labor movement and the state]. Busan: Yeuleum Press.

————. 1989. *Labor and the Authoritarian State: Labor Unions in South Korean Manufacturing Industries, 1961–1980*. Seoul: Korea University Press.

————. 2011. "Political Cleavages in South Korea." In *Consolidation of Democracy in South Korea*, edited by Hahm Chaibong, 24–71. Seoul: Academy of Korean Studies Press.

Chŏng, Kungno. 1995. *Han'guk haksaeng minju undongsa: 1956–1960 chŏn'gae kwajŏng chungsim* [History of the Korean students' democratization movement: Focus on developments, 1956–1960]. Seoul: Han'guk Hyŏndaesa Yŏn'guso.

Chun, Soonok. 2003. *They Are Not Machines: Korean Women Workers and Their Fight for Democratic Trade Unionism in the 1970s*. Surrey, UK: Ashgate.

Clark, Donald N. 1986. *Christianity in Modern Korea*. Lanham, MD: University Press of America.

————. 2002. "Protestant Christianity and the State: Religious Organizations as Civil Society." In *Korean Society: Civil Society, Democracy and the State*, edited by Charles K. Armstrong, 187–206. London: Routledge.

Cole, David C., and Princeton N. Lyman. 1971. *Korean Development: The Interplay of Politics and Economics.* Cambridge, MA: Harvard University Press.

Cole, Wade M. 2005. "Sovereignty Relinquished? Explaining Commitment to the International Human Rights Covenants, 1966–1999." *American Sociological Review* 70(3): 472–495.

Cole, Wade M., and Francisco O. Ramirez. 2013. "Conditional Decoupling: Assessing the Impact of National Human Rights Institutions, 1981 to 2004." *American Sociological Review* 78(4): 702–725.

Commission on Theological Concerns of the Christian Conference of Asia (CTC-CCA), ed. 1981. *Minjung Theology: People as the Subjects of History.* Singapore: Christian Conference of Asia.

Croteau, David, and Lyndsi Hicks. 2003. "Coalition Framing and the Challenge of a Consonant Frame Pyramid: The Case of a Collaborative Response to Homelessness." *Social Problems* 50(2): 251–272.

Cumings, Bruce. 1981. *The Origins of the Korean War. Vo1. I: Liberation and the Emergence of Separate Regimes, 1945–1947.* Princeton, NJ: Princeton University Press.

——. 1990. *The Origins of the Korean War. Vol. II: The Roaring of the Cataract, 1947–1950.* Princeton, NJ: Princeton University Press.

——. 1997. *Korea's Place in the Sun: A Modern History.* New York: W. W. Norton.

Davenport, Christian. 2005. "Repression and Mobilization: Insights from Political Science and Sociology." In *Repression and Mobilization*, edited by Christian Davenport, Hank Johnston, and Carol Mueller, vii–xli. Minneapolis: University of Minnesota Press.

Davenport, Christian, and Marci Eads. 2001. "Cued to Coerce or Coercing Cues? An Exploration of Dissident Framing and Its Relationship to Political Repression." *Mobilization* 6(2): 151–171.

Davenport, Christian, Hank Johnston, and Carol McClurg Mueller. 2005. *Repression and Mobilization.* Minneapolis: University of Minnesota Press.

Diamond, Larry, and Byung-Kook Kim, eds. 2000. *Consolidating Democracy in South Korea.* Boulder, CO: Lynne Rienner.

Dobson, William J. 2013. *The Dictator's Learning Curve: Inside the Global Battle for Democracy.* New York: Anchor Books.

Dong-A T'uwi. 2005. *Chayu ŏllon: 1975–2005 Dong-A T'uwi 30-yn palchach'wi* [Free press: 1975–2005, the 30-year footsteps of Dong-A T'uwi]. Seoul: Haedamsol.

Earl, Jennifer. 2003. "Tanks, Tear Gas, and Taxes: Toward a Theory of Movement Repression." *Sociological Theory* 21(1): 44–68.

——. 2006. "Introduction: Repression and the Social Control of Protest." *Mobilization* 11(2): 129–143.

Earl, Jennifer, Sarah A. Soule, and John D. McCarthy. 2003. "Protest Under Fire? Explaining the Policing of Protest." *American Sociological Review* 68(4): 581–606.

Eckert, Carter J. 1991. *Offspring of Empire: The Koch'ang Kims and the Colonial Origins of Korean Capitalism, 1876–1945.* Seattle: University of Washington Press.

Eckert, Carter J., Ki-baek Yi, Young Ick Lew, Michael Robinson, and Edward W. Wagner. 1990. *Korea, Old and New: A History.* Seoul: Ilchokak.

Em, Henry H. 1999. "*Minjok* as a Modern and Democratic Construct: Sin Ch'aeho's Historiography." In *Colonial Modernity in Korea*, edited by Gi-Wook Shin and Michael Robinson, 336–361. Cambridge, MA: Harvard University Asia Center.

Ennis, James G. 1987. "Fields of Action: Structure in Movements' Tactical Repertoires." *Sociological Forum* 2(3): 520–533.

Fendrich, James M. 1977. "Keeping the Faith or Pursuing the Good Life: A Study of the Consequences of Participation in the Civil Rights Movement." *American Sociological Review* 42(1): 144–157.

Forsythe, David P., and Susan Welch. 1986. "Human Rights Voting in Congress." *Policy Studies Journal* 15(1): 173–187.

Francisco, Ronald A. 1995. "The Relationship Between Coercion and Protest: An Empirical Evaluation in Three Coercive States." *Journal of Conflict Resolution* 39(2): 263–282.

———. 2005. "The Dictator's Dilemma." In *Repression and Mobilization*, edited by Christian Davenport, Hank Johnston, and Carol Mueller, 58–81. Minneapolis: University of Minnesota Press.

Gale, Richard P. 1986. "Social Movements and the State: The Environmental Movement, Countermovement, and Government Agencies." *Sociological Perspectives* 29(2): 202–240.

Gerth, H. H., and C. Wright Mills. 1946. *From Max Weber: Essays in Sociology.* New York: Oxford University Press.

Goedde, Patricia. 2011. "Lawyers for a Democratic Society (Minbyun): The Evolution of Its Legal Mobilization Process Since 1988." In *South Korean Social Movements: From Democracy to Civil Society*, edited by Gi-Wook Shin and Paul Y. Chang, 224–244. London: Routledge.

Goldstone, Jack A., and Charles Tilly. 2001. "Threat (and Opportunity): Popular Action and State Response in the Dynamics of Contentious Action." In *Silence and Voice in the Study of Contentious Politics*, edited by Ronald R. Aminzade, Jack A. Goldstone, Doug McAdam, Elizabeth J. Perry, William H. Sewell Jr., Sidney Tarrow, and Charles Tilly, 179–194. Cambridge, UK: Cambridge University Press.

Gutiérrez, Gustavo. 1973. *A Theology of Liberation: History, Politics, and Salvation.* Maryknoll, NY: Orbis Books.

Ham, Sok Hon . 1959. "Han paeum [One lesson]." *Sasangge Monthly* 7(10): 180–192.

Han, Sŭnghŏn. 2002. "Han'guk Aemnesŭt'i hoego: kŭ kollan kwa poram ŭi kwejŏk [Reflecting on Amnesty International Korea: Its trials and rewards]." In *Han'guk*

Aemnesŭt'i 30-yŏn! Inkwŏn undong 30-yŏn!: Kukche Aemnesŭt'i Han'guk Chibu 30-yŏn yaksa [30 years of Korea's Amnesty International! 30 years of human rights activities! 30-year historical outline of Amnesty International's South Korea Section], edited by Amnesty International South Korean Section, 142–147. Seoul: Amnesty International South Korean Section.

Han, Sunjoo. 1980. "Student Activism: A Comparison Between the 1960 Uprising and the 1971 Protest Movement." In *Political Participation in Korea: Democracy, Mobilization, and Stability*, edited by Chong Lim Kim, 143–161. Santa Barbara, CA: Clio Books.

Han, Yong-Sup. 2011. "The May Sixteenth Military Coup." In *The Park Chung Hee Era: The Transformation of South Korea*, edited by Byung-Kook Kim and Ezra F. Vogel, 35–57. Cambridge, MA: Harvard University Press.

Hankyoreh Newspaper. 2010. "'Chŭnggŏ ŏpsi kiso haran malssŭm inya' Inhyŏktang tamdang kŏmsa tŭl hangmyŏng ['Are you saying to prosecute without proof?' the insubordination of the prosecutors in charge of the PRP case]." April 18.

———. 2012. "Chang Chun-ha's Family Hopes to Know Truth of His Death After 37 Years." August 16.

———. 2013. "Forensic Reinvestigation Concludes Chang Chun-ha Was Murdered." March 27.

Henderson, Gregory. 1991. "Human Rights in South Korea, 1945–1953." In *Human Rights in Korea: Historical and Policy Perspectives*, edited by William Shaw, 125–169. Cambridge, MA: Council on East Asian Studies, Harvard University and The East Asian Legal Studies Program of the Harvard Law School.

Hoare, Quintin, and Geoffrey Nowell Smith. 1971. *Selections from the Prison Notebooks of Antonio Gramsci*. New York: International Publishers.

Hocke, Peter. 1998. "Determining the Selection Bias in Local and National Newspaper Reports on Protest Events." In *Acts of Dissent: New Developments in the Study of Protest*, edited by Dieter Rucht, Ruud Koopmans, and Friedhelm Neidhardt, 131–163. Berlin: Edition Sigma Rainer Bohn Verlag.

Hong, Joon Seok. 2011. "From the Streets to the Courts: PSPD's Legal Strategy and the Institutionalization of Social Movements." In *South Korean Social Movements: From Democracy to Civil Society*, edited by Gi-Wook Shin and Paul Y. Chang, 96–116. London: Routledge.

Hoover, Dean, and David Kowalewski. 1992. "Dynamic Models of Dissent and Repression." *Journal of Conflict Resolution* 36(1): 150–182.

Huntington, Samuel P. 1991. *The Third Wave: Democratization in the Late Twentieth Century*. Norman: University of Oklahoma Press.

Hyŏn, Yŏnghak. 1962. "Kyŏngje kaebal kwa kŭrisŭdoin ŭi ch'amyŏ [Economic development and Christian participation]." *Kidokkyo sasang* [*Christian Thought*] 58(October): 51.

———. 1985. "Minjung, konan ŭi chong, hŭimang [The suffering and hope of the min-jung]." *Sinhak sasang* [*Theological Thought*] 51: 863–874.

Im, Hyug Baeg. 2011. "The Origins of the *Yushin* Regime: Machiavelli Unveiled." In *The Park Chung Hee Era: The Transformation of South Korea*, edited by Byung-Kook Kim and Ezra F. Vogel, 233–261. Cambridge, MA: Harvard University Press.

Jennings, M. Kent. 1987. "Residues of a Movement: The Aging of the American Protest Generation." *American Political Science Review* 81(2): 367–382.

Jeong, Jooyeon. 2007. *Industrial Relations in Korea: Diversity and Dynamism of Korean Enterprise Unions from a Comparative Perspective.* London: Routledge.

Johnston, Hank. 2005. "Talking the Walk: Speech Acts and Resistance in Authoritar-ian Regimes." In *Repression and Mobilization*, edited by Christian Davenport, Hank Johnston, and Carol McClurg Mueller, 108–137. Minneapolis: University of Minne-sota Press.

Johnston, Hank, and Bert Klandermans, eds. 1995. *Social Movements and Culture.* Min-neapolis: University of Minnesota Press.

Jung, Hae Gu, and Ho Ki Kim. 2009. "Development of Democratization Movement in South Korea." Unpublished Manuscript. Retrieved on January 23, 2013, from http://aparc.stanford.edu/publications/development_of_democratization_movement_in_south_korea

Jung, Kyungja. 2013. *Practicing Feminism in South Korea: The Women's Movement Against Sexual Violence.* London: Routledge.

Kang, Jung In. 2002. "Reflections on Recent Democratization." In *Korean Politics: Striv-ing for Democracy and Unification*, edited by the Korean National Commission for UNESCO, 3–27. Elizabeth, NJ: Hollym Corporation.

Kang, Wi Jo. 1997. *Christ and Caesar in Modern Korea: A History of Christianity and Poli-tics.* Albany: State University of New York Press.

Katsiaficas, George. 2012. *Asia's Unknown Uprisings.* Vol. 1: *South Korean Social Move-ments in the 20th Century.* Oakland, CA: PM Press.

Keck, Margaret E., and Kathryn Sikkink. 1998. *Activists Beyond Borders: Advocacy Net-works in International Politics.* Ithaca, NY: Cornell University Press.

———. 1999. "Transnational Advocacy Networks in International and Regional Politics." *International Social Science Journal* 51(159): 89–101.

Khawaja, Marwan. 1993. "Repression and Popular Collective Action: Evidence from the West Bank." *Sociological Forum* 8(1): 47–71.

———. 1994. "Resource Mobilization, Hardship, and Popular Collective Action in the West Bank." *Social Forces* 73(1): 191–220.

Kim, Byung-Kook. 2011a. "Introduction: The Case for Political History." In *The Park Chung Hee Era: The Transformation of South Korea*, edited by Byung-Kook Kim and Ezra F. Vogel, 1–31. Cambridge, MA: Harvard University Press.

———. 2011b. "The Labyrinth of Solitude: Park and the Exercise of Presidential Power."

In *The Park Chung Hee Era: The Transformation of South Korea*, edited by Byung-Kook Kim and Ezra F. Vogel, 140–167. Cambridge, MA: Harvard University Press.

Kim, Byung-Kook, and Ezra F. Vogel. eds. 2011. *The Park Chung Hee Era: The Transformation of South Korea*. Cambridge, MA: Harvard University Press.

Kim, Byong-suh. 1989. "Modernization and the Rise of Religiosity in Korea: The Case of the Protestant Church and Sectarian Groups." In *Industrializing East Asia*, edited by the Asian Sociological Association, 152–168.

Kim, Chiha. 1970. "Ojŏk" [Five bandits]." *Sasangge Monthly* 205 (May 1970): 231–248.

Kim, Dong-One, and Johnseok Bae. 2004. *Employment Relations and HRM in South Korea*. Burlington, VT: Ashgate.

Kim, Eun Mee, and Gil Sung Park. 2011. "The Chaebol." In *The Park Chung Hee Era: The Transformation of South Korea*, edited by Byung-Kook Kim and Ezra F. Vogel, 265–294. Cambridge, MA: Harvard University Press.

Kim, Hyun-young Kwon, and John (Song Pae) Cho. 2011. "The Korean Gay and Lesbian Movement 1993–2008: From 'Identity' and 'Community' to 'Human Rights.'" In *South Korean Social Movements: From Democracy to Civil Society*, edited by Gi-Wook Shin and Paul Y. Chang, 206–223. London: Routledge.

Kim, Hyung-A. 2004. *Korea's Development Under Park Chung Hee: Rapid Industrialization, 1961–79*. London: Routledge.

Kim, Hyung-A, and Clark W. Sorensen. eds. 2011. *Reassessing the Park Chung Hee Era, 1961–1979: Development, Political Thought, Democracy, and Cultural Influence*. Seattle, WA: University of Washington Press.

Kim, Joo-Hong. 2011. "The Armed Forces." In *The Park Chung Hee Era: The Transformation of South Korea*, edited by Byung-Kook Kim and Ezra F. Vogel, 168–199. Cambridge, MA: Harvard University Press.

Kim, Joochul, and Sang-Chuel Choe. 1997. *Seoul: The Making of a Metropolis*. Chichester, UK: Wiley.

Kim, Myŏngsu. 2006. *An Pyŏngmu: sidae wa minjung ŭi chŭngŏnja* [An Pyŏngmu: Generations and witnesses of the minjung]. Seoul: Sallim.

Kim, Quee-Young. 1996. "From Protest to Change of Regime: The 4–19 Revolt and the Fall of the Rhee Regime in South Korea." *Social Forces* 74(4): 1179–1209.

Kim, Samuel S., ed. 2003. *Korea's Democratization*. Cambridge, UK: Cambridge University Press.

Kim, Sun-Chul. n.d. *Democratization and Social Movements in Korea: Defiant Institutionalization*. London: Routledge.

Kim, Sun-Gun. 1997. "The Shinto Shrine Issue in Korean Christianity Under Japanese Colonialism." *Journal of Church and State* 39(3): 503–521.

Kim, Sunhyuk. 2000. *The Politics of Democratization in Korea: The Role of Civil Society*. Pittsburgh, PA: University of Pittsburgh Press.

———. 2009. "Civic Engagement and Democracy in Korea." *Korea Observer* 40(1): 1–26.

Kim, Sunhyuk, and Eun Sun Lee. 2011. "'Dynamics of Contention' in Democratic Korea: The Role of Anti-Americanism." *Korea Journal* 51(2): 229–255.

Kim, Sun Joo. 2007. *Marginality and Subversion in Korea: The Hong Kyŏngnae Rebellion of 1812*. Seattle: University of Washington Press.

Kim, Taehyun, and Chang Jae Baik. 2011. "Taming and Tamed by the United States." In *The Park Chung Hee Era: The Transformation of South Korea*, edited by Byung-Kook Kim and Ezra F. Vogel, 58–84. Cambridge, MA: Harvard University Press.

Kim, Yong-Jick. 2011. "The Security, Political, and Human Rights Conundrum, 1974–1979." In *The Park Chung Hee Era: The Transformation of South Korea*, edited by Byung-Kook Kim and Ezra F. Vogel, 457–482. Cambridge, MA: Harvard University Press.

Kleiner. Juergen. 2001. *Korea: A Century of Change*. Hackensack, NJ: World Scientific.

Koo, Hagen. 1993. "Strong State and Contentious Society." In *State and Society in Contemporary Korea*, edited by Hagen Koo, 231–249. Ithaca, NY: Cornell University Press.

———. 2001. *Korean Workers: The Culture and Politics of Class Formation*. Ithaca, NY: Cornell University Press.

Koo, Jeong-Woo. 2007. "The Origins of the Public Sphere and Civil Society: Private Academies and Petitions in Korea, 1506–1800." *Social Science History* 31(3): 381–409.

———. 2011. "Origins of the National Human Rights Commission: Global and Domestic Causes." In *South Korean Social Movements: From Democracy to Civil Society*, edited by Gi-Wook Shin and Paul Y. Chang, 77–95. London: Routledge.

Koo, Jeong Woo, and Francisco O. Ramirez. 2009. "National Incorporation of Global Human Rights: Worldwide Expansion of National Human Rights Institutions, 1966–2004." *Social Forces* 87(3): 1321–1353.

Koopmans, Ruud. 1993. "The Dynamics of Protest Waves: West Germany, 1965 to 1989." *American Sociological Review* 58(5): 637–658.

———. 1997. "Dynamics of Repression and Mobilization: The German Extreme Right in the 1990s." *Mobilization* 2(2): 149–165.

Kwang, Cho. 2006. "Human Relations as Expressed in Vernacular Catholic Writings of the Late Chosŏn Dynasty." In *Christianity in Korea*, edited by Robert E. Buswell Jr. and Timothy S. Lee, 29–37. Honolulu, HI: University of Hawai'i Press.

Kwon, Jong Bum. 2011. "Exorcizing the Ghosts of Kwangju: Policing Protest in the Post-Authoritarian Era." In *South Korean Social Movements: From Democracy to Civil Society*, edited by Gi-Wook Shin and Paul Y. Chang, 58–74. London: Routledge.

Kyunghyang Shinmun. 1961. "Song Chiyŏng e kwandae chŏbun ŭl [Song Chiyŏng's generous suspension]." August 30.

———. 1975. "Yi Pyŏngnin ssi kusok hangŭi Kukche Samyŏn Ilbon wisŏ [Amnesty International Japan Committee's protest against Mr. Yi Pyŏngnin's imprisonment]." January 21.

———. 1979. "Kim Kyewŏn 'Kim Chaegyu obal sago' hŏwi pogo [Kim Kyewŏn's false report on 'the incident of Kim Chaegyu's accidental discharge']." December 04.

———. 2003. "Kinjo 9-ho sedae pisa: Karhyŏn-dong moim 6–inbang [The secret history of generation Kinjo No. 9: The Galhyeon Group of Six gathering]." December 25.

Lee, Byeong-cheon. 2006. *Developmental Dictatorship and the Park Chung Hee Era: The Shaping of Modernity in the Republic of Korea.* Paramus, NJ: Homa & Sekey Books.

Lee, Chong-Sik. 2012. *Park Chung-Hee: From Poverty to Power.* Seoul: Kyung Hee University Press.

Lee, Hahn-Been. 1968. *Time, Change, and Administration.* Honolulu: East-West Center Press, University of Hawai'i.

Lee, Jeongeun. 2001. "Han'guk esŏ ŭi inkwŏn kaenyŏm hyŏngsŏng kwajŏng [The process of the formation of the concept of human rights in Korea]." *Minjujuŭi wa inkwŏn* [Democracy and human rights] 1(2): 121–161.

———. 2009. "4.19 hyŏngmyŏng kwa inkwŏn: inkwŏn kaenyŏm e taehan insik kwa chedo ŭi pyŏnhwa [The 4.19 revolution and human rights: Conceptual and institutional changes regarding the concept of human rights]. *Minjujuŭi wa inkwŏn* [Democracy and human rights] 9(2): 129–156.

Lee, Jung-Hoon. 2011. "Normalization of Relations with Japan: Toward a New Partnership." In *The Park Chung Hee Era: The Transformation of South Korea*, edited by Byung-Kook Kim and Ezra F. Vogel, 430–457. Cambridge, MA: Harvard University Press.

Lee, Min Yong. 2011. "The Vietnam War: South Korea's Search for National Security." In *The Park Chung Hee Era: The Transformation of South Korea*, edited by Byung-Kook Kim and Ezra F. Vogel, 403–429. Cambridge, MA: Harvard University Press.

Lee, Myung-sik. 2010. *The History of the Democratization Movement in Korea.* Seoul: Korea Democracy Foundation.

Lee, Namhee. 2007. *The Making of Minjung: Democracy and the Politics of Representation in South Korea.* Ithaca, NY: Cornell University Press.

Lee, Timothy S. 2000. "A Political Factor in the Rise of Protestantism in Korea: Protestantism and the March First Movement." *Church History: Studies in Christianity and Culture* 69(1): 116–142.

———. 2010. *Born Again: Evangelicalism in Korea.* Honolulu, HI: University of Hawai'i Press.

Lewis, Linda S. 2002. "Commemorating Kwangju: The 5.18 Movement and Civil Society at the Millennium." In *Korean Society: Civil Society, Democracy and the State*, edited by Charles K. Armstrong, 165–186. London: Routledge.

Lichbach, Mark Irving. 1987. "Deterrence or Escalation? The Puzzle of Aggregate Studies of Repression and Dissent." *Journal of Conflict Resolution* 31(2): 266–297.

Liston, Robert A. 1988. *The Pueblo Surrender: A Covert Action by the National Security Agency.* Santa Barbara, CA: Liston House.

Loveman, Mara. 1998. "High-Risk Collective Action: Defending Human Rights in Chile, Uruguay, and Argentina." *American Journal of Sociology* 104(2): 477–525.

Marx, Karl, and Friedrich Engels. 1976. *Collected Works, 1845–1848: Volume 6*. New York: International Publishers.

Mason, Edward S., Mahn Je Kim, Dwight H. Perkins, Kwang Suk Kim, and David C. Cole, with Leroy Jones, Il Sakong, Donald R. Snodgrass, and Noel F. McGinn. 1980. *The Economic and Social Modernization of the Republic of Korea*. Cambridge, MA: Council on East Asian Studies, Harvard University.

McAdam, Doug. 1982. *Political Process and the Development of Black Insurgency, 1930–1970*. Chicago: University of Chicago Press.

———. 1983. "Tactical Innovation and the Pace of Insurgency." *American Sociological Review* 48(6): 735–754.

———. 1988. *Freedom Summer*. Oxford, UK: Oxford University Press.

———. 1989. "The Biographical Consequences of Activism." *American Sociological Review* 54(5): 744–760.

———. 1995. "'Initiator' and 'Spin-off' Movements: Diffusion Processes in Protest Cycles." In *Repertoires and Cycles of Collective Action*, edited by Mark Traugott, 217–239. Durham, NC: Duke University Press.

———. 1996. "Conceptual Origins, Current Problems, Future Directions." In *Comparative Perspectives on Social Movements: Political Opportunities, Mobilizing Structures, and Cultural Framings*, edited by Doug McAdam, John D. McCarthy, and Mayer Zald, 23–40. Cambridge, UK: Cambridge University Press.

McCammon, Holly J., and Karen E. Campbell. 2002. "Allies on the Road to Victory: Coalition Formation Between Suffragists and the Women's Christian Temperance Union." *Mobilization* 7(3): 231–251.

McCarthy, John D., Clark McPhail, and Jackie Smith. 1996. "Images of Protest: Selection Bias in Media Coverage of Washington D.C. Demonstrations." *American Sociological Review* 61(3): 478–499.

McCarthy, John D., and Mayer N. Zald. 1977. "Resource Mobilization Theory and Social Movements: A Partial Theory." *American Journal of Sociology* 82(6): 1212–1241.

Merrill, Karen R. 2007. *The Oil Crisis of 1973–1974: A Brief History with Documents*. New York: Bedford/St. Martin's Press.

Meyer, David S. 2003. "Political Opportunity and Nested Institutions." *Social Movement Studies* 2(1): 17–35.

———. 2004. "Protest and Political Opportunities." *Annual Review of Sociology* 30: 125–145.

Meyer, David S., and Catherine Corrigall-Brown. 2005. "Coalitions and Political Context: U.S. Movements Against Wars in Iraq." *Mobilization* 10(3): 327–344.

Meyer, David S., and Suzanne Staggenborg. 1996. "Movements, Countermovements, and the Structure of Political Opportunity." *American Journal of Sociology* 101(6): 1628–1660.

Minjuhwa Undong Kinyŏm Saŏphoe [Korea Democracy Foundation Documentary].

2006. *Yusin hŏnpŏp pandae undong* [The Anti-Yusin Constitution Movement]. Seoul: Korea Democracy Foundation.

Minjuhwa Undong Kinyŏm Saŏphoe [Korea Democracy Foundation]. 2009. *Han'guk minjuhwa undongsa: Yusin ch'ejegi, Vol. 2*. [History of the Korean Democratization Movement: The Yusin Period, Vol. 2]. Paju: Dolbegae.

Moon, Faye. 2006. "Heartaches No Longer, and Some That Linger." *More Than Witnesses: How a Small Group of Missionaries Aided Korea's Democratic Revolution*, edited by Jim Stentzel, 159–195. Seoul: Korea Democracy Foundation.

Moon, Seungsook. 2002. "Carving Out Space: Civil Society and the Women's Movement in South Korea." *Journal of Asian Studies* 61(2): 473–500.

———. 2005. *Militarized Modernity and Gendered Citizenship in South Korea*. Durham, NC: Duke University Press.

Moore, Will H. 1998. "Repression and Dissent: Substitution, Context, and Timing." *American Journal of Political Science* 42(3): 851–873.

———. 2000. "The Repression of Dissent: A Substitution Model of Government Coercion." *Journal of Conflict Resolution* 44(1): 107–127.

Mottl, Tahi L. 1980. "The Analysis of Countermovements." *Social Problems* 27(5): 620–635.

Muller, Edward N. 1985. "Income Inequality, Regime Repressiveness, and Political Violence." *American Sociological Review* 50(1): 47–61.

Nam, Hwasook. 2009. *Building Ships, Building a Nation: Korea's Democratic Unionism Under Park Chung Hee*. Seattle: University of Washington Press.

Nohlen, Dieter, Florian Grotz, and Christof Hartmann, eds. 2001. *Elections in Asia and the Pacific: A Data Handbook*. Vol. II: *South East Asia, East Asia, and the South Pacific*. Oxford, UK: Oxford University Press.

Oak, Sung-Deuk. 2013. *The Making of Korean Christianity: Protestant Encounters with Korean Religions, 1876–1915*. Waco, TX: Baylor University Press.

Ogle, George E. 1977. *Liberty to the Captives: The Struggle Against Oppression in South Korea*. Atlanta, GA: John Knox Press.

———. 1990. *South Korea: Dissent Within the Economic Miracle*. London: Zed Books.

———. 2006. "Our Hearts Cry with You." In *More Than Witnesses: How a Small Group of Missionaries Aided Korea's Democratic Revolution*, edited by Jim Stentzel, 67–103. Seoul: Korea Democracy Foundation.

Oh, Chang Hun. 1991. *A Study of the Dynamics of an Authoritarian Regime: The Case of the Yushin System Under Park Chung Hee, 1972–1979*. PhD Dissertation, Ohio State University.

Oh, John Kie-chiang. 1999. *Korean Politics: The Quest for Democratization and Economic Development*. Ithaca, NY: Cornell University Press.

Oliver, Pamela E. 1993. "Formal Models of Collective Action." *Annual Review of Sociology* 19: 271–300.

Oliver, Pamela E., and Gregory M. Maney. 2000. "Political Processes and Local Newspaper Coverage of Protest Events: From Selection Bias to Triadic Interactions." *American Journal of Sociology* 106(2): 463–505.

Oliver, Pamela E., and Daniel J. Myers. 2003. "The Coevolution of Social Movements." *Mobilization* 8(1): 1–24.

Olzak, Susan. 1989. "Analysis of Events in the Study of Collective Action." *Annual Review of Sociology* 15: 119–141.

Olzak, Susan, Maya Beasley, and Johan L. Olivier. 2003. "The Impact of State Reforms on Protest Against Apartheid in South Africa." *Mobilization* 8(1): 27–50.

Olzak, Susan, and Emily Ryo. 2007. "Organizational Diversity, Vitality and Outcomes in the Civil Rights Movement." *Social Forces* 85(4): 1561–1591.

Olzak, Susan, and S. C. Noah Uhrig. 2001. "The Ecology of Tactical Overlap." *American Sociological Review* 66(5): 694–717.

Opp, Karl Dieter, and Wolfgang Roehl. 1990. "Repression, Micromobilization, and Political Protest." *Social Forces* 69(2): 521–547.

Osa, Maryjane. 2003. *Solidarity and Contention: Networks of Polish Opposition*. Minneapolis: University of Minnesota Press.

Paine, Thomas. 1777. *The American Crisis*. Whitefish, MT: Kessinger.

Park, Albert L. 1996. "The Quest for Salvation: A Study on the Urban Industrial Mission and Its Relationship with the Korean Working Class." Honors Thesis, Department of History, University of Chicago.

———. 2015. *Building a Heaven on Earth: Religion, Activism, and Protest in Japanese Occupied Korea*. Honolulu: University of Hawai'i Press.

Park, Chung-Shin. 2003. *Protestantism and Politics in Korea*. Seattle: University of Washington Press.

Park, Mi. 2008. *Democracy and Social Change: A History of South Korean Student Movements, 1980–2000*. New York: Peter Lang.

Park, Min-na. 2005. *Birth of Resistance: Stories of Eight Women Worker Activists*. Seoul: Korea Democracy Foundation.

Park, Myung-Lim. 2011. "The *Chaeya*." In *The Park Chung Hee Era: The Transformation of South Korea*, edited by Byung-Kook Kim and Ezra F. Vogel, 373–400. Cambridge, MA: Harvard University Press.

Pedler, Anne. 1927. "Going to the People: The Russian Narodniki in 1874–5." *The Slavonic Review* 6(16): 130–141.

Piper, Nicola. 2004. "Rights of Foreign Workers and the Politics of Migration in South-East Asia and East Asia." *International Migration* 42(5): 71–97.

della Porta, Donatella. 1996. "Social Movements and the State: Thoughts on the Policing of Protest." In *Comparative Perspectives on Social Movements: Political Opportunities, Mobilizing Structures, and Cultural Framings*, edited by Doug McAdam, John D. McCarthy, and Mayer Zald, 62–92. Cambridge, UK: Cambridge University Press.

Rasler, Karen. 1996. "Concessions, Repression, and Political Protest in the Iranian Revolution." *American Sociological Review* 61(1): 132–152.

Rauschenbusch, Walter. 1918. *A Theology for the Social Gospel.* New York: MacMillan.

Robinson, Michael Edson. 1988. *Cultural Nationalism in Colonial Korea, 1920–1925.* Seattle: University of Washington Press.

Robinson, Michael. 2012. "Sasanggye and Post-Colonial Discourse in 1950s Korea." Paper presented at the "Korea in the 1950s" Conference, held at the Kyujanggak Institute for Korean Studies, August 16–17, 2012, Seoul National University.

Rucht, Dieter. 2004. "Movement Allies, Adversaries, and Third Parties." In *The Blackwell Companion to Social Movements*, edited by David Snow, Sarah A. Soule, and Hanspeter Kriesi, 197–216. Malden, MA: Blackwell Publishing.

Rupp, Leila J., and Verta Taylor. 1987. *Survival in the Doldrums: The American Women's Rights Movement, 1945 to the 1960s.* New York: Oxford University Press.

Schmid, Andre. 2002. *Korea Between Empires, 1895–1919.* New York: Columbia University Press.

Scott, James C. 1985. *Weapons of the Weak: Everyday Forms of Peasant Resistance.* New Haven, CT: Yale University Press.

Seo, Joong-Seok. 2007. *Contemporary History of South Korea—60 Years.* Seoul: Korea Democracy Foundation.

Shaffer, Martin B. 2000. "Coalition Work Among Environmental Groups: Who Participates?" *Research in Social Movements, Conflicts and Change* 22: 111–126.

Shaw, William. 1991. *Human Rights in Korea: Historical and Policy Perspectives.* Cambridge, MA: Council on East Asian Studies, Harvard University and The East Asian Legal Studies Program of the Harvard Law School.

Shin, Gi-Wook, and Paul Y. Chang, eds. 2011. *South Korean Social Movements: From Democracy to Civil Society.* London: Routledge.

Shin, Gi-Wook, Paul Y. Chang, Jung Eun Lee, and Sookyung Kim. 2011. "The Korean Democracy Movement: An Empirical Overview." In *South Korean Social Movements: From Democracy to Civil Society*, edited by Gi-Wook Shin and Paul Y. Chang, 21–40. London: Routledge.

Shin, Gi-Wook, and Kyung Moon Hwang. eds. 2003. *Contentious Kwangju: The May 18 Uprising in Korea's Past and Present.* Lanham, MD: Rowman & Littlefield.

Skocpol, Theda. 1985. "Bringing the State Back In: Strategies of Analysis in Current Research." In *Bringing the State Back In*, edited by Peter B. Evans, Dietrick Rueschemeyer, and Theda Skocpol, 3–42. Cambridge, UK: Cambridge University Press.

Smith, Jackie, John D. McCarthy, Clark McPhail, and Boguslaw Augustyn. 2001. "From Protest to Agenda Building: Description Bias in Media Coverage of Protest Events in Washington, D.C." *Social Forces* 79(4): 1397–1423.

Snow, David A., and Robert D. Benford. 1988. "Ideology, Frame Resonance, and Participant Mobilization." *International Social Movement Research* 1: 197–217.

Snow, David A., E. Burke Rochford Jr., Steven K. Worden, and Robert D. Benford. 1986. "Frame Alignment Processes, Micromobilization, and Movement Participation." *American Sociological Review* 51(4): 464–481.

Snow, David A., Rens Vliegenthart, and Catherine Corrigall-Brown. 2007. "Framing the French Riots: A Comparative Study of Frame Variation." *Social Forces* 86(2): 385–415.

Sŏ, Namdong. 1975a. "Yesu, kyohoesa, Han'guk kyohoe [Jesus, church history, the Korean church]." *Kidokkyo sasang [Christian Thought]* 201(February): 53–68.

———. 1975b. "Minjung ŭi sinhak: Kim Hyŏnghyo Kyosu ŭi pip'an e tapham [Minjung's theology: A response to professor Kim Hyŏnghyo's criticism]." *Kidokkyo sasang [Christian Thought]* 203(April): 85–90.

Sohn, Hak-Kyu. 1989. *Authoritarianism and Opposition in South Korea*. London: Routledge.

Song, Kidŭk. 1984. "Sŏ Namdong ŭi minjung sinhak [Sŏ Namdong's minjung theology]." *Kidokkyo sasang [Christian Thought]* 316(October): 22–23.

Staggenborg, Suzanne. 1986. "Coalition Work in the Pro-Choice Movement: Organizational and Environmental Opportunities and Obstacles." *Social Problems* 33(5): 374–390.

Stentzel, Jim, ed. 2006. *More Than Witnesses: How a Small Group of Missionaries Aided Korea's Democratic Revolution*. Seoul: Korea Democracy Foundation.

Strang, David, and Sarah A. Soule. 1998. "Diffusion in Organizations and Social Movements: From Hybrid Corn to Poison Pills." *Annual Review of Sociology* 24: 265–290.

Suh, Doowon. 2009. *Political Protest and Labor Solidarity in Korea: White-Collar Labor Movements After Democratization (1987–1995)*. London: Routledge.

Sung, Wan-kyung. 2012. "The Rise and Fall of Minjung Art." In *Being Political Popular: South Korean Art at the Intersection of Popular Culture and Democracy, 1980–2010*, edited by Sohl Lee, 188–202. Seoul: Hyunsil.

Sunoo, Harold Hakwon. 1976a. *Repressive State and Resisting Church: The Politics of CIA in South Korea*. Fayette, MO: Korean American Cultural Association, CMC.

———. 1976b. "The Story of Kim Chi Ha." *Worldview* 19(6): 18–22.

Tajfel, Henri, and John C. Turner. 1986. "The Social Identity Theory of Intergroup Behavior." *Psychology of Intergroup Relations*, edited by Stephen Worchel and William G. Austin, 7–24. Chicago: Nelson-Hall.

Tarrow, Sidney. 1993. "Cycles of Collective Action: Between Moments of Madness and the Repertoire of Contention." *Social Science History* 17(2): 281–307.

———. 1998. *Power in Movement: Social Movements and Contentious Politics*. Cambridge, UK: Cambridge University Press.

Tashakkori, Abbas, and Charles Teddlie. 1998. *Mixed Methodology: Combining Qualitative and Quantitative Approaches*. Thousand Oaks, CA: Sage.

Taylor, Verta. 1989. "Social Movement Continuity: The Women's Movement in Abeyance." *American Sociological Review* 54(5): 761–775.

Thomas, Daniel C. 2001. *The Helsinki Effect: International Norms, Human Rights, and the Demise of Communism*. Princeton, NJ: Princeton University Press.

Thomas, Owen C. 1983. *Introduction to Theology*. Harrisburg, PA: Morehouse.

Tilly, Charles. 1978. *From Mobilization to Revolution*. Boston, MA: Addison-Wesley.

———. 1995. *Popular Contention in Great Britain, 1758–1834*. Cambridge, MA: Harvard University Press.

Titarenko, Larissa, John D. McCarthy, Clark McPhail, and Boguslaw Augustyn. 2001. "The Interaction of State Repression, Protest Form, and Protest Sponsor Strength During the Transition from Communism in Minsk, Belarus." *Mobilization* 6(2): 129–150.

Van Dyke, Nella. 2003. "Crossing Movement Boundaries: Factors That Facilitate Coalition Protest by American College Students, 1930–1990." *Social Problems* 50(2): 226–250.

Vogel, Ezra F. 1991. *The Four Little Dragons: The Spread of Industrialization in East Asia*. Cambridge, MA: Harvard University Press.

Weede, Erich. 1987. "Some New Evidence on Correlates of Political Violence: Income Inequality, Regime Repressiveness, and Economic Development." *European Sociological Review* 3(2): 97–108.

Weiss, Meredith L. 2006. *Protest and Possibilities: Civil Society and Coalitions for Political Change in Malaysia*. Stanford, CA: Stanford University Press.

Wells, Kenneth M. 1990. *New God, New Nation: Protestants and Self-Reconstruction Nationalism in Korea, 1896–1937*. Honolulu: University of Hawai'i Press.

———. ed. 1995a. *South Korea's Minjung Movement: The Culture and Politics of Dissidence*. Honolulu: University of Hawai'i Press.

———. 1995b. "Introduction." In *South Korea's Minjung Movement: The Culture and Politics of Dissidence*, edited by Kenneth M. Wells, 1–9. Honolulu: University of Hawai'i Press.

White, James W. 1993. "Cycles and Repertoires of Popular Contention in Early Modern Japan." *Social Science History* 17(3): 429–455.

White, Robert W. 1989. "From Peaceful Protest to Guerrilla War: Micromobilization of the Provisional Irish Republican Army." *American Journal of Sociology* 94(6): 1277–1302.

Whittier, Nancy. 1997. "Political Generations, Micro-Cohorts, and the Transformation of Social Movements." *American Sociological Review* 62(5): 760–778.

———. 2004. "The Consequences of Social Movements for Each Other." In *The Blackwell Companion to Social Movements*, edited by David A. Snow, Sarah A. Soule, and Hanspeter Kriesi, 531–551. Malden, MA: Blackwell.

Wotipka, Christine Min, and Kiyoteru Tsutsui. 2008. "Global Human Rights and State Sovereignty: State Ratification of International Human Rights Treaties, 1965–2001." *Sociological Forum* 23(4): 724–754.

Woolley, John T. 2000. "Using Media-Based Data in Studies of Politics." *American Journal of Political Science* 44(1): 156–173.

Yi, Chaeo. 2011. *Han'guk haksaeng undongsa: 1945–1979-yŏn* [History of Korean student movements: 1945–1979]. Seoul: P'ara Puksŭ.

Yi, Sanghŭi. 2005. "1960-yŏndae sŏngjang chŏllyak ŭi chŏnhwan kwa nodong t'ongje kije ŭi pyŏnyong kwajŏng" [Shifts in growth strategies and the process of transforming labor control mechanisms in the 1960s]." In *1950–60-yŏndae Han'gukhyŏng palchŏn model ŭi wŏnhyŏng kwa kŭ pyŏnyong kwajŏng* [The prototype of the Korean development model and the process of its transformation], edited by Kong Cheuk and Cho Sukkon, 299–337. Paju: Hanwul.

Youm, Kyu Ho. 1996. *Press Law in South Korea*. Ames: Iowa State University Press.

Yun, Hyon. 2002. "AI Han'guk Chibu ŭi ch'angnip chŏnhu [Before and after the foundation of the AI Korea Branch]." In *Han'guk Aemnesŭt'i 30-yŏn! Inkwŏn undong 30-yŏn!: Kukche Aemnesŭt'i Han'guk Chibu 30-yŏn yaksa* [30 years of Korea's Amnesty International! 30 years of human rights activities! 30-year historical outline of Amnesty International's South Korea Section], edited by Amnesty International South Korean Section, 137–141. Seoul: Amnesty International South Korean Section.

Zoh, Byoung-Ho. 2004. *Democratization and Evangelization: A History of the Christian Student Movements in Korea: 1884–1990*. Seoul: Tanggulshi.

Zwerman, Gilda, and Patricia Steinhoff. 2005. "When Activists Ask for Trouble: State-Dissident Interactions and the New Left Cycle of Resistance in the United States and Japan." In *Repression and Mobilization*, edited by Christian Davenport, Hank Johnston, and Carol Mueller, 85–107. Minneapolis: University of Minnesota Press.

INDEX

Abelmann, Nancy, 3, 102, 195, 205
Abramowitz, Stephen I., 52
academic freedom, 35, 158, 180
Acheson, Dean, 18
Act on Special Measures for National Security, 43, 251n15
Act on the Establishment of Free Export Zones, 251n15
Adesnik, A. David, 207, 208, 213
advertisement repression, 121–24, 149, 162, 182, 192, 197, 245
AFP, 121
African Methodist Episcopal Church, 82
Ahn Byung-Mu, 82, 94, 107, 184, 186, 197, 254n7
Ahn, Sang Nim, 83
AKC. *See* Amnesty Korean Committee
Alinsky, Saul, 100
Allen, Horace, 253n2
alliances and coalitions, 206–7, 208–9, 256n2; formal coalitions, 181–88, 192, 208; intragroup vs. intergroup, 179, 186, 187, 192, 257n4; and movement solidarity, 175–81; relationship to repression, 175–76, 177, 179, 180–81, 182, 186, 188–93, 199; solidarity statements, 179–81, 186, 192, 199
Almeida, Paul D., 8, 9, 177
Alves, Maria Helena Moreira, 177
Amnesty International, 16, 89, 126, 134, 161, 165, 166, 168, 169–70, 189, 256n8

Amnesty Korean Committee (AKC), 161, 167, 168–70, 244
An Chaehwan, 184
An Ch'ihwan, 258n12
An Ch'ungsŏk, 184
An P'ilsu, 184
An Yangno, 68
Andrews, Kenneth T., 147
Anglican Church, 86
Annual Congress of PEN International (1970), 168
Annual National Prayer Breakfast Committee, 106
Anti-Communist Law (ACL), 10, 34, 35, 38, 65, 92, 106, 186, 243, 245, 250n6, 253n13
Appenzeller, Henry, 253n2
Armstrong, Charles K., 2, 92, 192, 195
Army Security Command (ASC), 25, 32, 33, 37, 204
Asahi Shimbun, 121
Asia Pacific Forum of National Human Rights Institutions, 209–10
Asia Watch, 165
Asset Management Corporation, 132
Associated Press, 121
Association of Family Members of Democracy Movement Practitioners, 35
Association of Family Members of Prisoners of Conscience, 95, 96, 171, 176, 190, 208

one million signatures petition campaign,
186–87, 245
"on-the-job-site" movement, 58, 207
Opp, Karl Dieter, 8, 199
Osa, Maryjane, 8, 192

Pae Yŏnwŏn, 220, 249n2
Paek Kiwan, 62, 121
Paek Nakchŏng, 133, 186
Paek Nakchun, 184, 250n7
Paek Namŏk, 22
Paine, Thomas, 1
Pak Ch'anggyun, 184
Pak Ch'anwŏn, 178
Pak Chin'gwan, 239
Pak Chonggyu, 203
Pak Hansang, 74, 129
Pak Hyŏnch'ae, 72
Pak Hyŏnggyu, 75, 79, 85–88, 94, 100, 104, 121,
140, 175, 185, 219, 220, 254nn4,5; arrested, 84,
88, 92, 96–97, 105, 170, 197, 239, 245; Easter
Sunday protest, 83, 85, 87–88, 89, 105, 170,
206, 239, 245, 253n3
Pak Kyŏngsŏ, 82, 95, 101, 102, 104, 106, 145, 220
Pak Min'gi, 257n3
Pak Nohae: Nodong ŭi saebyŏk, 210–11
Pak Pongnang, 186
Pak Sangnae, 184
Pak Tongsun, 250n4
Pak Wŏlryong, 104
Pak Wŏnsun, 130, 138
Pak Yonggil, 240
Pak Yŏnggŭn, 258n12
Pak Yŏngnok, 241
Pak Yŏnhŭi, 184
Park, Albert L., 80, 84
Park Chung Hee, 4–5, 6, 7–8, 9–11, 15–16,
19–29, 31, 32–45, 49–50, 51, 53, 54, 61, 62–77,
79, 84, 87, 90, 145, 158, 162, 175, 177–78,
180–81, 182, 188, 191–93, 195–96, 200, 209,
212, 249n1, 250nn5,8; assassination of, 12, 33,
108, 201, 202, 203–4, 246, 250n6, 257nn2,3,
258n4; coup of 1961, 5–6, 16–17, 25, 33, 49, 63,
84, 114, 127, 131, 195, 204, 243, 248n9, 249n2,
251n16; and death of wife, 36; democratic
interlude (1961–71), 4, 6, 15, 16–20; economic
policies, 5, 10, 15, 17, 19, 20, 21, 25–26, 29,

55–56, 57, 81, 84, 95, 105, 106, 112, 123, 146,
149, 201–2, 209, 248n1, 251nn14,15, 257n5;
Good Harvest Project, 23; military government, 5–6, 15, 16–17, 114, 195, 249n3; policies
regarding Japan, 10, 17, 19–20, 32, 44, 50,
51–52, 53, 57, 62, 63, 66, 72, 74, 115, 123, 128,
131, 195, 201, 243, 249n6, 257n1; policies
regarding judiciary, 127–29, 133–34, 197–98;
policies regarding labor unions, 42–44,
251n13, 252n2; policies regarding media,
114–16, 117–18, 119–20, 121–27, 162; policies
regarding national security, 10, 17, 25, 26–29,
34–35, 66–67, 105; Vietnam War policies, 10,
17, 18–20, 27, 44
Park, Chung-Shin, 81, 83, 84, 90, 91, 92, 93, 103,
108–9
Park Geun-hye, 258n13
Park, Gil Sung, 26
Park, Mi, 3
Park, Min-na, 188, 189, 247n5
Park, Myung-Lim, 9, 15, 75, 76, 102, 108, 181,
203, 209, 248n9
Peace Market Laborers' Human Rights Prob-
lem Council, 167
Pederson, Eric Karup, 170
Pedler, Anne, 258n7
People's Movement Coalition for Democracy
and Reunification (PMCDR), 193, 207, 208,
237–39
People's Revolutionary Party (PRP), 72, 97;
PRP case (1964), 129, 243, 253n12; PRP case
(1974), 3, 34, 49, 73–77, 84, 98, 100, 112, 130,
133–34, 141, 162–63, 169, 170, 171, 188, 246,
253nn12,13, 256n4
Piper, Nicola, 159, 209
PMCDR. See People's Movement Coalition for
Democracy and Reunification
Poland's Solidarity Movement, 192
politicians, oppositional, 12, 19, 25, 61, 90, 96,
126, 135, 136, 150, 151, 153, 154, 157, 158, 184,
198. See also Kim Dae Jung; Kim Young Sam;
New Democratic Party (NDP); Yun Posŏn
Pŏpchŏng, 88, 142, 184
Prayer Meeting for the Recovery of Human
Rights, 162
Presbyterian Theological Seminary, 91
Prisoners of Conscience Fund, 170

The authorized representative in the EU for product safety and compliance is:
Mare Nostrum Group
B.V Doelen 72
4831 GR Breda
The Netherlands

www.ingramcontent.com/pod-product-compliance
Lightning Source LLC
Chambersburg PA
CBHW020500270326
41926CB00008B/684